COLONIAL CRAFTSMEN
And the Beginnings of American Industry

The original tin lantern that signaled Paul Revere.
Now owned by the Concord Antiquarian Society.

*Forging anconies with the tilt hammer at Hammersmith on the
Saugus River in Massachusetts, about 1650*

COLONIAL CRAFTSMEN

And the Beginnings of American Industry

WRITTEN AND ILLUSTRATED BY

EDWIN TUNIS

WORLD PUBLISHING
TIMES MIRROR
NEW YORK

1972 PRINTING

PUBLISHED BY THE WORLD PUBLISHING COMPANY
2231 WEST 110TH STREET, CLEVELAND, 2, OHIO
PUBLISHED SIMULTANEOUSLY IN CANADA BY
NELSON, FOSTER, AND SCOTT LTD.
LIBRARY OF CONGRESS CATALOG CARD NUMBER: 65-13076
ISBN 0—529—03438—7
W

WORLD PUBLISHING
TIMES MIRROR

PREFACE

ARTISANS still make some things almost as their colonial forerunners made them, even though they use mechanical aids unsuspected by the colonials. Some trades, like weaving, are now widely practiced as handicrafts while the mechanical aids have taken over the main business of production. Many trades exist only as machine work and some, like hornsmithing, have vanished entirely from our part of the world. Let's not weep sentimentally over them; hard-rubber and plastic combs are better in every way than horn combs and they are also cheaper.

This is no how-to-do-it book; it is intended to be read for the interest that old ways may have. It describes working methods broadly, skipping many details. Rather than try to crowd in slight sketches of all the trades and enterprises, fairly full descriptions are given of the important ones. Those left out are some of the very simple jobs—like lime burning, for instance—that needed no special skill, and a few skilled trades—like glovemaking—in which the application of the skill is too obvious to need explaining. A few trades, like shipbuilding and coachmaking, are here in bare outline because they are too important to omit but too complex to cover fully.

The ways to do things are often lost. A small example: a master carpenter showed the author how to form a neat bead on the edge of a board, using as a cutter only the head of a common wood screw set in a block. Some apprentice of his may remember that and pass it on, but it isn't likely to be recorded elsewhere than here. Such has usually been the way in the crafts—do it, show it, but don't write about it. This has done nothing to make this book an easy job.

The richest mine of facts about early trades is Denis Diderot's great *Encyclopédie*, written, illustrated, and published in eighteenth-century France. Though it has been an invaluable guide and last resort, other sources, sparse and scattered though they are, have been preferred to it. This isn't mere cussedness. The *Encyclopédie* describes French ways and it became quickly obvious that colonial American methods were seldom exactly those Diderot describes. The settlers followed their native traditions: English, Scottish, German—with only a leaven of French Huguenot.

Unless he can qualify as a limner, the author is not expert in any of the trades described. He has certainly missed some things entirely and failed, in spite of his best efforts, to understand others. He will welcome being corrected by any reader who can do it, asking only that the informant include a reference that can be checked.

Parts of some illustrations are reconstructed from descriptions but "on colonial principles," that is, they are based on the known solutions of similar problems. Extensive reconstructions are noted in the captions.

Acknowledgments

GATHERING the information needed for this little work was no simple matter of digesting a few dozen monographs. It required long digging in museums and in the remoter stacks of libraries. Among the assembled bits and pieces baffling blanks occurred that ordinary sources would not fill. To do so took the able help of all the kind people listed below. Some of these people are associates of large organizations, some are personal friends, some are collectors, some are specialists who generously answered questions:

Mr. Maurice H. Annenberg; Miss Alice Baldwin Beer, Curator of Textiles, Cooper Union Museum for the Arts of Decoration; Mr. Hugh Benet; Mr. Don H. Berkebile, Division of Transportation, Smithsonian Institution; Mr. William L. Browne, American Institute of Dry Cleaning; Professor Verne E. Chatelain, Department of History, University of Maryland; Miss Grace Rogers Cooper, Curator of Textiles, Smithsonian Institution; Mr. Halbert Nelson Cox; Mr. Allan C. Davis; Mr. Christopher Demuth; Dr. Jackson P. English; Mr. Douglas A. Fisher, United States Steel Corporation; Mr. Perry W. Fuller; Mr. John R. Gerwig, Jr.; Mr. Gerry Gilmarten, Snuff Information Center; Dr. George E. Hardy, Jr.; Mr. Earl J. Heydinger, Acting Superintendent, Hopewell Village National Historic Site; Miss Eugenia Calvert Holland, Assistant Curator, Maryland Historical Society; Mr. James W. Holland, Regional Historian, National Park Service; Mrs. Willard C. Holloway; Miss Elsa von Hoenhoff, Enoch Pratt Free Library; Mr. J. Paul Hudson, Museum Curator, Colonial National Historic Park, Jamestown; Miss Margaret Jacobs, Enoch Pratt Free Library; Mr. H. Lee Hoffman; Mr. John D. Gordon, Arents Collection, New York Public Library; Mrs. Howard W. Kent, Concord Antiquarian Society; Mr. John D. Kilbourne, Assistant to the Director, Library and Archives, Maryland Historical Society; Mr. Stanley Kolker, Cigar Institute of America; Mr. Maurice L. Long; Miss Beatrice Marriott, Health Sciences Library, University of Maryland; Mr. John N. Pearce, Assistant Curator, Division of Cultural History, Smithsonian Institution; Mr. Joseph R. Prentice, Superintendent, Harpers Ferry Historical Site; Mr. Edward M. Riley, Director of Research, Colonial Williamsburg; Mrs. Paul Sais, Assistant Curator, Bucks County Historical Society, Pennsylvania; Dr. Alta Schrock, President, Council of the Alleghenies; Mr. Richard C. Sheridan; Mr. Donald Stewart, Curator, U.S.S. *Constellation*; Miss Ellen Watson, Enoch Pratt Free Library; Mr. John D. Weaver; Mr. Peter C. Welsh, Associate Curator, Department of Civil History, Smithsonian Institution; Mrs. Lura Whiteside Watkins.

Special thanks are due my friends: Helen Chittick, for aid in research; Paul Downing, for checking the section of wheelwrights and coachmakers, which he could do as no one else could; Dorothy Brown, for typing the manuscript twice over—accurately; and to my wife, Lib, for occasionally posing in strange attitudes and for giving suggestions and criticisms without which the illustrations would be worse than they are.

Many thanks are also due The Macmillan Company for permission to redraw and print weaving patterns from *The Shuttle Craft Book of American Weaving* by Mary Meigs Atwater, New York, 1951; and Yale University Library for permission to reproduce its unique proof of Abel Buell's type face.

CONTENTS

COLONIAL
CRAFTSMEN
And the Beginnings of American Industry

Yankee trading brig, about 1750

I.

NEW WORLD, NEW WAYS

HAND CRAFTS changed little during the whole period here very loosely called "colonial," which, for our purposes, is extended from the first settlements to about 1830 when the industrial revolution was developing the muscles that would change the nation. The gradual growth of those muscles is part of this account, though most of it is concerned with the ways of professional artisans in small shops. Details of work and tools are hard to pin down for the first ninety years after Jamestown, and especially for the first fifty years. So you are reading about the eighteenth century here except where other dates are given.

British restrictions and the newness of the country strongly affected the development of crafts and the beginnings of American industry. These forces are briefly and incompletely sketched in this chapter along with some other matters that applied to all of the crafts.

At first the Southern colonies could export tobacco, pine tar, and turpentine—later they added rice, indigo, and cotton—to earn profits in the form of credit in England for buying most of their needs at about three times the normal English prices. So the planters made few things for themselves and needed to have few things made for them locally. Artisans who went south found the pickings slim.

Except for timber, the best of which was commandeered by the British navy, the colonists north of the Mason–Dixon line had at first no export products that England wanted and therefore no credit and no money. They had to make for themselves whatever things they needed. Some of them used skills they learned in Europe; others learned skills they had never expected to need.

The Northern colonist in the 1630's cut and hewed the timber for his house and with the help of his neighbors set it up and pegged it together. He brought little furniture with him, so he built his stools, tables, and beds himself. The settler's wife kept pace with him; she made her own soap and candles, and ground corn by hand for bread. As soon as flax could be grown and sheep raised, she spun linen and wool and wove them into cloth which she sewed into garments for her family. Two earlier books by this writer, *Colonial Living* and *Frontier Living*, discuss the homespun crafts.

As soon as the settlers became a little prosperous, they began to pay the more skillful of their neighbors to make things for them. They paid in goods rather than in money. While any surplus household product might well be sold or bartered, the making of no one thing occupied the whole time of any one householder. As soon as one did, it was a workshop craft. Real skill at any trade comes only with years of full-time work. When we think of the early artisan, we visualize a lone worker bent over his bench personally carrying out every step in the creation of each article he made. There were many such, but most had at least one journeyman helper and an apprentice or two.

British Restrictions

England encouraged her colonists to produce whatever would best serve the interests of her subjects at home and made laws to discourage any colonial production that competed with home trades. Since the American settlers were also loyal subjects, they increasingly resented this discrimination and it finally undermined the loyalty of most of them. England's attitude wasn't considered odd at the time, however shortsighted it may seem now. It was the practical application of a theory known as "mercantilism" which holds that a nation is more important than its parts—or its colonies; that it should try to make everything it uses; that it should strive to sell abroad but not to buy there; and that it should fill its vaults with all the coin it could lay hands on—and keep it.

Some causes and effects of the practical application of the theory went about like this: Wood, often in the form of charcoal, was used as fuel on both sides of the Atlantic Ocean in the seventeenth century and in most of the eighteenth. English forests had been used up, so America was to supply the mother country with fuel and with timber. English ironworkers wanted pig iron from the colonies, smelted here with American charcoal, but they wanted no such nonsense as colonial ironworkers making pots, pans, hinges, and tools from the pig. Such things were to be made overseas, shipped back, and sold for cash. So with wool. The English were sheep raisers and cloth weavers; their European market fell off in the seventeenth century. Obviously the colonies would take up the slack. As late as 1774, the last control law forbade export to this country of tools for making wool cloth. By that time, the colonies north of the Mason-Dixon line were absorbing two-thirds of Britain's colonial trade.

In 1660, the British government published a list of "enumerated articles" which colonials might ship only to British ports. This was contained in the first of the Navigation Acts. Some variation of the list remained in force until the Revolutionary War. It usually included tar, pitch, turpentine, hemp, masts, and spars—all for the navy—and cast pig iron, wrought bar iron, potash, pearl ash, hides—all raw materials for British artisans—and tobacco, which didn't grow well in England.

According to the mercantile system, the colonists were supposed to import only from England, including items like tea which the English imported themselves, and the Americans were expected to pay cash for nearly all they bought. Unfortunately, few legal ways were left for them to get their hands on any money. So they took illegal ways to get it; and what they got, they did their best to keep. They, too, were sound mercantilists. One way they got it was by trade with known pirates; another was by coastal smuggling. But the principal way was by the illicit trade of American ships with interdicted foreign ports. For example, some southern tobacco went quietly to Holland and to France and was bartered for cheese, for printed cottons, for silk, for brandy—all salable for cash in world ports. Rhode Island rum went to Africa to pay for slaves to be sold in the West Indies to buy molasses to make more rum. Molasses was cheaper than rum or slaves, so the ship captain turned over to the owner a satisfactory take of Dutch florins and Spanish dollars. Boston and Salem, avoiding slaves, worked out other successful "three-cornered" trades. Most Americans admired such evasions of the law and abetted them. The fact that John Hancock, when he signed the Declaration with such a flourish, had a price on his head in London as a smuggler did not hurt his position as a respected Boston merchant.

Specialists

A few trained craftsmen came early to America, in fact, on the first boats: Blacksmith James Reed to Jamestown in 1607 with the original group of settlers; Cooper John Alden to Plymouth in 1620 on the *Mayflower*. No one has celebrated Reed in verse, but it was probably he who beat out Captain John Smith's "little chissels" from the bog iron they dredged out of ponds near Jamestown Island.

Every succeeding boat brought artisans of some sort. Those who worked at their trades at all had to farm a little on the side. Quite a few of the settlers who came to Salem and Boston after 1628 had been weavers in England. Some of them worked with imported material until something had been raised that could be spun and woven. Such people had many new skills to learn, even farming itself.

Once life in the colonies showed signs of becoming ordered, people's natural aptitudes led them to full-time work at some trade. Practice improved their skills; so a man who began as a housewright might end as a joiner, paneling the inside walls of houses and building neat staircases. His son might push *his* skill further, becoming a cabinetmaker. He would be apt to move from the home village, to venture a shop in a larger town. A man couldn't get far in a hamlet where most of the surrounding farmers bought absolutely nothing but salt and nails, and quite often made their own nails.

Naturally, most craftsmen—and the best of them—gathered in the coastal commercial centers: Boston, Newport, New York, Philadelphia, with a few, not of first rank, in the south at

Annapolis, Williamsburg, and Charleston. In Boston as early as 1647 there were professional weavers, feltmakers, furriers, ropemakers, brick- and tilemakers, three kinds of leatherworkers, six kinds of woodworkers, and seven kinds of metalworkers. Most of the other towns didn't exist in 1647. The count of a list of men attainted of treason in Philadelphia during the Revolution shows thirty-five different trades. Since there were no Tories named on the list, and there must have been some insurgents who weren't caught, probably more trades than that were practiced there. By the way, merely calling a man "carpenter" or "chandler" didn't mean that he still worked at his trade. Whatever he did later, he remained John Smith, carpenter, or William Jones, chandler, for life.

A country artisan usually owned his house and farm, and worked at his trade in a shop out back. In a town of some size, the shop was on the first floor of a house that was likely to be rented. If his trade was a dirty one or if it required a forge, the craftsman's workshop was in the back yard and only the sales room was behind the front door. The family lived and slept on the upper floor or floors, and cooked and ate in the cellar or in a kitchen built on to the house.

Status

Social position was a great matter to our ancestors but it wasn't so rigidly fixed as it was in England. A smart, industrious American could get ahead not only financially but socially as well, particularly if he joined the "right" church and married the right girl. As a result, craftsmen penetrated every social level, but in the main, "substantial artisans" stood near the middle of the social structure. Such men were also called "mechanicks," defined as those whose work made "more use of the Hand and the Body than of the Mind." Semi-skilled laborers such as sawyers were inferior mechanicks. When the artisans became the moving spirits of the Sons of Liberty in the early 1770's, the Tories called them all—from Paul Revere down—base mechanicks.

Except for the voice the New England town meeting gave to every householder in strictly local affairs, the run of citizens had no chance of choosing their government. In most of the colonies only those who owned at least fifty acres of land or fifty pounds' worth of personal property could vote, a privilege that had little chance of affecting their welfare. The thirteen colonies were actually run by thirteen cliques of wealthy gentlemen strictly for their own benefit. In part, the people approved of this: tradition and education made the gentry the natural rulers, but, though some of them preferred reform under the Crown, the substantial artisans wanted the right to pick their own gentlemen. It was to gain this point that most trades workers plumped for Independence.

How important were these artisans? How many of them were there? The careful estimates of careful men put them at about eighteen per cent in a total 1770 population of a shade over two million—a solid 360,000. Eighty per cent of Americans were farmers, widely scattered and hard to organize. That other two per cent were gentlemen. The mechanicks were grouped in towns and villages close to the sources of news and were all known to one another in any one locality. They could organize and, not very convincingly disguised as "Mohocks," they could heave a couple of cargoes of tea into Boston's Fort Point Channel.

The Apprentice System

In England a labor surplus made any apprenticeship there a very desirable thing. The master was in a strong position. He could demand that a boy serve seven years; he could rigidly enforce discipline; and, in addition to the menial services he demanded of the novice, he could exact a cash premium from the parents who "bound out" the boy.

At no time was there enough labor in early America. Masters gladly took apprentices at no charge, both the voluntary kind whose parents offered them and the compulsory kind, the orphaned and the illegitimate, who were bound out by the town to ease the poor rates. Few Americans served seven years; five or four were more usual, and sometimes the boy shortened that term by running away as Ben Franklin did.

Somebody was always advertising in the newspapers for a missing apprentice.

The contract, called the indenture, enjoined the boy to behave himself and "faithfully his said Master shall serve, his secrets keep, his lawfull [sic] commands at all Times readily Obey . . ." The master agreed to teach the apprentice his "mystery"—this word still appeared in legal documents but wasn't much used in speech; it

meant simply trade, nothing weird—to feed him, lodge him, dress him, and keep his clothes washed. At the end of his term the lad became a journeyman and was given "custom of country"—usually a new suit, four shirts, and two necklets. Compulsory apprentices didn't come off quite so well.

Normally a master agreed to allow his apprentice to attend an evening school at the parents' charge or sometimes at the master's; in fact, some masters personally taught their 'prentices to read, write, and cipher. Most towns had evening schools. They were privately run and gave only "useful instruction," avoiding the Latin and Greek offered by the public schools. In addition to the three R's, some evening schools taught "Merchants accompts" and even went on into higher mathematics and surveying.

Bad masters were all too frequent, though the courts sturdily backed any abused apprentice who could manage to get a case before them. On the other hand, the boys did little to make life easy for "the Old Man." They seldom had been consulted when they were indentured and many lacked any interest in, or aptitude for, the trade they learned. So, in addition to the habit of vanishing in the night, they tended to be lazy and wild. It's no pleasant description that a New York printer left us, early in the 1730's, in his advertisement for a runaway: ". . . pretty much pitted with the Small Pox, wears his own hair, and is much bloated by drinking, to which he is most uncommonly addicted."

Journeymen

The English guilds required a journeyman to submit a "master-piece" before he could hope to start in business for himself. An echo of this survived in America. A master sometimes demanded an "apprenticepiece," often a miniature, before he would countersign the indenture to make the novice a journeyman. The apprentice was then free to work at his trade wherever he pleased. The master hoped to keep him in the shop and often did, but just as often the new journeyman took to the road, working awhile where his fancy led him to tarry or where he ran out of funds.

On any job he took, the journeyman had to put in twelve hours of hard work six days a week; in some trades it ran to fourteen, even sixteen, hours. This was more tiring physically than eight hours of work at a machine, but it was also more interesting. It didn't make a robot of a man. He knew what he was doing and why he was doing it; he performed the whole process of what he was making, from start to finish. He could take pride in his work.

The journeyman who wasn't stupid, or wasn't a dedicated bum, had always ahead the goal of working for himself. Wages were high and usually included board and lodging, so it wasn't too hard to save money. As soon as he accumulated a few pounds, he could set up as a master in his own shop. The average wage of a journeyman in all trades stayed fairly constant through the eighteenth century; abut 1760 it seems to have been near fifteen shillings a week and keep. The chancy method of averaging several old estimates and inflating the result up to date makes fifteen shillings worth $20.50 in today's money.

Some enterprises required the co-operative efforts of a number of men. Slaves worked in many group industries—more of them in the

South, of course, than in the North—and at other trades, also. They became skilled iron founders, brickmakers, carpenters. A Southern plantation owner would often hire a white journeyman cooper, carpenter, or blacksmith, and keep him just so long as it took an intelligent slave to learn his trade. Some slaves were apprenticed and became expert weavers, tailors, joiners, even cabinetmakers; and in Charleston, Williamsburg, and Annapolis, their owners hired them out at a lower wage than a white journeyman would accept.

Masters

The independent craftsman had his troubles. He was not only a manufacturer, he was also a retailer and up against strong competitors with whom he often carried on bitterly sarcastic wars of words at a personal level in the newspapers. He was chronically short of help; one of the causes of the newspaper feuds was the raiding of one man's labor force by the other. The whole of his work force commonly lived under the master's roof as one big, but not necessarily happy, family. It was the master's responsibility to settle the disputes of his men, to spring them from "gaol" when they got into trouble, and to see to it that they showed up at the church on Sunday.

The master was his own purchasing agent, hunting out scarce raw materials and haggling over prices. He discussed custom work with buyers, laid out and supervised the work of his helpers, and in his spare time did his own part of the work at the bench. His wife ran her complicated household and was almost invariably—and ably—the sales department. Widows often kept little shops of their own and many of them successfully continued their late husbands' pursuits.

In small towns and, for some specialties, everywhere, there simply was not enough demand to support full-time work. The artisan had to have a side line or two. Even quite large and successful operations did this. There was either a second related trade, as when a cabinetmaker made coffins and conducted funerals, or a related business, as when a bookbinder was also a bookseller and possibly sold buttons and buckles, too. Benjamin Franklin sold books and stationery in his highly successful printshop, and also made ink to sell to printers in other colonies.

The master was faced with matters of credit and collections in addition to his other responsibilities. Credit accounts ran on for years and, if they were ever paid up, the creditor had to accept all sorts of things instead of cash. This custom was so universal that artisans often advertised their willingness to take "country pay," that is—farm produce. Old advertisements reveal such oddities as a silversmith offering for sale a cheese or some hams; he was only trying to turn his assets into cash.

In England no craftsman could set up in business until the guild of his trade licensed him. Even then he was supervised by the guild, which could legally condemn inferior workmanship and materials. Early efforts to start guilds in this country all died on the vine. There was no place for them in the ferment of the New World; they belonged to an old and rigid way of life, supported by a vast excess of labor. The Moravian Brethren at Bethlehem, Pennsylvania, and at Wachovia, North Carolina, did manage to maintain a successful guild system under their strict religious discipline. It lasted some twenty-five years—until 1762.

Quality and Honesty

Though the frayed joke about the antique chair that collapses under a guest has its origin in fact—joints do loosen and wood does dry out—much old furniture is worth cherishing not only because it is beautiful but also because it is sturdy. This would seem to suggest that all handmade articles were strong and beautiful. But that is far from the truth. There was plenty of sloppy workmanship and enough of bad taste, but most of the examples of both have disappeared for obvious reasons. Good stuff, too, has been lost through accident and ignorance, but some survives that is sound and fine, and a little of it is almost unequaled.

Dishonest manufacturers and tradesmen exist today and national as well as local regulations try to keep them in line. The control ordinances were all local in early times, but their number leaves no doubt that cheating and adulteration were as rife in the three centuries preceding this one as they are now. False weight, undersized casks, misrepresented goods, constantly plagued buyers and officials. Honest craftsmen sometimes waged one-man campaigns within their own trades by publicly printing names and facts in their advertising.

Prices

The Quakers "had a concern" that the price of merchandise should be its cost plus an honest profit; their goods were for sale at such a price—no more, no less. Until this radical idea was gradually accepted, all sales involved contests of wits between buyer and seller, contests that wasted time and usually ended in a draw.

The long lists of early commodity prices given in scholarly studies need not be repeated here. It seems better to concentrate on an article of food and one of clothing which have stayed nearly the same in form through the years: cheese and shoes. In Salem, in 1630, ordinary rat cheese had a value in today's money of twenty-two cents a pound; by 1775, it had fallen to nine cents a pound; a 1964 quotation from the local store on the same kind—real cheese, not "processed"—is $1.00 a pound. A Salem goodman paid $1.23 in 1630 for a pair of good shoes lasted to his size and sewn together by hand; such a pair was up to $1.64 by 1700, and cost twice that during the Revolutionary War when all prices rose. Comparable machine-made shoes, though the leather isn't as good, now cost ten dollars or more. Admittedly these are vague comparisons which would be sharper if they were based throughout on how much labor was needed to pay for the cheese and the shoes.

A brass mold, made about 1800, for casting silver or pewter buttons four at a time, complete with pierced shanks. When the pivoted halves meet, the bevels on them form a trough to receive the molten metal which runs into the button-shaped cavities and hardens there.

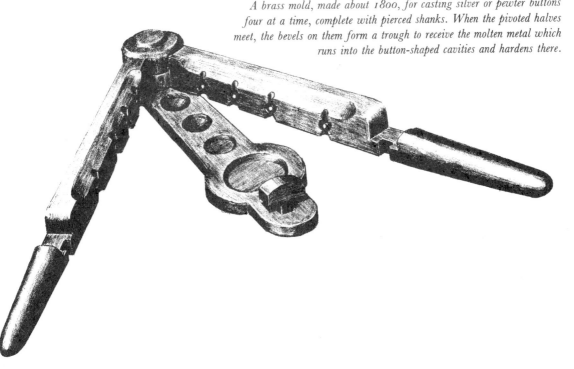

2.

COUNTRY WORK

IT IS almost true that there were no villages in the Southern plantation country. Even a county seat might be no more than the court house, a church, a blacksmith shop, and perhaps an "ordinary"—an inn where one ate what was put before him. In time the big plantations became nearly self-sufficient, villages themselves in effect. Small planters turned to the plantation workers for things they couldn't do themselves.

In the North the earliest villages were set up deliberately by the authorities, some of them so soon that the settlers' feet were hardly dry from wading ashore. Even as far south as Maryland, a few settlements owed their being to edict. But villages commonly appeared spontaneously where they were needed; often they grew up around grist mills. Overland travel was arduous; overland hauling was worse; so settlements always started near navigable water. Large ships could get to some inland villages and in time many of those became towns and cities. Those on smaller streams depended upon long narrow boats called gundalows. These had lateen sails to use when they could, but men pushed them with poles when the wind failed.

Planned New England villages spread themselves about open commons where the householders grazed livestock; elsewhere, settlements grew in a familiar pattern—a High Street, the main street, with three or four cross streets. Completely innocent of paving, these were rutted and either muddy or dusty. Time and use extended them into the countryside as roads that eventually joined those of neighboring centers. In the seventeenth century, while some houses were whitewashed, none were painted; few were in the first half of the eighteenth century. Grass grew in the streets and weeds flourished along fences; the lawnmower was unborn and lawns were mown as fields were—with scythes.

Small places seldom displayed shop signs to tell strangers where to buy: the residents knew and few strangers inquired. Only the ordinary was likely to be marked. Farmers came to the village on Saturday to trade and confabulate and on Sunday to church. As they prospered, these men and their wives found more and more articles and services that they needed to buy in the village, and their needs attracted residents to the place to fill them.

In so sparsely populated a center, strict craft specialization wasn't possible; almost everybody doubled in brass. The miller might also run the general store; the doctor, if there was one, might own a sawmill, might be the local slave trader, or might even do a little barbering on the side. So with the artisans, almost all of them had to work at more than one trade or have some kind of secondary activity—if it was only operating a ferry. Not all who served the local farmers lived in the village or near it. Each spring brought a tide of itinerants who went directly to the farms to sell their wares or to ply their trades.

The Blacksmith

He has been called the most important of American artisans because few men had the ability to do his work for themselves and because he was essential to many enterprises. He will turn up later in special aspects of his trade. It is largely as a specialist, calling himself anything but blacksmith, that he survives today. Mostly, the village smithy is gone, along with its famous chestnut tree, but a few old shops still do country work.

One of them carries on not far from where this is being written. Though only a father and his son have worked there, the forge fire has burned for more than a hundred years. The present smith has lost most of his hearing, but none of his skill. Wearing the leather apron of his ancestors, he stood recently at his forge, heating a two-inch-thick bar. A waiting farmer wagged his head. "Old man's failin', gettin' pretty feeble." As he spoke, Mr. Brent swung his glowing bar across the hardy and halved it with three hammer blows. Try it.

The forge, not the building, made the smithy. Stone more often than brick was used for forge,

chimney, and even the hood that spread above the fire. The base of the structure was a flat-topped masonry block two and a half feet high, with the square fire hole on top, a little in front of its center. A grate, set in the hole, held charcoal, and the opening continued a foot or so below it as an ash pit, reached through an iron door on one side of the base. Another hole entered from the back, just below the level of the grate. Cemented into this was a tapered nozzle called the "tue iron" after the tuyère of a smelting furnace, through which an air blast blew the fire to intense heat.

Sledge and flattening hammers

Today Mr. Brent's tue iron delivers a gale from a motor-driven fan; even portable forges have hand-cranked fans. The early smith blew his fire with a bellows large enough to need a whole ox hide for its lung. Closely spaced big-headed nails attached the leather to the pitch-smeared edges of the two wooden leaves of the bellows. These leaves were more than an inch thick. Round on their wide ends and tapering toward the tue iron, they were some six feet long and three and a half feet across their widest dimension. The usual but by no means invariable way of rigging a bellows was to attach its upper leaf to the underside of a crossbeam set between two posts. Raising the lower leaf pleated the leather and expelled air to blow the fire; released, the leaf fell again by its own weight. As it fell, it inhaled through a six-inch hole in the

Hardy

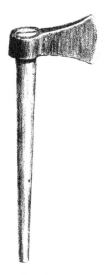

17th-century felling ax

wood. A square of heavy leather, tacked on the inside along one edge only, covered the hole and acted as a flap valve. The handle end of a long shaft, hung in reach of the man at the forge—often it was literally a shaft taken from a discarded cart—swiveled near its thick end above the bellows. A light chain or a leather thong connected that end with a lug on the lower leaf of the bellows. When the smith pulled the handle down, he blew his fire; when he released it, the lung sucked air. Most blacksmiths set a helper, known as the blower-and-striker, to do the pulling.

The anvil stood about four feet in front of the forge, a convenient reach with long tongs. It was a heavy mass of forged iron resting on the butt of a log set in the earthen floor. It commonly lined up with the left-hand edge of the forge as the smith faced the fire. The anvil has hardly changed its essential shape in two thousand years: a spreading base, a rectangular core for flatting, a tapered beak over which iron can be bent, and a square hole in the core for the tangs of various tools, the most important being the hardy or hack iron, a short chisel that cuts upward as the smith hammers hot iron down upon it.

Once he had his anvil, the blacksmith could make all his other tools. He could also make for the farmer a hoe, a plowshare, or a cowbell.

Early 18th-century felling ax

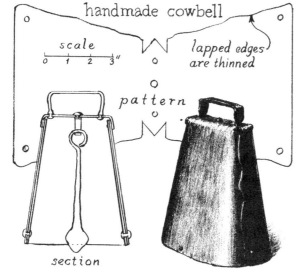

handmade cowbell

scale
0 1 2 3"

lapped edges are thinned

pattern

section

He could make an awl for the cobbler, a scraper for the tanner, a plane blade for the joiner.

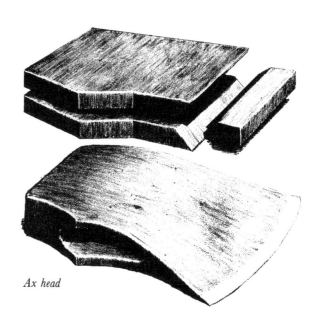

Ax head

Probably he made nothing finer than the American ax. The ax of the earliest settlers had a long narrow blade and a straight handle. The head was iron, hardened as well as could be managed; it had no poll or hammer end whatever. Somewhere around 1700, the Americans added a square poll without changing the shape of the blade. This ax was still iron. Steel was rare and costly even in the 1780's when it began to be used for the cutting edges of axes. It was then that the blade was widened and shortened, helpful curves were added to the helve, and it became, to Europeans, "the American ax." Its shape has been slightly modified and its whole head is now forged steel. In the early 1800's, English ironmongers often falsely labeled their axes "American" to sell them more readily.

To make an ax head, the 1780 blacksmith cut two flat pieces of iron to its approximate shape. He made the two identical except for bevels, opposed on the blade edges to form an acute V-shaped channel when the two halves were joined back to back. Into the fire went the poll ends of the two pieces; the blower pumped; the smith poked the coal. A word, and blower became striker as the smith seized both pieces together and moved them, white-hot and incandescent, to the flat top of the anvil. The striker hit them repeatedly with a sledge, and the softened metal fused, welding the two halves of the poll into one piece.

The American ax

The welding was repeated on the blade end, but the men were careful not to close the seam where the eye for the helve would be and not to disturb the channel along the edge. Into it they inserted a sliver of hot steel and welded it there. The ax head was now a flat blank. Heat and hammer blows thinned it and gave a slight arc to its margin. A tapered swage, driven between the two layers, opened and shaped the narrow eye. The whole ax head was then heated red hot and plunged into cold water. This hardened the iron, but it made the steel brittle, so the smith tempered it. He heated the edge, watching its color as it warmed. Pale straw color deepened with more heat to a strong yellow, then darkened to brown. When purple spots appeared in the brown, the steel had reached 510° F., and the smith quenched it again in water. It was still hard—only scissors, razors, and files were harder—but it was now also tough.

The helve of this ax was hickory or ash, both strong and springy, shaped by hand to nice, experience-tested curves. An expertly made ax handle is slender; it has a slight whip that seems to lighten the work of using it. Robert Frost has described it better. Such a helve is a rare thing now. The slotted head-end of the handle fits the eye and a thin wedge, driven into the slot, expands the handle in the eye and holds it there.

Shoeing

Forge tongs

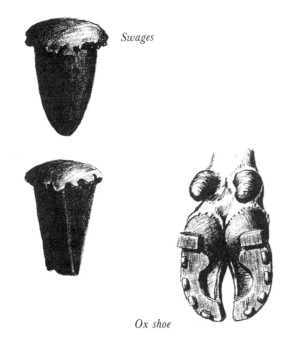

Swages

Ox shoe

The country blacksmith was invariably a farrier. This word is used now only to designate a shoer of horses, but in earlier times, a farrier also shod oxen and was expert in the diseases of animals, though not, of course, a trained veterinarian. Any good smith could also pull an aching tooth for a neighbor. Most of the smith's practice *was* horseshoeing, however. He made all his shoes complete from the bar, shaping them, turning down the heels, turning up the little toe piece, and punching holes in them for nails. He made his own shoeing nails, too, from eked-out rods of soft Swedish iron.

The smith selected the right size shoes for each horse, reshaped them at the forge to a perfect fit and pressed each one, hot, against the horny wall of the hoof, burning it to complete contact. This created a lot of smoke but didn't hurt the horse. The nails were driven through the punched holes in the shoe and upward through the hoof wall, then nipped off, and "clinched over."

Ox shoes are made in two pieces because of the animal's cloven hoofs. A horse stands easily on three legs while the smith holds the fourth between his knees to fasten a shoe in place, but an ox has to be held up in an elaborate sling because three of his small feet will not support his great weight.

The Cooper

Though a farmer could hollow out a tree trunk to make a useful barrel called a gum, it was a long laborious job, and since he needed many barrels and also tubs and pails, he bought them from the village cooper whenever he could. He stored flour, corn meal, and threshed grain in dry or "slack" barrels; in wet ones, he kept molasses, maple syrup, cider, beer, salt meat, and salt fish; rum and gunpowder went into kegs. Coopers made all three kinds and, in addition, made wash tubs, pails, and piggins, which were small pails with one stave left much longer than the rest, shaped to serve as a handle. There's not much you can do with a piggin in the twentieth century.

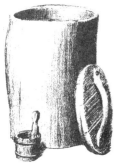

A gum and a piggin

It's a fair guess that in the South there were more coopers than any other kind of artisan. Tobacco was pressed into coopered hogsheads. These were slack and cylindrical, without the bulging midriff of a barrel, hence they required no expert workmanship. Plantation slaves learned to make them. But the South had other needs for barrels, strong watertight ones. Professionals made them in the towns for shipping rice, indigo, tar, turpentine, rosin, molasses, and salt meat.

The northern and middle Atlantic farmers rived oak barrel staves as winter work and tried to supply the cooper with at least enough to pay for the barrels he made for them. Barrel staves and larger pipe staves in the rough were among the earliest exports of the colonies. The froe they used for riving was a splitting tool, a thick wedge-shaped blade which they drove downward along the grain of the wood. The illustration on page 24 shows one in use. An 1836 account mentions curved froes for riving staves. The writer hasn't tried one, or even seen one, but he has split a lot of wood and he doubts that a curved froe will do what is hoped for it. Wood has its own ideas about how it will split.

Drawknives

outside

inside

The cooper, working on a shingle horse, cut the necessary transverse arc into a barrel stave with curved drawknives, one for the outside and one for the inside. An ordinary drawknife served to rough out the angled sides of the staves. These had to be finished precisely and beveled to the radii of the barrel. The job needed experience and a sharp eye. The cooper did it by pulling the stave edges across the blade of a fixed jointer plane more than five feet long. It was set, sloping and blade-up, on legs. The barrelmaker stood a set of shaped staves on end inside a stout truss hoop, adjustable and held to size by pegs in matching holes. Confined at their lower ends, the tapered staves flared outward at the top like the petals of an opening flower. The rope of a cooper's windlass, passed around their tops, bent them and pulled them evenly together when the crank was turned, and the first of the permanent hoops went on their upper ends to hold them.

Cooper's jointer

The cooper then removed the rope and drove the hoop downward with a mallet and a wooden drift to tighten the staves against one another. Smaller hoops went on above the first and the barrel was turned bottom-up to complete the hooping.

The ends of the staves stayed rough until they were hooped; then the cooper trimmed off the too long ones with his hand adz and smoothed all of the ends with a sun plane, curved sideways to do the job. A special planelike cutter called a howel, riding the newly evened ends and guided by a curved fence bearing against the inner curve of the barrel, beveled the "chines" on the inner edges of both ends. Barrels had heads, and the cooper cut grooves just inside the ends of the barrel below the chines to hold them. The tools for this were guided by the barrel itself, as the howel was. First, there was a curious little saw with an arched blade set with only a few coarse teeth. These made a shallow cut which the croze, again guided by the barrel's curve, gouged out to a V-shaped groove. The name croze was given to the groove also.

Assembling the staves of a barrel

Sun plane

Hand adz

Kerfing saw

or chestnut. The cooper notched these with nice judgment on opposite ends and edges so he could lap them and hook them together, tucking the nibs between hoop and barrel where the squeeze would hold them in place. The staves of wet barrels were almost an inch thick, but those for slack or dry barrels could be much thinner and of softer wood; nor did slack barrel hoops have to be so tough—birch or cedar would do.

The staves of pails and churns were usually cedar. A pail tapered from top to bottom and a churn from bottom to top. The cooper made them much as he made a barrel and put their bottoms into a croze, but since neither bulged in the middle, both were easier to make.

The White Cooper

He was found in towns rather than in villages but he, too, was called cooper, so he shall be dealt with here. He made grain measures, firkins, sieves, and boxes out of wide strips of bass or poplar shaved thin. These strips he rolled into cylindrical drums and riveted in shape with tacks. Bands of the same material surrounded the ends as hoops. Bottoms for boxes and measures were thin wooden disks tacked into place and lids were similarly made. The bottom of a sieve or temse could be covered with crossed wires or with a piece of stiff sheepskin perforated with a red-hot iron point. White coopers also made military drums. Though it was certainly not coosering, they made small fireplace bellows, too, and shaped thick wooden soles for the clogs that farmers wore in the field.

Croze

To make the heads, the cooper doweled together the edges of a couple of boards, used big compasses to scratch out two circles on the resulting wide surface, and then sawed them out. His hand adz served to bevel the heads all the way around on both sides. Then he sprung them into their crozes with mallet blows. This finished the job, except for a bunghole in one head and usually a spy hole in one side of the barrel. These he bored with a cross-handled auger and reamed to a taper with a pod auger. Tapered plugs were made to close them.

By 1800 and perhaps earlier, riveted iron hoops began to be used on some wet barrels. Before that, hoops were thin strips split out of hickory

Compass

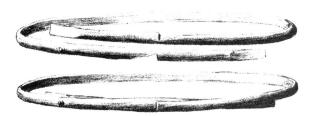

Temse

Pod auger

Hewing and adzing

logs right on the spot. He often did so long after sawmills were common, simply because it was easier than hauling to the mill and back. A "balk line" along the top of the log showed the hewer how much wood to remove. He snapped it on with a stretched string charged with keel (red ocher). The log lay, braced, across two others to keep it clear of the ground and the hewer started his work by scoring across the bark rather deeply along its right side. He did this with an ordinary felling ax, standing on the timber to work. The same ax split off two-foot slabs between the scores.

An inch or so of wood remained outside the balk line and the hewer "stood down" on the ground to remove it with his broadax. Once more he scored the face of the wood across the grain with a series of back cuts, as he called them. Then, with the log on his left, he "hewed to the line," not splitting but cutting the wood away with downward strokes. He had to hold his broad blade parallel to the line for this and, to save his knuckles, the short helve of the ax was doglegged to the right. The blade of a felling ax is ground on both sides so that its edge is on the center line, but the broadax is ground only on one side, so its bezeled edge slopes one way, like that of a chisel.

An expert squared a sixteen-foot timber in a couple of hours. The surface he left was somewhat irregular and the marks of the back cuts showed on it. If its use in the building would conceal it entirely, it was finished no further. But if it was to be an exposed post or beam, as many were exposed in the seventeenth century, the builder carefully dressed its surface with an adz. This tool can be described as a hoe-shaped chisel with a straight ax-length helve. A dangerous tool to use, since it was kept as sharp as a chisel and the user, standing on his work, cut toward his toes.

The Housewright

In a large town the carpenter who framed the house was one man and the joiner who did the finish work on it was another, but in the country, the same man usually did both jobs and also did glazing, masonry, and coffinmaking. The trades of housewright and joiner are separated here chiefly to keep their tools distinct.

Through most of the seventeenth century, houses in America were like the late Gothic dwellings that were still being built in northern Europe. Such a house was fairly satisfactory for the American South but not for the North. Its dense walls and thin roof leaked heat; its huge chimney removed much warmth along with the smoke from a cavernous fireplace which itself trapped heat instead of radiating it into the room.

Changes of taste in England after 1650 only slowly reached the colonies and, when they did arrive, they took a long time to affect the appearance of ordinary houses. Country carpenters worried not at all about taste or styles. They did their work as they had learned it and they taught their sons the same ways, so houses changed slowly. Even after 1700, when a more formal style, the one we casually call Colonial, began to spread, the methods of building remained the same. They hardly changed even by the 1840's when modern balloon construction was introduced. Balloon building—light timbers nailed together—really took hold only after it served for quick reconstruction following the Chicago Fire of 1871.

Oak timbers framed the early American house. The carpenter hewed them square from

Broadax

Chalk-line reel

Adz

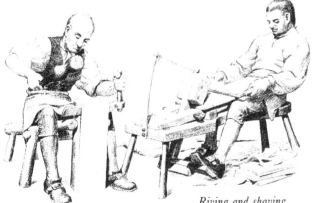

Riving and shaving

The housewright cut all the timbers for a house to size, and jointed and assembled them on the ground, a whole side at a time. Then he called in a gang of men to raise the frame with long poles called pikes. Pikes are still used to set up utility poles. But before he could joint and assemble, the carpenter had to cut his timbers to length with a cross-cut saw. The one he used most was narrow-bladed and framed like a modern bucksaw; he also had a wide-bladed saw of standard shape, but its handle would look odd to a modern workman.

Mortise and tenon

Most of the posts needed to have tenons on both ends, and the carpenter had to allow for them in his measurements. A tenon is a projecting tongue of wood to be inserted into a matching mortise cut into the timber to which the tenoned piece is to be joined. Since each mortise and tenon made a fitted pair, the carpenter scratched an identical number on each with a hook-bladed tool called a race knife. Once the two were joined, he used a cross-handled auger to bore straight through both pieces and then pinned them together with a "trunnel" (tree-nail) driven into the hole. His apprentice put in endless hours shaping treenails with a hatchet.

The housewright called on the blacksmith for the parts of his tools that had to be iron; all other parts he made himself. His square was all wood, brought to accuracy with an ancient formula: if the base is six parts, the altitude eight, and the hypotenuse ten, then the base-altitude angle will be ninety degrees. The carpenter made his own level, too—an arched affair with a plumb bob hanging under the crown to a mark on the base exactly below the suspension point. A fancier one had a guarded recess for the bob so it wouldn't swing around too much. The spirit level was invented about 1660, but it had to wait seventy years for glass tubes accurate enough to make it practical.

25

Wooden mallets and short-handled mauls served for treenail driving, but the eighteenth-century carpenter had a claw hammer for driving and pulling iron nails. Its head lacked the extended eye of a modern hammer and hence frequently "flew off the handle." Curiously, the adz always had such an extension.

The builder stiffened his house frame with corner braces angled between posts and beams, and spaced vertical studs from sill to girt between the posts. When the frame was up, he filled the spaces between studs with nogging. Sometimes this was stone and clay; more often it was brick in lime mortar. This nogging was probably exposed on the outside of some very early houses as it was on English half-timber houses. In the colder climate of America, an outside covering of clapboards was soon added. As time passed, the nogging gave way to a layer of sheathing boards under the clapboards which, by trapping air, made a warmer house. Outside walls stuffed with dry seaweed were not unknown.

Seventeenth-century clapboards were split radially from four-foot logs with a froe and put on rough. Later, sawmills cut them in longer pieces and planes dressed them smooth. Roof shingles, too, were split with a froe and at first were also put on rough as shakes. Again refinement set in. Old men tapered the shakes into true shingles, holding them on shingle horses and shaving them with drawknives. Sheathing a roof with boards before putting on shingles is quite a new idea. Our ancestors fastened enough horizontal strips called purlins across the rafters to give them "nailing" and let it go at that. Daylight often showed through cracks in the roof.

Corner of a house frame

Auger

Handsaws

Square

Level

Clawhammer

The Sawyers

Small studding timbers, and boards for flooring and wainscoting, were sawn from logs that had first been squared with a broadax. Sawyers, working by hand in pairs, cut most of them well into the eighteenth century. Sawyer was a recognized craft, but there's evidence that its journeymen did more with their arms than with their brains.

Though small batches ripped at building sites were often sawn on high trestles in the medieval way, most sawyers worked in narrow pits with the timber resting on transverse rollers. Permanent pits were lined with brick and had level sills let into their top courses for the rollers to ride on. Holes through the rollers allowed them to be turned with a bar to move the balk endwise. The leader of the team, the top sawyer, stood on the timber and guided the saw along a snapped-on line. He also pulled the saw up so that the pitman below could pull it down again for the cutting stroke. The pitman swabbed the saw occasionally with linseed oil. Each cut was stopped a little short of the end of the timber. This kept the planks in place so the top sawyer would have something to stand on until the last one was sawn.

Common pit saw

The whipsaw, or sash saw, with a thin narrow blade stretched in a wooden frame, goes back at least to Roman times. Though called common,

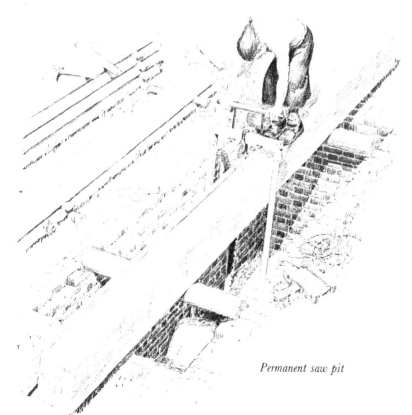

Permanent saw pit

the thicker wide-bladed pit saw, with a "tiller" handle at the top and an easily removable "box" handle at the bottom, seems to have been still something of a novelty in 1700. The whipsaw cut more freely, but the broad saw held to its line more steadily and could be conveniently pulled from the kerf.

Water-powered and wind-powered sawmills duplicated the action of a sash saw, with a crank and a connecting rod—known as a pitman, of course—to move the saw up and down. As it moved, it hit the operating arm of a ratchet wheel which inched the timber carriage against the saw teeth. Such mills operated in New England at least as early as 1633. Gang saws, with two or three blades set parallel in the sash to cut several boards at once, appeared in Maine in 1650. There was no further improvement in sawmills until the circular saw was introduced in 1814. The whole countryside came to look at the "round saw" that the clockmaker Eli Terry installed in his factory in 1816.

The Joiner

John Alden was ship's cooper on the *Mayflower*. Perhaps there was something about Priscilla Mullins that led him to jump ship and set up as joiner and, no doubt, as carpenter, too, in the wilderness. No known work of his survives, but he was the first of many. A joiner worked hard. His boards didn't come to him all dressed from a planing mill, but rough-sawn from the pit; he had to dress the showing faces of them with planes, by hand. The razor-sharp blade of a plane projects just slightly and evenly from a slot in the flat sole of the tool which, riding the surface of the board, keeps the edge from digging in and cutting too deeply. The plane thus removes a shaving of constant thickness. Any forming of an edge, from a simple half-round bead to a molding three or four inches wide, the joiner had to cut with a specially shaped plane. As a result, he usually owned—quite literally—a barrelful of wooden planes. Except for their irons (blades), he made them himself—of maple, as a rule. He shaped the block, long or short, according to its purpose, and pierced it with a hole, wide at the top and tapering downward to the blade slot at the bottom. At the back of the

26

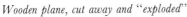

Wooden plane, cut away and "exploded"

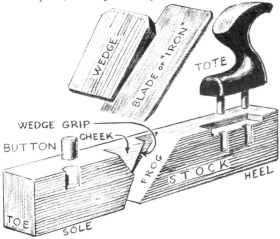

hole he cut a sloping "frog" to receive the blade and the wedge that held it. Wedges were the wing nuts and set screws of early times. Striking the top of the plane's stock near its front would loosen the wedge for changing the depth of cut, and a tough plug was inset there to take the blows. The handle of a plane, called the "tote," stood behind the blade; it was originally merely a hook for hanging up the tool. The cap iron, or back iron, which curled shavings to keep the blade from clogging, was added only some ten

STANDARD BLOCK PLANES

JACK PLANE *for rough work: 17 inches long; blade edge curved slightly; always set "rank" (deep)*

TRYING PLANE *or* SHORT JOINTER *used for smoothing boards and "shooting" (squaring) edges: 20 inches long*

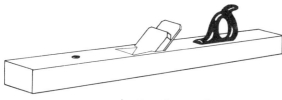

LONG JOINTER *for smoothing floors and dressing long boards: 30 inches long*

SMOOTHING PLANE, *7 inches long, boat-shaped, for trimming*

years before Mr. H. Knowles, in 1827, made the first cast-iron plane stock, with a screw to hold a slotted blade. The first back iron was merely an old blade face-down.

The joiner's four standard planes appear on this page. The jack plane, which gouged wood down to size, had a slightly curved blade; this made it cut faster but it left tool marks to be removed by the trying plane or short jointer. The long jointer took high spots from floors after they were laid; its great length kept it from creating hollows. The ill-named "smoothing" plane was for tight corners and small work. Most of the planes that filled the joiner's barrel were rabbet planes with profiled cutters and soles for special shapes. A rabbet plane was narrow as a rule and had a guiding fence along its left-hand side.

Rabbet plane

Joiner's clamp

Marking gauge

Molding plane

The early joiner covered a fireplace wall, or most of it, with vertical wainscot boards and constructed all interior partitions of them. Sometimes he carried the wainscot full height around the window walls, too, but there he more often reduced it to chair-rail height and plastered the wall above, even if the plaster had to be clay because there was no lime. These wainscot boards were shiplapped. At first the joiners contented themselves with a simple bead on one edge, but soon they went into elaborate moldings, using a plane that took so wide a cut that an apprentice had to tow it with a rope while the master pushed and guided it. The joiner first roughed out such a big molding with smaller planes.

A job like this had to be held firmly on the workbench. Vises were known but hard to come by because the wooden screws that tightened them had to be carved by hand and few were competent to do it. The joiner used a catch

All-wood brace with fixed bit

Bow drill

Hold-down and catch

against the end of a board to resist the plane's push and a hold-down to keep the board from slipping sideways. Both went into holes in his workbench. The catch was merely a tanged iron block with one sharp edge to bear against the wood. The hold-down, or hold-fast, was shaped like the figure 7; its head part reached over the board, its tail angled into the square oversized bench hole and was jammed tight in it by a hammer blow.

17th-century staircase

Shiplap and bead

The carpenter–joiner had stairways to build. Even the earliest seventeeth-century houses used their attics as sleeping quarters for boys. The narrow stairs to these were at one time entirely enclosed behind wainscot, but before 1650 artisans opened them up and provided handrails capping short balusters which stood on a slanting stringpiece that hid the ends of the steps. The joiner probably turned the balusters himself on a spring-pole or back-action lathe in his shop. He operated this by pressing down on a foot treadle to spin the lathe and then allowing the spring of an overhead pole to raise the treadle again. Rotation was discontinuous, but men who have run such a lathe say it is easy to get used to this and good work can certainly be done on one.

Making window frames and sash was also part of a joiner's work. Up to 1700, windows were all small casements, about a foot wide and two feet high, glazed with leaded glass. Most people placed the sashes in pairs or triplets and hinged not more than a third of them to open. The

Dovetail joint

much-flawed glass was less than a sixteenth of an inch thick. It was cut into small panes called quarrels and was held between calmes, strips of lead, which were heated with the glass in place to make them grip it. Many of these casements still served in 1776, but almost none of them survived the Continental Army's requisitions of lead for bullets.

Early houses in Philadelphia and the Wren Building at Williamsburg, built in the late 1600's, had "modern" sliding sash windows with larger panes of glass held in wooden muntins instead of in lead. As they became increasingly popular, joiners had to learn to make the special frames they required. Only the lower sash moved as a rule and it had to be propped to stay open; very few windows had sash weights. The joiners put tenons on the ends of muntins and held the corners of the sash together with dowels.

Village joiners frequently made simple furniture that involved no fancy curved pieces, but they justified their name by "joining" the parts with ingeniously planned mortises and tenons and with nicely accurate dovetails. Since houses rarely had clothes closets, the joiner's principal product was chests: at first simple, lidded boxes; then boxes with a drawer or two under them; then boxes that were all drawers. Panels, carving, and painted decorations ornamented the earlier ones. Few of these men ever signed their work, but in Hartford, sometime in the late 1600's, one of them did scratch inside a box he made: "Mary Allyns chist cutte and joyned by Nich. Disbrowe."

Spring-pole or back-action lathe

Small post mill

The Miller

He was a custom miller in small villages because he custom-ground each farmer's grain, taking part of it as toll. He was thus distinguished from the "merchant" miller who bought grain and sold flour. It was a small village indeed that had no mill. As has been said, the mill was usually a prime reason for the settlement. Nor are such mills extinct; one of them lacks less than twenty years of three centuries' continuous toll-taking. In most cases the choice of the mill site depended on the existence of a head of water—that is, a stream with enough fall and enough volume to turn a water wheel. In the flatlands along the coast streams ran sluggishly, and though the rising tide was sometimes caught and held by a dam to run a mill part time, wind power was likely to be more satisfactory than water in those parts.

Windmills dotted the lowlands from Cape Cod at least as far south as Virginia; a few of them still stand. The four arms or vanes of such a mill, which the wind turned to rotate a shaft at the top of the structure, were exactly like those still used in Holland. Four long spars radiated from the outer end of the shaft. Each spar provided a spine for a light wooden grid which extended along both sides of its full length and was set to face the windstream at a slight angle, as are the vanes of a pinwheel. To offer resistance to the wind, each vane had a sail made of two long strips of linen, one on each side of the spar, lashed to the grid. The miller could reef these in a high wind by twisting their outer ends and so reducing their area. To do this, he stopped the mill with one vane at its bottom position where he could reach the sail. A helper pulled a rope that cramped a hickory brakeband on a seven-foot wheel fixed on the windshaft inside the mill.

No early American mill seems to have had a flyer to keep its sails automatically facing the wind. When the wind changed, the miller's apprentice, if he was strong enough, trundled the tail pole around to a new position. The ground end of the tail pole served as the axle of a wheel which gradually wore a circular trace around the mill. If it was a tower mill, built on a solid base, the 'prentice turned only a cap on the top of the tower, but if it was a post mill, supported by one huge central stanchion, he rotated the whole building.

Water mills were less flighty than windmills. Their power came always from the same direction and the miller could commonly control the amount of it. Commonly but not always. Very primitive mills in the back country where streams ran steeply often took power from the natural fall of water. The miller set a simple turbine, called a tub mill, below a natural cataract which turned it horizontally on a vertical shaft. The upper end of the same shaft ran the millstones. Sometimes the miller backed the blades of an undershot flutter wheel—the simplest possible paddle wheel—into such a fall. Neither it nor the tub mill delivered much power.

Flutter wheel

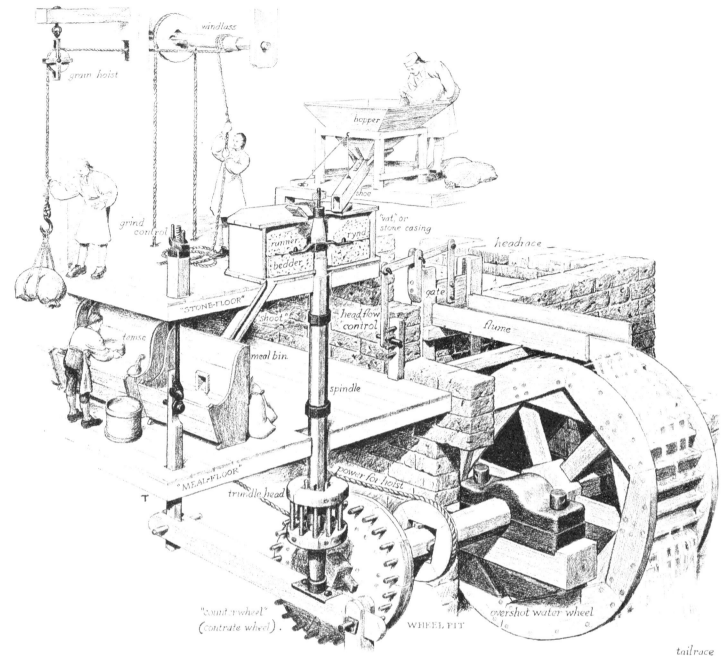

The mechanism of a country gristmill, driven by an overshot water wheel.
The hopper platform would normally stand on the "stone-floor" inside the mill
instead of floating in the air over the millrace, as it does here.
It is put where it is for compactness and clarity.

The best and most widely used form was the overshot wheel to which water came by way of a nearly level ditch, called the head race, from a dam some distance upstream. On small streams the dam stored water overnight for running in the daytime. While water over the dam's crest ran off rapidly downhill, the water in the race flowed sluggishly to a gate which the miller raised to release a controlled flow into the buckets of his wheel. He needed only enough water to keep the buckets filled, since it wasn't the speed of the flow but the weight of the full buckets, overbalancing the empty ones, that turned the wheel. An overshot wheel was often as much as twenty feet in diameter and, where the head was great enough, it might be equally wide. A good many were enclosed to minimize freezing. Wheels of this kind made about two and a half revolutions a minute and the big ones yielded real horsepower. They not only ran grist

30

mills but every other kind of mill and did it so effectively that the industrial revolution might have happened without steam.

The heart of a grist mill was its grinding stones. A wooden "counterwheel" or contrate wheel, wedged on the horizontal drive shaft, ran the trundle head, a small wooden lantern gear. The trundle-head shaft, usually called the spindle, turned six or eight times as fast as the water-wheel shaft. This vertical spindle passed through the central holes of both grinding stones without affecting the fixed bedder at all, but it turned the runner or upper stone. This was true whether the spindle came down from above in a windmill or up from below in a water mill. In either case, an iron rynd, fixed on the spindle, crossed the funnel-shaped hole in the runner and had its ends firmly anchored in the upper surface of the stone. Again, in either case, the lower bearing of the spindle rested on a beam which the miller could raise or lower to adjust the cut of his stones minutely, according to information gathered by his celebrated miller's thumb feeling the texture of the meal. The device could also separate the stones entirely to keep them from grinding each other, and so prevent their setting fire to the place as they sometimes did.

Grain dribbled from a hopper and was guided by a spout, called the shoe, into the hole in the runner. It was moved outward by centrifugal force as the stones ground it. Leaving their edges, the meal was confined by a wooden casing, the vat, that covered the stones. It could escape only down a "shoot" or chute that led to a wooden bin on the floor below. Silk bolting cloth was hard to come by, so in the most primitive mills the grind was sifted and resifted by hand in a temse. By the late eighteenth century most mills had bolters to which "little leathern buckets fastened to a strap" raised the mixed flour and bran by power taken off the main shaft. The bolter was a sixteen-foot-long, gently inclined reel, usually octagonal, covered with a series of bolting cloths of increasingly coarse mesh; sometimes the lowest one was fine wire screen. The ground meal entered the high end. As the reel revolved slowly, the finest flour fell through near the head into its own chute; common flour dropped at the mid-point; shorts or "canal," a mix of coarse flour and fine bran, left near the

foot; coarse bran fell out of the open lower end.

Ordinary granite, quarried in full-size chunks from a local hillside, did very well for grinding rye flour, buckwheat, and corn meal, but for grinding wheat flour nothing equaled a French burr. It could be made sharper and would stay

Millstone dresser

sharper than any other stone. Hence, these burrs were imported early and late. The French quarried them in smallish lumps from beds of softer stone, shaped them to fit together, and bound them with heavy iron bands into the thick disk shape of all millstones.

RUNNER rotates →

BEDDER fixed

The miller had to shut down occasionally to recut the dulled grooves in the working surfaces of his millstones with a very hard chisel-headed hammer called a millbill. Itinerant stone dressers also did the work, taking six to eight days to resharpen a pair of stones. The grooves had what might be called a check-mark profile, one side nearly vertical, the other sloping. They were arranged variously but always in such a way that the upper ones would shear across the lower, with the steeper edges opposed to achieve a cutting action. The commonest arrangement was in groups of straight grooves, each group parallel to a tangent of the central hole: the bedder was just slightly concave; the runner was convex but was almost imperceptibly flatter than the bedder. This made the stones bear hardest at their outer edges and therefore grind finest there.

Though the water mill needed no aiming, its miller and his helpers had little time to loaf. When grain arrived in a cart or wagon or in a sack slung over a horse, they had to hook a rope

Wooden grain scoop

to it and haul it to the top floor of the mill. This was a hand-over-hand job in many small mills, with only a single pulley to help, but it wasn't too hard to rig a windlass using power from the water wheel. They had to keep the hopper full and to watch the grind and change the gap between the stones as needed, sometimes no more than the thickness of paper. Even when there was no hand sifting to do, the meal had to be measured, tolled, and bagged in the presence of the customer. A man wanted his own grain ground, not just an equivalent amount of some other fellow's grain. So the miller had to tag each man's sacks and grind them separately when that man's turn came. The strict first-come-first-served turn was each man's legal right and he was pretty stuffy about it. On a Saturday the miller often had to referee a scrap—when he wasn't personally involved in one.

Unfortunately custom millers long bore a poor reputation for honesty. "Wel coude he stelen corn, and tollen thryes," Chaucer wrote of one of them. As a result, early laws named specific and severe penalties to keep millers in line. Their toll dishes and peck measures were inspected and stamped and they were enjoined "to grind according to turn and well to grind the grain." Typical is a North Carolina act of 1777: a miller could take as toll one-eighth part of wheat and one-sixth part of corn, with a fine of twelve shillings, payable to the person injured, if he took more. Some tricky millers had a small extra chute from the vat to a concealed bin. Even an honest miller might put a square housing over his round stones and take what profit accumulated in its corners.

The Tanner and Currier

When the wind was wrong, nearly every village in early America was within smelling distance of a tanyard. Leather still remains indispensable for shoes, belts, and saddles, but it formerly had many other uses for which no substitutes existed—no rubber, no plastic, no "leatherette." Men wore high boots for riding and outdoor work; nearly all who worked in the open and many who didn't wore leather breeches, buckskin usually; artisans wore leather

Fleshing knife

Dehairing knife

Scraping

aprons because they gave good protection and were tough. Harness was made of leather, of course; so were carriage tops, whether rigid or folding, and carriage curtains for bad weather. Coach bodies rode on slings called thorough-braces, made of layers of thick oxhide. Even when springs became common, carriage bodies hung from them on straps. Thus, every hamlet had work for a tanner, who was his own currier and often made shoes, harness, and saddles in addition; or it could work the other way—the shoemaker had to do his own tanning in order to get material.

Many men tanned hides at home but not necessarily well, and after a farmer had ruined Old Bess's hide, he was glad to divide the next one with the tanner so as to have some boots that didn't crack. But, as with his grain, he wanted his own back again. The tanner had to mark every fell to assure this. In addition to the half of the leather he got for his work, the tanner also got the hair, which he sold to plasterers to hold their lime mortar together, and the offal, which he sold to peddlers who resold it to gluemakers.

The tanner made a distinction between hides, which were cow or bull or ox, horse, or, rarely, buffalo or moose; and skins, which were calf, sheep, pig, deer, or, again rarely, goat. Tanning cured all hides and some skins, but the thinner and more delicate skins were tawed. Tawing will get attention presently; little of it was done in country yards. The tanner first prepared his hide. He split it down the middle into "sides" to make handling easier and trimmed away worthless ends; then he gave it a long soak in water to soften it. The hair could be loosened by further soaking in limewater, but small tanneries

32

did this by simply stacking the wet hides for some days and letting them "sweat." Sweating was actually the beginning of rot, but it wasn't allowed to go far enough to hurt the leather. The hide was next thrown over a slanting "beam" and scraped with two-handled knives: on the flesh side to remove fat and tissue, and on the grain side to take off not only the hair, but also the outer layer of skin, the epidermis. A thorough washing followed. What was washed was the under skin or corium, fibrous and permeated with gelatin. The slow combining of tannic acid with the gelatin toughened a hide into leather and preserved it. Speeded-up modern tanning, using minerals, does not yield as good leather as did the old method.

A tannery used a lot of water, so it was always on a stream in which the hides could be washed and soaked. Water was needed for at least a half dozen vats sunk to ground level and separated by walkways. A tan vat was six feet long, four deep, and from four to six wide. To tan the best sole leather, the kind that would end up pliable, the cleaned hide was first soaked in a weak infusion of bark called ooze. The tanner gradually strengthened his ooze over several months before he started the real tanning. When the time for that arrived, he filled a dry vat with one-inch layers of bark alternated with layers of hide, then flooded the vat and kept it full while the hides lay in it, for as long as a year. From time to time he handled or turned the sides, using a slender

Spud for removing tanbark

Bark mill

Tree bark was the source of tannin. Of the many trees that yielded it, black oak was the best, with hemlock a close second. Some men made an occupation of supplying tanneries, cutting the trees and stripping them during the time of corn planting, when the bark came off easily, and grinding it to the required wheat-grain size in the other months. A tanbark mill was no more than a vertical post, arranged to rotate and supporting a heavy pole which served as axle tree for a thick stone wheel. The wheel's corrugated edge crushed the bark as an ox or a blindfolded horse, hitched to the pole's outer end, trundled the stone around a circular wooden trough which kept the bark in the path of the wheel. The mill ground two "floorings" a day—about a cord and a half. Large tanneries had their own bark mills.

pole with a big hook on one end. It was a back-breaking job.

An expert knew by "feel" when the process was complete and he could fish the heavy leather out and load it on a long cart for hauling, first to the stream for washing, then to the drying racks. These were no more than horizontal poles, often in the open but better covered by a shed.

The dried leather was thumped with a heavy club to toughen and compact it. In 1768, Governor Moore of New York wrote that American tanners "have not yet arrived at the perfection of making sole leather." He must have meant that they made poor sole leather. It's utterly incredible that all colonial shoe soles were imported.

Sole leather came from the butt of a bovine hide, the thickest part near the backbone. The

33

Skiver for splitting hides and skins

Tanyard

Pin for removing bloom

Slicker

thinner belly parts of cowhide made uppers for heavy shoes and boots. Calfskin provided uppers for dressy footwear. Being thinner than cowhide and needing to be more pliable when finished, the process of tanning it was different. After soaking, scraping, and washing, calfskins lay for a week or ten days in a solution of hen or pigeon dung and were turned frequently. They were then tanned in ooze of increasing strength and handled every day for up to six months but were never layered in bark like cowhides. Buckskin was tanned this way, too, but might instead be tawed as whitleather—white leather, that is, for gloves and clothing.

Sheep and goat kips (skins) were always tawed. Again the soaking, scraping, and washing, followed by long immersion in a solution of alum and salt. These light skins, including calf, were finished by currying. The currier began his operation with the skin wet. His object was to make the leather soft and pliable and to give it a good surface finish. His first task was to remove any roughness or thick spots from the flesh side. He used a fluted pin to remove the yellowish bloom from the grain side. Then he scoured both sides with the edge of a smooth stone set in a handle. To do this he stood at the high end of a smooth and steeply sloping stone slab. He repeated the operation with an iron slicker, made like the scouring stone, to burnish the surface. He next stuffed the leather with a mix of tallow

and neat's-foot oil beaten in with a mallet, and hung it up to dry. Since drying stiffened it, it was bruised by beating or stomping, and then rubbed and worked in the hands.

Curriers in large centers specialized, particularly after the Revolution. Some dressed only thick leather, which they blackened and waxed, for shoes and harness; others concentrated on glove leather; others on bookbinding leather; still others on hard leather for drumheads and sieves. The book men tanned their own calfskins with sumac leaves and turned out a far more durable product than can now be had anywhere. They also used a big knife, called a skiver, to split the grain layer off a sheepskin, calling it, too, a skiver.

Curriers

Fulling mill

The Fuller

Woolen cloth, whether home-woven or professionally woven, needed fulling to cleanse it of grease and compact its fibers and to raise the nap on its surface. A household could get through part of the procedure by giving a fulling party. The neighbors sat in a circle and stamped on the soap-saturated cloth with their feet, but they didn't do a very good job. It did the floor no good and the final surfacing didn't get done at all. The date of the earliest American fulling mill shows the importance of professional work. Set up in 1643 by John Pearson at Rowley, Massachusetts, it kept on fulling until 1809. The word "mill" indicated power of some kind, probably ox power at first, since water wasn't harnessed to fulling mills until late in the eighteenth century.

Proper fulling began with a thorough washing of the cloth in hot water and soap to remove dirt and some grease; then it went into the beating trough with fuller's earth and was "thumped" mechanically for hours. It was the thumpers that made the establishment a mill. The illustration of them is based on a plate in *The Young Millwright and Millers Guide*, issued by the Delaware mechanical genius, Oliver Evans, in 1795, but its principle was far older than that. Quite similar mills had stamped ores and beaten paper pulp for three hundred years. Some fulling mills used vertical pestles falling into a simple trough,

but they were raised and dropped by the same kind of tappet arms (cams) that moved Evans's mallets, as he called them. His innovation was shaping the beaters and the trough to turn the cloth constantly as it was beaten.

Fuller's earth is an absorbent clay, most often of a greenish color. It took nearly all of the natural grease from the wool, and then had itself to be washed out of the cloth. The fuller stretched the wet fabric on tenter frames to get rid of wrinkles and to maintain its width. When it had dried, he hung it over rods and curried its surface thoroughly. He made his implement for this by mounting on a handle half a dozen or more dried seed pods of the fuller's teasel (*Dipsacus fullonum*) used for this purpose since man first wove wool. The pod is covered with hooked spines and no substitute has yet equaled it for raising the nap of cloth. It doesn't raise it evenly, however, and the fuller had to trim off the shagginess with extremely long-bladed shears. He moved the cloth over a horizontal wooden cylinder and did his shearing along its top.

*Fuller's teasel
(actual size)*

Fuller's shears

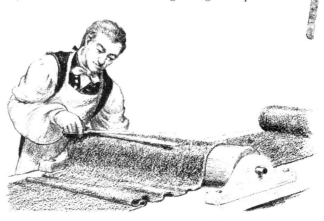

35

Fullers sometimes cleaned clothing as a side line, using fuller's earth, ox gall, and—of all things—egg yolks to remove grease spots. As early as 1716, an anonymous writer mentioned the ability of "oyl" (spirits) of turpentine to dissolve grease, but it didn't come into general use as a solvent until about 1800. Even then it was used only for spotting and it left the garment smelling like a paint shop. Some European fullers ran laundries but no evidence has been found that any did so in this country. They were probably all dyers, using colors of vegetable origin such as logwood for brownish red; peach-wood (brazilwood) for red and purple; quercetin bark (black oak) for yellow; and, of course, indigo for blue, the most widely used of all early dyes. A mix of logwood and quercetin yielded black. Colonial dyers understood the use of mordants not only to fix their adjective dyes but also to vary their colors.

Wayfaring chandler

The Itinerants

Any reader older than fifty may remember the dressmakers that families "had in": widows or elderly maidens who stayed a week or two fitting, snipping, stitching—and talking. None of the colonial itinerants seem to have been women, but most of them operated the same way. From April to October, when traveling was least bad, they moved from farm to farm, often on a regular route to known patrons, staying as long at each place as the work lasted, and taking their pay in the surplus materials of their craft or in any other portable product the farmer offered. Only rarely did they compete with local workers; they were the perhaps not overskilled outriders of trades that centered in large towns. Because of this, it seems better to leave their methods for later and to cover here only the circumstances of their work.

Cat whipper's folding bench, about 1800

The Cat Whipper

A maker of shoes was a cordwainer in the seventeenth and early eighteenth centuries. Just when and why he became a shoemaker, while the repairer remained a cobbler, is open for guessing. However, our ancestors often called a cobbler a "botcher," with no reflection on his skill. The shoemaker who worked his way through the country at both trades was generally known, especially in derision by his urban colleagues, as a cat whipper. Probably he moved from place to place—on horseback as a rule. But the cat whipper who owned the folding bench in the illustration must have had a chaise or a gig; the thing is too bulky for a saddle bag, though he may have trundled it in a wheelbarrow; some did transport their equipment that way. Once artisan and farmer had come to terms, which might take half a day—people enjoyed such discussions and never hurried them—the shoemaker settled in the kitchen to retail news to the housewife and to resole and

36

patch all the shoes that "still had wear in 'em." Then, using leather that had "grown up" on the place, he replaced the hopeless ones, and if he had no last the right size, he whittled one from a hunk of white pine. He could build both shoes of a pair over the same last; they were identical—not left and right. He placed the last across his knees for working and kept it there with a strap passed under a stick he held down with his feet. Though the cat whipper's shoes were of the heaviest kind, he sewed their soles on with linen thread. Wooden pegs for holding soles were invented by Harvey Bailey about 1825.

Winding warp onto spools from a swift

The Weaver

The farmer sheared his sheep in the spring and washed the wool. His women carded it into "slivers" by dragging it between paddles studded with wire hooks and then, for the rest of the year, spun the slivers into yarn by twisting them together on the big wheel at which they stood to work and which they turned with a wooden wheel finger held in the hand.

The farmer pulled up his flax by the roots in midsummer, retted (rotted) it in water, fragmented its hard sheath and core on a heavy wooden flax brake, then scutched or swingled it by slashing at it with a wooden blade to get out the larger chips. The women then took over the fibers and dragged them through coarse iron combs called hatchels to remove the rest of the splinters. Seated at the little wheel turned by a treadle, they spun the cleaned linen into yarn during the rest of the year.

Country families north of Wilmington, Delaware, nearly always owned a loom, and come spring they had plenty of spun yarn on hand. If the wife in such a family was worth her salt, she could weave and did, but she had other things to do and a large family needed a lot of yard goods. So the traveling weaver was welcomed. While the women worked at the quilling wheel winding warp on spools for him, and weft on quills, he sat for weeks in the family's loom, webbing plain fabrics or stripes or checks, the only patterns most looms were equipped to weave. The linen made shirts, work smocks, shifts, towels, and big napkins; it took three strips to make a sheet, since the linen was only thirty inches wide. The wool made blankets, again in strips, and outer clothing. Sometimes the weaver combined the two fibers, a woolen weft on a linen warp, to make linsey-woolsey, almost as warm as pure wool and much more durable.

The Tailor

A farmer could sometimes patch a shoe, but he could seldom make shoes; his wife might weave and she could patch an elbow or make a linen shirt, but she was seldom able to tailor a coat very well. So the tailor followed the weaver and squatted cross-legged on the kitchen table stitching breeches, long coats and short roundabouts, cloaks, which were capes for men, and riding hoods, which were full-length hooded capes for women. The styles of these things changed slowly and never was the tailor heard to say, "They're not wearing that this year."

Tailor's shears

The Chandler

A colonial housewife never threw away any fat. She rendered it and stored it in pottery crocks. In very early days the family burned it in grease lamps for light, but it was a smelly, smoky light and candles were better. The mistress could make "taller dips" by repeatedly dipping wicks into hot tallow and cooling, between dips, what adhered. Some families owned tin molds that would cast as many as a dozen candles. The traveling chandler brought along his own big molds that cast six dozen at once. He strung them up with the loosely spun tow-linen candle-wick that the house provided, melted down some of the harder fat, and cast a year's supply of candles. The softer fat the chandler turned into soap by boiling it, outdoors, with lye. As he boiled, he stirred with a wooden paddle, always in one direction because of a superstition that the soap would fail if he didn't.

The Tinker

Sometime between snow and snow, a tinker showed up with his "pig" over his shoulder and his charcoal brazier on his back. His stay was short—only a night or two. A day's work was usually enough to plug a family's leaky basins, put new handles on old dippers, and recast pewter spoons that had been broken. A tinker might mend a larger pewter article like a plate or a bowl, but he could seldom recast it, not only because the molds were too heavy to tote around the country, but also because he had no equipment for cleaning up a cast after he made it.

Below is a tinker's pig with the principal tools he carried in it. Solder and rivets rode in the boxes on its ends. Circling from the two hammers, a light one and a heavy one, there are: tongs for holding metal over a fire, tin snips, a hand vise, a double-ended soldering iron, and a snarling iron, the use of which is explained in the later section on silversmithing. The tinker made his pig himself, for though he could turn a hand at almost anything, he was first of all a tinsmith.

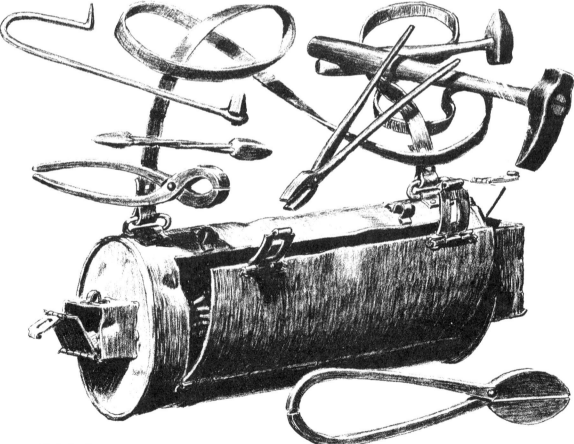

Tinker's pig

3.

TOWN SHOPS

NEARLY all colonial centers large enough to call towns had good harbors and hence were ports of entry for merchant ships. Some such towns are now great cities; others, whose harbors silted up, sleep peacefully. Few towns were planned in advance as Philadelphia and Annapolis were, so main streets took the most traveled directions and cross streets filled in at random. The older parts of Boston, New York, and Baltimore retain more than traces of this.

Though some small shops clustered around market squares where countrymen sold produce from wagons, there was no special shopping district. Retailers as well as artisans set up shop in their houses, regardless of where the houses were. No regulation interfered—zoning is a twentieth-century idea—though early New Yorkers did force the tanners out of town. A journeyman starting out for himself would tend to stay in the neighborhood he knew, not far from his old master. As a result some streets became asso-

ciated with one trade and were even named for it, as was Pewter Alley in Philadelphia.

Shops may be roughly divided into four kinds: those of craftsmen who did bespoke work, that is, custom work to order; these are the subject of the chapter following this one. Those of retailers who simply bought and sold, those of artisans who offered "salework" on a take-it-or-leave-it basis, and those of specialists who performed some direct personal service for the public are dealt with in the present chapter. Entirely outside these categories were the shopless hawkers who offered goods and services through the streets, calling their wares as they went: wood sellers, charcoal burners, rag buyers, broom sellers, chimney sweeps, scissors grinders. The butchers sold meat from carts, the fishwives sold from baskets. Hunters brought in game in barrels or hanging from poles over their shoulders. The milkman brought around big copper cans and ladled his milk into the customer's

The butcher

pannikin. The tale of the deaf housewife who thrust her ear trumpet through her barely opened door and got the milk in it was a stock colonial jest.

Some workers needing no salesroom simply did things in a shed somewhere, as the cooper, the joiner, and the blacksmith did. Such a one was the pump-log borer—his trade seems to have no generic name—who made wooden pumps and wooden pipes by boring holes lengthwise through logs. He used a cross-handled auger with a long shank capable of extension by added sections. His skill consisted of keeping the hole straight all the way through. Wooden pipes of this kind were joined by inserting a tapered end into a recessed one and sealing the joint with hot mutton fat. Such pipes carried the earliest public water supplies. Boston got the first ones in 1652; most were laid in the late 1700's and continued to serve well into the nineteenth century when pressures became too great for the joints.

In large towns, even in the seventeenth century, sheer necessity forced the paving of a few main streets with cobbles, often glacial pebbles, and some individuals laid brick or plank sidewalks in front of their properties. Towns, nevertheless, offered as much mud and dust as did country villages. Boots were the only practical wet-weather footgear for a man on foot or on horseback. Ladies on spring shopping tours took along their pattens or clogs and teetered on them from carriage to shop door. Sedan chairs were popular partly because they delivered the passenger dry-shod on the doorstep.

Large windows of small panes made most shops unmistakable in a street. Frequently these windows, with sides one pane wide, projected from the wall, sometimes straight out and sometimes angled; they were rarely bowed because curved frames were costly and hard to make. Many shops, perhaps the majority, had the large window set flush with the wall, and some made

Pipe auger and wooden pipe

out with ordinary house windows. However, any shop could be identified for what it was by the sign swinging from a bracket over the walkway or hanging in a frame set on top of a post that stood in the walkway.

In a day when many people were completely illiterate, a shop sign had to be something recognizable and readily described—an identification and an address. Indeed, since there were no street numbers, householders gave their addresses in relation to signs—"Adam Gummidge, near the King of Prussia in Race Street"; someone at the inn would point out Adam's house. Perhaps the majority of signs were painted boards, but a great many were solid objects associated with the owner's business, or replicas of the objects, enlarged, carved, and painted. Certain articles associated themselves with certain trades; thus the farrier hung out a horseshoe, a big one; the wheelwright displayed a cartwheel; the shoemaker, a big wooden boot—a chain of shoe stores does so now; the tailor, shears, again enlarged. Of fourteen early bookbinders whose emblems are recorded, ten displayed the Sign of the Bible; two of them strove for distinction by adding, one a dove, the other a crown. Examples may still survive of two signs common up to thirty years ago: a huge pair of eyeglasses to designate an optician, and a gargantuan gilded molar over the door of a dentist.

Though taverns hung out a tankard or a jug, most of the better inns used painted signs often bearing the presumed portrait of some worthy by whose name the place was known. In 1776, all the "King Georges" hastily changed their names but not necessarily the portraits. What didn't look much like the King wouldn't look much less like General Greene. A few craftsmen displayed on their signs the heraldic arms of their trade's English guild. They had no legal right to do so, and heraldry didn't make good signs because the symbols were strange to most Americans and they had no ready words to describe them.

Women ran many shops retailing dry goods and notions, books, stationery, music, and so on. It has been mentioned that widows successfully continued their husbands' craft shops; having been long involved in the business, they were able to oversee journeymen's work. Women of

40

sound earthy qualities ran grog shops and ordinaries and operated cookshops which were the delicatessen-caterers of the time. Women also practiced some minor trades. They were milliners and "mantua makers" (dressmakers), displaying imported "fashion dolls" to show the latest London styles. Women ruled paper for bookkeeping and music notation. Women, as well as men, made stays (corsets), stiffening them with whalebone, the preparation of which was a separate minor trade. Both sexes made gloves, not in standard sizes but to order, with the fingers neither too long nor too short.

Except where a widow continued a business, grocers were usually men, perhaps because the grocers of London boasted a guild to which, heaven forfend, no woman belonged. Back in the mid-1300's, "grossers" wholesaled spices and foreign produce; they gradually moved into retail trade and, in the 1600's, the spelling changed. The stock of an eighteenth-century grocer would be lost in a supermarket. He sold only goods that didn't readily spoil, but its variety is surprising: tea; coffee in the bean only; chocolate; cocoa; sugar in beehive-shaped loaves which the customer broke up—three such loaves are the symbol of the London Grocers Company; treacle (molasses); spices much in demand by gentlemen for flavoring beer and wine mulled by thrusting into it a red-hot square-ended poker called a loggerhead. (When gentlemen were "at loggerheads," they had

seized the nearest weapons to settle a dispute.) Some grocers sold wine, brandy, rum, and whisky, but there were vintners or wine merchants who specialized in those commodities. The grocer's staple foods were confined to dried legumes with perhaps corn meal and flour and dried fruits. Wealthy men imported oranges, lemons, grapes, pineapples, coconuts, and even bananas for their own use; ships also brought oranges and grapes from the Mediterranean for sale to the general public at Christmas.

Loggerhead

The Barber and Wigmaker

With all respect to modern mechanized tonsorial parlors—which, note, are still called barber *shops*—their eighteenth-century predecessors, with four or five journeymen and apprentices to help, were much more versatile establishments.

To begin with, the barber shaved not only the faces but also the heads of his wig-wearing customers, or rather he set an apprentice, a little shaver, to do it. Though few men shaved more than once a week, nearly all were at least technically clean-shaven. Only pirates and backwoodsmen wore beards.

In medieval days, the barber-chirurgeon performed all kinds of surgery. By Henry VIII's time, though the two trades made one guild, surgeons were forbidden to perform "barbery"

Barber's shop

Fleam

Great wig

Ramillies wig

Tye wig

Bag wig

Bob wig

and the barber's surgery was limited to tooth pulling and bloodletting from an arm vein, an operation thought to relieve many human ills. The barber-pole symbol, still with us but disappearing, had its origin in the blood-reddened staff grasped by the patient when he was bled. A white bandage spiraling around it completed the design. American barbers in the eighteenth century still pulled teeth and let blood; in fact, you could find a barber to bleed you in the 1830's, and leeches to reduce black eyes can be found in strategically located barber shops today.

When King Louis XIII of France found his regal grandeur impaired by a bald head, he bought a wig. All his courtiers put them on and merely changed the wigs' style to match the luxuriant natural ringlets of the next Louis. The English Charles II and all his gay companions wore big wigs in the 1660's, and presently men who never saw the court were wearing them also. Preachers first blasted wigs from the pulpits and then ended up preaching in wigs. Even American Quakers wore them, and men who clung to their own hair dressed it to look as wiglike as possible. We associate white wigs with George Washington, but though his friends and neighbors wore them, he carefully powdered his own hair.

Wealthy men often put their house servants and coachmen into wigs, and bought them for their male children above the age of seven. Though some gentlemen avoided wigs, many plain citizens wore them; a Williamsburg barber recorded the sale of one to a plasterer. Second-hand wigs came into this country from Europe in barrels and poor men bought them on a grab-bag basis.

Not all wigs were white. The most expensive were made of human hair left in its natural color. Wigs were designated brown, light-flaxen natural, chestnut, yellowish, auburn, gray, black, white, and grizzle which was black-and-white. Horsehair, cow tails, linen, and silk thread made the cheaper wigs.

These headpieces attained their largest size as periwigs (*perruques*) or great wigs in the early 1700's when they crested high on top and fell in long curls down the back and over the shoulders. At this time, a gentleman turned out in silk stockings, satin breeches, deep-cuffed velvet coats, and embroidered waistcoats—a costly outfit worth just about as much as the wig that went with it. Such wigs were not only uncomfortable—all wigs are—but they were a fearful nuisance in any kind of physical activity. Military men, particularly, had to pin them up or tie them out of the way. These restraints affected the styles and soon there was a rash of long-tailed wigs like the "Ramillies," short-tailed wigs like the "tye" and the club, two-tailed wigs, wigs with silk bags for tails, and wigs with no tail at all like the bob. "Tailed" wigs had a bow of ribbon at shoulder level; usually the ribbon was black, but sometimes it was brightly colored or striped. In general, wigs grew smaller as the eighteenth century aged. They began to disappear not too long after the Revolution, though some elderly men clung to them into the 1800's. Better the old wig than a bald pate.

Even small wigs were expensive and so was their upkeep. Men paid their barbers by the year the equivalent of $400 to keep one wig properly dressed. Dressing consisted of careful cleaning and combing, and of curling by rolling the hair in curl papers on small heated cylinders of pipe clay. In dressing a new wig the curlers were sometimes rolled cold and the whole wig was baked in an oven, and sometimes the oven scorched the wig. All wigs were powdered; even colored ones had their original tint maintained with brown, black, or light-flaxen natural powder.

The barber made a wig to fit the head that would wear it, measuring the skull roundabout, fore and aft and athwartship, and making a net cap called the caul to correspond. He made this over a wooden wig block to which he could tack it temporarily, and finished it off with a drawstring or a buckle in the back to help its wearer keep it in place. The hair for the wig the barber cleaned, combed through a fine-toothed hackle, and then held by its root ends in a special vise to roll it on his pipe-clay curlers. He next patiently knotted those ends onto triple strands of silk, producing a kind of fringe. This he attached to the caul, beginning at the nape and stitching the strands to the net in lines a quarter of an inch apart, so that the fringes of curled hair hung in layers. Some wigs had short hair on the sides; others had long sides rolled into sausage curls. A final dressing and powdering, and the addition of whatever ribbons fashion demanded, made the wig ready to wear.

Very large towns like Philadelphia and Boston could support hairdressers who catered exclusively to women; in smaller places the barbers "made curls" for the wives and daughters of their customers. Fashionable women took to wigs in the 1760's when coiffures became too large and elaborate for home dressing and powdering. They abandoned them in the late 1780's when sympathy for the French Revolutionists changed styles. Both women and men got their wigs off as quickly as possible at home, the men covering their shaven heads with silk turbans, the women with what came to be called mob caps.

The Baker

New Amsterdam had a bake shop by 1648 and by the eighteenth century every town large enough for an inn had a baker. Price regulation of bread was taken as a matter of course from the first; also the kind—rye, coarse, or white—and the weight, standard loaf *eight* pounds, were fixed by law. Bakers were sometimes compelled to initial their loaves, so their shortcomings could be brought home to them. Officials needed to be watchful. London bakers cheated so consistently on weight that they were made to give the "baker's dozen" of thirteen rolls to assure the customer of his money's worth. One of the duties of the mayor of Philadelphia was weighing the bakers' loaves once a month. A curious New York law forbade a baker to sell sweet cakes unless he also had bread for sale.

The miller sold his tolled flour to the baker, who resifted it into the big wooden trough where he mixed his dough. Kneading a couple of hundred pounds at a time called for strong arms. The trough had a cover to be closed when the mix was left to rise. Apprentices cut chunks from the risen dough and brought them to size on a balance scale, then moved them to a floured table where they shaped them into loaves. When the table was filled, they covered the loaves with a cloth and left them for the second rising.

There was no lack of warmth to raise the bread. The big brick oven radiated so much heat that bakers went about their trade nearly naked, though they wore close caps to keep flour out of their hair and hair out of the flour. The oven was a large-scale version of the fireplace cubbyhole in which women baked at home. It was preheated the same way, too, by a roaring fire

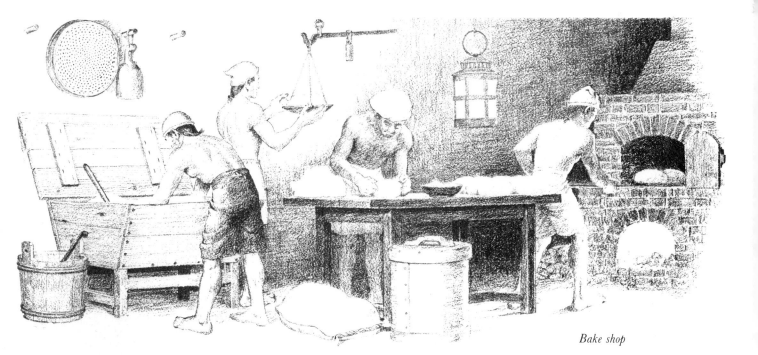

Bake shop

of dry wood built right in it. When the masonry was hot clear through, the baker raked out the coals, swept the ashes from the oven floor, and slid his round loaves onto it with a flat shovel called a peel. He used no pans whatever. When he had filled the oven, he closed its iron door, shut off its flue with a damper, and let the heat in the bricks bake his bread. This took longer than it does with constantly added heat and it produced a harder, thicker crust. Bread is still baked this way in rural Europe and people from there say it is unmatched for flavor. A man could do a day's work on two or three pounds of such bread made with natural unbleached flour.

Quite a few of the workrooms and ovens seem to have been in cellars. Much work was done at night and in the small morning hours so as to have the bread fresh-baked for the day's trade. While the bread was in the oven, the baker mixed his sponge (dough) for the following night's baking, and the apprentices cleaned up and fed the yeast culture, the barm, by mixing into it a thin paste of flour and mashed potatoes. The barm was thus kept alive indefinitely. Perhaps because of the knowledge of fermentation he gained from it and because he had a large oven for roasting malt, an early colonial baker was often a brewer also, though many people made beer at home. With increased population, brewing became a separate trade.

Baker's peel

A colonial baker's odd hours and unconventional work clothes kept him from often minding store; his wife or his daughters sold the bread and rolls. A colonial roll was quite a thing. You remember Ben Franklin, arriving in Philadelphia, bought for three pennies "three great puffy rolls" and, eating one, carried the other two *under his arms*. Notice Ben made no mention of a package. A customer who wanted to keep the bread clean on the way home brought a napkin to put it in; paper was far too scarce for wrapping anything that didn't have to be held together. Bakers, by the way, didn't make pies; those came from the pie woman, who made nothing else. Some of the money the bake shop took in was for custom work—dough prepared by housewives who brought it to the shop to be baked. It's safe to assume that they marked their loaves to make sure of getting the same ones back. The baker sometimes did another curious custom job. When

the barber had trouble curling certain hair for wigs, he rolled it on curlers and sent it to the baker to be enclosed in rye dough and baked.

The Apothecary

If the likeness between barber and surgeon still showed, the difference between apothecary and physician was almost invisible in America through most of the eighteenth century. The apothecary mixed medicines; he prescribed them and also visited the sick and applied poultices and blisters to relieve the most unlikely ailments. The physician did the same, mixing his bitter drafts on the spot. Everyone assumed that medicines had to taste bad to be effective. Most doctors imported their drugs personally and prepared them with the help of apprentices. Quite a few set their apprentices to making up doses for the public and selling them in a shop, with no more than an over-the-counter diagnosis —by the apprentice.

Both professions were entirely open to private enterprise: "anyone at his pleasure sets up for physician, apothecary, or chirurgeon. No candidates are examined or licensed." The Connecticut Assembly considered licensing but decided against "any monopoly in the practise of medicine." The public's confidence in any kind of patent medicine or any quack "doctor" was boundless, as it still is; but government then gave people no protection, in spite of themselves, as it does now. Any colonial gathering attracted "Indian physicians" and vendors of snake oil by dozens. Even Ben Franklin advertised in 1730: "Seneca rattlesnake root (*Polygala senega*) with direction how to use it in pleurisy."

Many patent medicines originated in England, and American apothecaries advertised them in the earliest newspapers. "Scotch Pills," "Bateman's Elixir," and "Godfrey's British Oyl," dosed Bostonians within a couple of months of their first assaults on the bodies of Londoners. We find comedy in the extension of drug stores into department stores and restaurants, but early apothecaries used as much advertising space to offer paint, varnish, linseed oil, paint brushes, and window glass as to sell remedies. True, none offered food, cooking utensils or furniture.

44

The twentieth-century pharmacist complains that the end use of his extensive knowledge is counting pills out of big bottles into little ones. A trained eighteenth-century apothecary had no way to learn much that is basic to his modern counterpart, who never needs to learn much that the earlier man regarded as basic. Christopher Marshall, an honest Irish Quaker, started an apothecary shop at the "Sign of the Golden Ball" on Chestnut Street, Philadelphia, in 1729. It was the first in the town and for years it was the only dependable one. Marshall not only had to mix his medicines; he had to gather many of the simples in the fields and woods, dry them, and extract their essences with various graters and squeezers and alembics, or in a kettle on the hearth. The United States had no pharmacopoeia until 1820, no college of pharmacy until 1841, and no pharmaceutical code of ethics until 1856. The earlier men used English texts, but they adopted many native roots and herbs, such as mayapple, sassafras, bloodroot, and slippery elm, which were used by the Indians. Botanists supplied respectable Latin names for these: for instance *euonymos* for "whaoo."

The apothecary bought liquid drugs from the druggist, the wholesaler, in large pottery or glass demijohns protected by burlap wrappings which were sometimes stuffed with sawdust. He used these containers for reserve storage, keeping active supplies in bottles on his shelves. His shelf bottles were not only glass but also glazed pottery to match the wide-mouthed jars in which he kept dry materials. When he compounded a prescription, either a physician's or his own, the "pharmaceutist" reached down the drugs he needed from the shelves behind him and measured, weighed, and mixed them on the shop counter.

Early medicine liked its mixtures complex even though but one ingredient of the lot might, with luck, be the effective agent. Compounding a prescription might take half a day of mortar-and-pestle grinding, filtering, measuring, and weighing. Here are the ingredients of a kind of soothing syrup known as *elixir paregoricum*: opium, honey, licorice, benzoic acid, camphor, oil of anise, potassium carbonate, alcohol.

Apothecaries had to import small glass bottles for dispensing liquids in the early days when glass works never seemed to get going. The bottles were usually stoppered with wooden pegs and a bit of sealing wax. Corks, known and

Stone mortar and pestle

Grater made from a pewter dish studded with short nails

Powders

45

used in Europe, reached America only in small quantities. The apothecary rolled some pills and even silvered some, but he never saw what we call a capsule. Many drugs he sold as powders in folded papers, sometimes wrapping each dose separately.

Away from the centers, the village stores stocked a few drugs to be purchased and dosed at the discretion of the buyer; they were linaments, healing ointments, purgatives, emetics, and "blood thinners." Farther still from civilization, the circuit-riding preacher carried similar nostrums in his saddlebags and made shift to comfort the body as well as the soul.

The wedge of separation between medicine and pharmacy was started when Dr. John Morgan founded the Medical School of the College of Philadelphia in 1765. Morgan had studied in London, Edinburgh, and Paris, and had returned convinced that doctors should not sell drugs.

Apothecary jar, porcelain

The Hatter

AN ACT to prevent the Exportation of Hats out of any of His Majesty's Colonies or Plantations in America, and to restrain the Number of Apprentices taken by the Hat-makers in the said Colonies or Plantations, and for better encouraging the making of Hats in GREAT BRITAIN.

Act of Parliament, King George II, January 13, 1731

Apothecary jar, Delft

The "Hat Act" limited each hatter to only two apprentices, each to serve a full seven years. In America so long a term would eliminate all apprentices, but the Act made little actual trouble since, beyond a spate of indignant discussion, no one in the colonies paid any attention to its prohibitions. In the next year, 1732, both Boston and New York made ten thousand hats and the trade went on from there; even Charleston exported hats and, by 1774, Philadelphia, leading all others, had forty-three master hatters. Beaver hats led in money value if not in numbers. Rather strangely, considering the climate, most of the export demand for them came from the West Indies. But then "Lord"

Timothy Dexter of Newburyport successfully sold warming pans there.

Man has covered his head with something as far back as recorded history goes, always, one suspects, with the fear that he looked faintly ridiculous. A wrong-sized hat is a clown's basic prop. A bareheaded man now attracts no attention on the street, but for three centuries before this one, people would have assumed he had lost his hat or his mind. In the seventeenth century men even dined in their hats and wore them in church. Wig-wearing ended this, except with Quakers. Plenty of men wore caps in the eighteenth century and in summer nearly all wore wide-brimmed straws, but then, as now, most hats were felt.

Hats can be felted from any kind of soft fur. Beaver was preferred for two hundred years because of its beautiful, soft sheen, and the preference almost did the beavers in. Otter, seal, muskrat, and rabbit served, in descending order, for cheaper grades. These made fur hats. When a colonial hatter spoke of a felt hat, he meant one felted from wool, usually sheep's wool, but in later years much llama wool was imported. The cocked or three-cornered hat was popular everywhere in the western world through most of the 1700's because it fitted under the arm when a man didn't want to muss his wig—he wouldn't think of leaving it at home. It was actually a low-crowned hat with three sides of its wide, round brim rolled up against or sometimes over its crown. A hard rain relaxed the rolls and demanded a reblocking job. Men who couldn't afford reblocking left their brims flat after the first disaster. A heavy dew would unroll a wool hat, leaving its edges gaily undulant. Though it persisted for some ten years and though the President had nothing to do with the change, the end of the cocked hat began about when George Washington was inaugurated. Wigs went out and gentlemen of fashion started wearing stiffened top hats with rather low, belled crowns and a rolling curl to the sides of the brims. By 1820, the crown was eight inches high and the curled brim, dipping fore and aft, had flattened slightly.

The hatter bought beaver pelts and started his work by removing the fur from them. Using his thumb against the blade of a dull knife, he first pulled all the long guard hairs, the visible part of natural fur, and sold them for whatever he could get. He wanted the soft "muffoon," the under fur, and he shaved it from the skin with a sharp semi-circular knife such as harnessmakers use for cutting straps.

Planking at the battery

The hurl

A journeyman weighed out enough fur to make each hat, divided it into two equal parts, and bowed each part separately in a hurl, which was a table enclosed on three sides. His bow or "stang," as he called it, was seven feet long and heavy enough to need suspending from the ceiling. He repeatedly twanged its taut sheep-gut string with a knobbed bowpin as he passed it through the pile of fur. The vibration crossed the fibers over one another and their natural scales hooked them together. When he had thoroughly stirred a pile, the hatter patted it into a round-topped triangle about three feet on a side, and flattened it with a slatted wooden hatter's basket. It was then a batt. The bowman placed this on a stack of its fellows alternated with wet linen separators. These, called in-layers, were

the same shape as the batts but slightly smaller. The batts were compacted by the moisture they absorbed. Later, hatters used brown paper in-layers.

A second man took pairs of batts from the stack and, as he kneaded them with the linen still in place, he worked their side and top edges together so that the two joined into an approximately conical hood. Hoods were fulled by boiling for six to eight hours during which they shrank and thickened. Then they went to the battery. This was a large kettle filled with a mild acid solution kept boiling by a fire underneath it in a brick firebox. A drainboard, sloping downward toward the center, surrounded the kettle. Hatters around the board snatched the hoods, one at a time, from the boiling vat, dipping their hands into very cold water before each snatch to avoid scalding themselves. This needs skill—it is best not to try it. They rolled each hood with a tapered wooden roller and planked it by beating it with a club or with a block called a glove held on the hand by a string. Planking, along with repeated dipping in the kettle, shrank the felt violently and at the same time compacted and thinned it. At the end, it was half its original size and was ready to be blocked.

Wool hat

Beaver, about 1790

Beaver, about 1810

Blocking

Blocking was a job for a master. His wooden block, held by a peg on a circular bottom board, was the size and shape of the crown of the finished hat. With his scarlet hands and a tool called a runner-down, the hatter shaped the hot, saturated hood to fit over the block and spread it out on the board to form the brim. Another wooden tool, called a tolliker—there were tollikers of many shapes—flattened the brim and took the wrinkles out of it.

Bell-crowned hat block

A day's production of shaped hats went on to racks in a mildly warm oven to dry overnight. Next day each hat had its brim trimmed and then had its surface smoothed with a pumice stone. A finisher next ironed the hat and raised the nap on its surface, using a paddle closely studded with short wires. Like the cloth fuller, he sheared off inequalities and then carefully brushed the nap all in one direction.

The addition of a leather sweatband stitched inside, a ribbon around the crown, and sometimes a binding on the edge of the brim finished the hat except for a final blocking if the brim was to be cocked. For this, the hat was lightly steamed and placed on a block; its brim was rolled upward, tied in place with tapes attached to the block, and left to dry.

The process described is that for beaver hats. Variations on it were required for hats of lower-grade fur and of wool. Very cheap hats had to be rolled in cloth to stand the planking operation, and wool hats had to have glue or varnish added to make them felt. After they had shrunk, cheap hats often had "flakes" of fur matted on their surfaces with a wet brush to make them look better.

Something like quantity production developed in the early nineteenth century, with each man

putting in full time at one or two operations. A bell-crowned hat block of that time had to be made in five pieces to get it out of the hat. When the square center piece was withdrawn, the other pieces could move into its space. The crown block stood on the center peg of a separate mold which gave shape to the curly brim. These hats were hardened with shellac while they were on the blocks. They were dyed on the blocks, too, and ironed on them after dyeing. Some hats were drab, that is, natural color, and women, children, and coachmen often wore white ones. But the vast majority for two hundred years were "as black as your hat." To achieve this color, a seven-foot wooden disk, studded with pegs and hung on an axle, dipped its lower third into a dye vat and carried with it the hat blocks set on its pegs. Turning the disk gave the hats repeated dippings and dryings.

Silk hats appeared about 1831. They were so much shinier and lighter in weight than any hat ever seen that everybody wanted one. That saved the beavers, though beaver hats didn't disappear entirely until the Civil War.

The Eyeglass Seller

Friar Roger Bacon, who died in 1294, first suggested looking through lenses in order to see better. So far as is known, he didn't try it, but someone did about six years later. Within seventy-five years spectacles were common enough—and uncommon enough—to be mentioned in wills, but the oldest surviving pair dates from about 1500. The Chinese are said to have invented spectacles independently, and it is also said that a Chinese manuscript mentions their introduction by Spanish Jesuits.

All of these ancient glasses had convex lenses and served only to help the elderly and the naturally far-sighted to read. Crude as they were, they allowed the gradual reduction of the size of letters in both written and printed books. Almost nothing was known of optics and absolutely nothing of the functioning of the eye. Selection of lenses was by guess, with the usual quackery and magic involved. So people who couldn't afford them told one another that glasses could make the blind see, that they

Hat dyeing in the 1830's

Convex lens (halved)

Concave lens (halved)

changing. He put his fabulous wits to work and had both pairs cut in half horizontally; then he mounted the distance halves above the reading halves in the same frame to make what he called "double" spectacles—bifocals.

Franklin's lenses and most others of his time were ground from ordinary window glass, selected for as few bubbles as possible and a minimum of the wavy lines called striations. Nobody thought this was good, and the few who could afford them had lenses ground from rock crystal, which is more nearly transparent than common glass and has no irregularities in it. Crystal lenses were advertised in Philadelphia in 1758. Optical glass as clear and perfect as crystal wasn't made in Europe until 1807 and wasn't made successfully in the United States until 1912.

Up to the early part of the present century, the same process that shaped those for the first pair ever made was still used to grind spectacle lenses. Though this is called grinding, it was actually rubbing against abrasives—a machinist would say lapping.

Grinding a convex lens

The grinder selected the clearest piece of glass he could find and chipped it roughly to size by tapping around its edge with a hammer or by breaking off bits with pliers. He attached a working handle to one face with hot pitch and used the handle to rub the other face laboriously over an iron matrix shaped to the curve of the lens he wanted to make. A dish-shaped matrix yielded a convex lens; a mushroom-shaped one, a concave lens. High-powered lenses might require a series of matrices with progressively shorter radii. The abrasive that cut away the unwanted glass was wet sand, coarse at first and finer toward the end of the job.

Matrix for a concave lens

When the first face of the lens reached its final shape, the grinder transferred his handle to it and ground the other side. He polished both sides on the matrix with dry tripoli powder (rottenstone) or, in later years, with wet jeweler's rouge which was found to be faster. With a common grindstone, he beveled and smoothed the edge where it would be gripped by the frame of the spectacles.

In 1825, the English astronomer George Airy realized that he wasn't using one of his eyes at all, that is, he was subconsciously disre-

enabled the wearer to look into the future, and that illiterate people could read at sight with them. Though the eighteenth century boasted itself "The Age of Reason," some of this nonsense carried over into it.

By then—in fact, after 1590—short-sighted people could buy concave lenses that helped them to see things at a distance, and people troubled by bright light could get "Venetian green glasses" to reduce glare. No eighteenth-century physician imagined that prescribing lenses could ever be a part of his trade. Nobody knew any way of testing eyes to find out what lenses they actually needed, but lenses did come in graduated strengths and the purblind could select the pair that seemed to serve the purpose. Before you scoff at such ignorance, remember that this is done every day in twentieth-century "ten cent" stores. Modern stores selling glasses that way are prohibited from making suggestions to the customer, but the eighteenth-century eyeglass seller, presenting his trayful, hesitated not at all. He even scratched on the lenses the ages for which he thought each would be most useful. A sustained effort has failed to discover if anyone at this time realized that one of his eyes saw better than the other and tried to even things up with unmatched lenses.

The crystalline lenses of the eyes of elderly people flatten and harden so that the muscles can no longer change the lenses' shape to accommodate for near and far vision. This reaches a point where even the far-sighted need glasses for seeing distant objects sharply. The only solution of the 1700's was two pair of spectacles, the only solution, that is, until 1786, when Benjamin Franklin became annoyed by the nuisance of

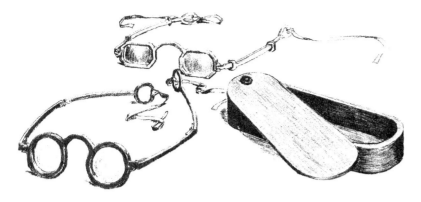

garding what it saw. Thousands of people had done this same thing for ages. Airy investigated and found that his bad eye saw horizontal lines better than vertical lines. The lens of that eye was deformed; he had astigmatism. Being an astronomer and used to lenses, Airy had a cylindrical lens ground to correct the defect. Such a lens is the shape of a slice taken lengthwise from the side of a cylinder, quite a large cylinder in the case of a spectacle lens. It "sees" better one way than the other. By 1860, such lenses were mounted loose in circular frames so that the user could rotate them to the position that helped him most.

Cylindrical lens

The use of noses and ears for supporting spectacles doesn't seem to have presented itself to anyone in the eighteenth century. Lenses were large and round, or small and oval, but the stout frames of both kinds were joined by bridges that soared over the nose without touching it. Temples ran straight back and had rings on their ends for tapes which tied them together at the back of the head. Small wonder that Franklin became tired of changing his glasses. Usually the temples were extended so that they almost met at the back. They were either hinged in the middle or arranged to telescope so the spectacles would fit into their case, which was usually a wooden box with its lid pivoted at one end. Most frames seem to have been made entirely of metal: iron, brass, pewter, silver, gold. Tortoise-shell or horn rims were almost a quarter of an inch wide and had metal bows and temples.

Telescoping temple

The Cutler

All cutting implements from saws to razors had to be made by hand and they all needed

steel. Probably the colonists imported small quantities of steel even in the seventeenth century and certainly they reworked old tools for some of their cutlery. Shops sold English blades, but it's doubtful that any American specialized in the craft until steel was made here. Connecticut produced a little of it in 1728, and a practical steel furnace began operation on High Street in Philadelphia about 1730. At this time founders were still convinced that the quality of the product depended on the kind of "liquor" in which they quenched the hot metal.

Colonial founders made steel by piling wrought-iron bars in ground-up charcoal and cooking them slowly for a week or ten days, a process called cementation. In the first furnaces the piles were covered with sand or clay to exclude air and so keep the charcoal from burning away. Later ones heated the iron and charcoal in long air-tight pots over a fire maintained without forced draft. The iron absorbed carbon as it cooked and was hardened by it. Because cementation raised blisters on the surface of the metal, the product was called blister steel. Its great fault was a lack of uniformity; it was hard on the outside, but soft on the inside.

Such steel edged the American axes and was welded to iron to make edges of plane blades and ordinary knives. When the founder reheated blister steel and "drew" it under a water-powered tilt hammer, he compacted it and improved its texture, calling it tilted steel. When he further heated it, cut it up, welded the pieces side by side, and redrew it, mixing the hard and soft parts, he improved it still further as shear steel, so called because it was good enough to make big and little shears. The English version of this steel was better than the American.

Before 1740, only India made anything better than shear steel. This cast or crucible steel,

Razor

known as wootz, was the steel of the famous Damascus swords. English diemakers paid weight-in-gold prices for wootz steel; little of it ever reached this country. In 1740, Benjamin Huntsman, an English clockmaker seeking to make cheaper springs, successfully melted blister steel in a crucible, using a wind furnace—one with bellows—and cast it. Liquefying gave it an even texture throughout. Due to a lack of the proper clay to make crucibles that wouldn't crack, no such steel was cast on this side of the Atlantic until 1832.

In the second half of the eighteenth century, American cutlers probably used Sheffield-cast steel for razors and scalpels. Yankee-made shear steel would do for swords, penknives, scissors, cold chisels, and the best wood chisel and plane blades. Tilted steel made augers and saws. Skilled blacksmiths could make some woodworking tools that required more refinement than an ax, but nicely finished articles were beyond their reach. Actually the cutler was a specialized blacksmith who concerned himself not only with the exact temper and qualities of steel but also with niceties of shape, smoothness, and polish. He had a tremendous demand to supply. The colonists had never been able to get all the cutlery they wanted and certainly the Indians never had.

The cutler shaped his metal hot, just as the blacksmith did, with hammer, forge, and anvil, and he tempered it the same way, quenching it first to make it very hard and then drawing it to color by reheating. A good cutler didn't make his knife all of one hardness. He held the spine of the blade over the forge and watched closely as the heat drove the yellow color upward toward the cutting edge. Just before it reached the edge, he quenched the blade again. This left a tough,

springy body to support a hard strip which, ground sharp, would stay sharp. If he made the whole knife as hard as the edge, the blade would be brittle and would shatter if it were dropped.

The next step was grinding, not only the edge but the whole surface of the blade, to remove roughnesses. The cutler's grindstone was the usual thick sandstone disk, revolving edge-up with its lower half in a water trough or with a drip can suspended above it. For hours at a time an apprentice turned the crank of a five-foot wooden drive wheel rope-belted to the small pulley of the stone. The same rig and power served the polishing wheels: first a wooden one, then a pewter one. That was as far as most work needed to be finished, but razors and surgical instruments got a final high polish with crocus powder (iron oxide) on a wheel covered with buff leather. French cutlers traditionally performed the grinding and polishing operations while lying prone on a sloping board above the wheel. Americans don't seem to have found this striking posture necessary.

An examination of plain colonial knives, such as paring knives and hunting knives, shows handles applied by two methods, but no assertion is made that they are the only ways the job was done. Both kinds had a soft steel tang, as long as the handle, attached to the blade. For one way the cutler flattened the tang and shaped it to the silhouette of the handle; than he applied a slip of wood, ivory, or bone, on each side of the tang, drilled two holes through everything, and riveted the slips in place with brass studs. The handles of clasp knives had such riveted slips on them. The other way required a squared tang passed lengthwise through a section of deer horn or wood and "upset" over a metal washer where it emerged. Both methods are still used.

51

Dress sword

Clasp knife, 1777

The Stuart snuffmill

The Tobacconist

Early Americans not only grew a lot of "sot weed," they also consumed a lot of it. Though the leaf can be chewed or smoked just as it comes from the curing barn, the user needs less fortitude if the stuff is processed a bit further before he gets it. Large factories attend to this now, but in the 1700's and most of the 1800's, small shops did the work in back rooms. They sold it out of their front doors direct to consumer, or out of the back doors, in bulk, to the general stores of neighboring villages. This or that tobacconist might get enough local reputation to have his name mentioned in connection with his products, but he offered them under no brand name. He merely sold tobacco at so much an ounce.

"Hand" of tobacco

The tobacconist bought his raw material, still in the grower's 500-pound hogsheads, from a local factor. The grower tied his cured weed into fan-shaped hands, a dozen or so leaves with their stems tied together. He placed the hands carefully flat and spread them evenly before he applied the heavy pressure needed to squeeze them into their casks. The tobacconist untied the hands and cut the central rib or stem from each leaf. He put the stems aside to grind into the cheapest snuff he made and sorted the leaves according to their intended use.

Thread tobacco

Whatever their final form, the tobacconist moistened his leaves and stacked them in a two-foot heap to sweat—that is, to ferment—for a couple of weeks. Then he flavored the tobacco according to the tastes of his customers and to how they would use it. Pipe and chewing tobacco had molasses added to it and sometimes licorice or vanilla. When the leaf had partially dried, the apprentices twisted it into "thread" on a tobacco wheel, which was actually a drum reel turned by a crank. Thread tobacco was leaves twisted into a lumpy strand about as thick as a finger. The dealer might cut the thread into fixed penny and two-penny lengths, or he might sell it by the yard, as it were, cutting off as much as the customer wanted. All tobacco products were aged several months or else pressed into kegs and heated for a few days to try to achieve the same curing.

Plug tobacco had molasses or honey mixed with it for flavor and to make it hold its shape when it was compacted under pressure into a hard mass. It got its name from the way it was originally made. This was to drive the tobacco into a hole bored in the end of a log, using a maul and a wooden plunger for the driving. The hole was thus literally plugged; the plug was recovered by splitting the log.

If the user chewed, he merely sliced off a "chaw" from plug or thread and distorted his cheek with it. If he smoked, he cut off a bit and crumbled it in his palm with his thumb before packing his pipe. The tobacconist also cut leaf into narrow strips to make shag pipe tobacco which he sold at higher prices in papers, usually cones, with the large ends folded down and held with sealing wax.

The birth date of the corncob pipe seems to evade detection. No evidence appears to show that the Indians smoked them, but it's hard to see why they didn't. The soft center of a cob is easily removed and hollow reeds for stems were

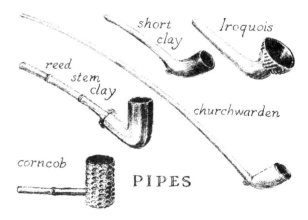

PIPES

common. The first man who broke his clay pipe and couldn't get another would obviously invent the corncob pipe. The Iroquois did use clay pipes; most other Indians carved pipes from soft stone. Nearly all colonial men and many women smoked clay pipes, long or short, with clay stems or with reed stems. They didn't often smoke them while they were working, walking, or riding; they waited until they were seated in comfort near a fire or a candle where they could get a light. Matches were unknown, and to light a pipe with flint and steel was beyond anybody's patience.

Smoking tongs for lighting a pipe with ember

Good inns and taverns provided long clay churchwarden pipes for their guests. If you wanted a smoke, you picked up a pipe, broke an inch off the stem for sanitation, filled the bowl from a box of tobacco on the bar, and lighted it with a hot coal held in smoking tongs. The usual charge was a penny. When the sixteen-inch stem of a churchwarden became clogged with tar, you simply put the pipe into the fire and left it overnight. The clay became red hot, all the tar burned away, and in the morning the pipe had cooled to its original whiteness.

Cigarettes were unknown east of New Mexico, but after 1762, when Israel Putnam brought in three donkey loads from Cuba, wealthy gentlemen smoked Havana cigars. Much more pungent ones, rolled in small shops out of Maryland and Kentucky tobacco, became increasingly popular with less prosperous men. The first cigar factory started in Connecticut in 1812, women rolled the common kind of cigars at the rate of fifteen hundred a day.

Gentlemen took quantities of snuff and so did ladies, though not so publicly. One may guess that, as with chewing tobacco, the popularity of snuffing started because of the difficulty of getting a light. However that may be, most men kept snuff always within reach—in crocks, in bottles, or in silver or pewter-mounted ram's horns, called mulls, at home, and in pocket boxes abroad. In the seventeenth century the boxes

were large enough to hold a bit of twist tobacco and were made with a lidded grater on one side. The later pocket boxes for ready-ground snuff were smaller but much more pretentious. A snuffbox was a status symbol and every man carried the most expensive one he could afford; some had a different box for every day. Said the *Tatler:* "I will . . . find out the shape of the fellow's snuff box, by which I can settle his character." The boxes were of all sorts of materials: gold, silver, tortoise shell, horn, brass, pewter, papier-mâché, and wood; they were often enameled and ornamented with miniature paintings surrounded with real or paste jewels.

An elaborate ceremonial went with snuffing, and gentlemen made a great ado of bowing their snuffboxes at one another. Snuff was a great icebreaker. Before he opened it, the snuffer tapped the top of his box three times to dislodge any powder that might stick to the lid. Some placed a pinch on the back of the hand that held the box and sniffed it from there, but most conveyed the pinch directly to a nostril, spilling part of it on their lace neckbands. The coats of the fashionable were constantly sprinkled with wig powder and their laces with snuff. The snuffer invariably sneezed and his companions invariably said, "God bless you."

Ram's-horn snuff mull

Snuff is still sniffed, though with little ritual, but a lot more of it is dipped. It's curious that two ways of using the same powder should stand so far apart in elegance. For, if snuffing was formal and graceful, dipping is as vulgar a performance as has ever been seen in public. The dipper pulls forward his lower lip and pours snuff onto it; then, with a well-chewed brush-ended snuff stick, he rubs the tobacco well into his gums. Many have now abandoned the stick and are content merely to "soak" snuff by tucking a little in a cheek. There are no positive colonial production figures, but it's safe to assume they were lower than the thirty-five million pounds of snuff that this country now produces yearly. Apparently snuff-taking is America's great hidden habit.

Pocket snuffbox

The Dutch made snuff in the eighteenth century and shipped it over here in delftware crocks, but American tobacconists produced the bulk of what was sold. The strongest and cheapest was Scotch, made of stems ground fine.

Glass snuff bottle and a lady's snuff spoon

The mortar of the Stuart mill

Demuth's "Old Man"

Early cigar-store Indian

Tobacconists ground small quantities of snuff in their shops in hand mortars. The demand became so great that, by 1750, snuff millers were grinding it with water power, either between ordinary millstones, like flour, or in large mortars. The father of the portrait painter, Gilbert Stuart, ran a snuff mill, now restored, in Rhode Island. His water wheel drove a heavy pestle in a mortar shaped like an inverted cone. Pot mulls ground snuff a little later. In these, a vertical shaft turned three steel rollers against the sloping corrugated iron sides of the pot. Six such rollers, clustered around a single drive shaft, are still grinding maccoboy in New Jersey as they have ground it since 1812.

Scotch snuff—a type, not an importation—was dry and was often adulterated with lime. Even more elegant snuffs were extended a little with pearl ash (refined potash) or with hellebore, which was poisonous enough to serve as an insecticide. The better snuffs received all sorts of fancy names according to various scents the makers added to them. Lemon and verbena went into some, and some snuff was salted. Basically there were two kinds: the fairly common rappee, generally called rap, which was dark, strong, and moist, and was flavored with bergamot, a powerful mint; and maccoboy, also moist, but lighter and more delicate,

normally scented with attar of roses. "Maccoboy" is a corruption of the snuff's place of origin, Macouba, in the island of Martinique.

The early tobacconist sold moist snuff in earthen crocks holding from one to twenty-five pounds. Of dry Scotch snuff, he packaged the larger quantities in the dried bladders of cows and calves and the smaller in sections of the esophagi of the same animals. He called these weasands, and small packages of snuff are still called that.

A few shops that sell tobacco only still carry on. Demuth's, in Lancaster, Pennsylvania, has sold it for nearly two centuries, and still owns the wooden figure of an eighteenth-century gentleman extending his snuffbox, carved for the first Christopher Demuth to stand outside his shop door. Though this is the oldest surviving one, such figures were not unusual as shop signs, but most tobacco shops then used swinging boards, with a painted Indian as the favorite symbol. The use of carved wooden Indians on tobacco-shop doorsteps seems to have started in Baltimore about 1775. Ship carvers made them from sections of old white-pine masts. The idea spread slowly, and by the mid-1800's a tobacconist with no wooden Indian had no prestige, either. The figures are nearly all gone now. Museums have the few survivors.

Horn spoon

The Hornsmith

The Manhattan telephone book lists no hornsmiths and only two workers in tortoise shell. But the art isn't a lost one. Workers in horn still function in Europe and Asia; it's simply that, in America, anything once made of horn is now plastic or glass. The processes of working horn and tortoise shell differ only as much as the natural shapes of the substances are different. The same tools are needed and similar articles can be made from both materials. Commercial tortoise shell is the overlapping plates of the

54

carapace (upper shell) of the tropical hawksbill turtle. Plates from a large specimen measure as much as eight by thirteen inches. Their substance is less fibrous than horn, and harder and more brittle. The mottled brown and amber colors are handsomer than the yellowish gray of horn and the shell takes a far higher polish. Colonial smiths used immeasurably more common cow horns than costly shells. Good gunpowder carriers could be made out of cow horns left in their original shape and no smith was needed to make them, but for almost everything else, the horns had to be opened and flattened.

The hornsmith first sawed off both ends, the small end because it was solid, the large end because it was gristly. After soaking the horn several days, he boiled or roasted it until it was soft. Sometimes he boiled it in oil, though just why isn't clear. Once soft, he could slit it from end to end and flatten it between heated iron plates to which he applied pressure with a screw press. The hornsmith "tempered" the flattened sheets by plunging them still hot into cold water. Softened horn is surprisingly malleable, and it was even possible to weld two pieces together in the hot press. Pressing not only clarified it, but

Flattening horn

equalized its thickness somewhat. Scraping to remove bumps and smooth the surfaces made the fan-shaped blanks ready for fabricating.

The smith sold some horn blanks to other craftsmen for use in their trades, along with other materials. Silversmiths and pewterers used horn as well as tortoise shell for the tops and bottoms of snuffboxes to which they gave metal sides and hinges; eyeglass sellers made some spectacle frames of horn; buttonmakers punched disks out of horn scraps. The smith himself made horn spoons by cutting out shapes and pressing them in hot iron molds. But most of his horn he made into combs.

He sawed out the rectangular comb blanks, somewhat wider than most modern combs and not tapered as they often are. The smith clamped one long edge of his blank in a wooden vise tightened with a wedge, and, seated with his work at eye level, made two cuts with a fine saw for each tooth. This left a thin slug of horn between each pair of teeth to be removed with a narrow chisel. The teeth of a colonial comb were coarse enough and were spaced widely enough to serve a horse, and they were never finer at one end of the short comb than at the other. The freshly cut teeth were sharp-edged and rough and the smith had to round each one with knife and scraper. That done, he buffed the comb all over with brick dust on a wheel. Sometimes he stained it to look as much like tortoise shell as possible, and finally he gave it a hand polish with vinegar and rottenstone.

Sometime around 1800 combmakers began to use a device called a twinning saw to cut teeth in two combs at once. This probably wasn't a circular saw thick enough to remove all the unwanted material from between the teeth, since a

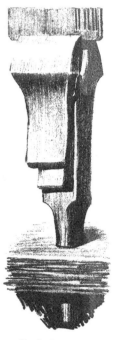

Comb vise

device invented ten years later and obviously slower than such a saw would have been was considered a major improvement. This was "Mr. Thomas's tooth cutter which uses chisels to cut one side of two teeth at a blow and removes slugs at the same time."

Soon after glassmaking was well started (1740), most lanterns had glass sides. Before that, if their walls were anything better than tin with holes punched in it, they were thin sheets of horn. Coppersmiths or tinsmiths made the bodies of such "lanthorns." The hornsmith soaked the horn for them in water two weeks—it took a month in winter—and the water loosened the growth layers enough to let him split them off with a thin chisel. They were about a thirty-second of an inch thick, and polishing both sides gave them a yellowish semi-transparency.

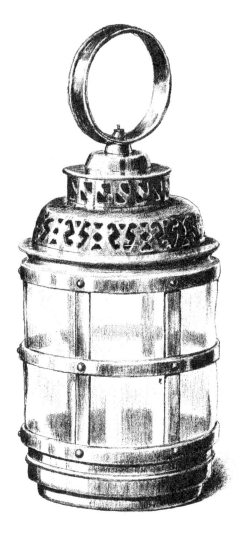

Brass and horn lantern about 20 inches high.
Few of these survive. This one is probably English.

4.

BESPOKE WORK

EVEN in the largest towns bookbinders, painters, engravers, and such other highly specialized craftsmen as ivory carvers—they made billiard balls, gaming pieces, toothpicks, walking-stick heads—needed a secondary trade to boil the pot. Our friend the cutler sometimes made locks and did "various other small Jobbs in the Iron Way." On the other hand, workers at more common trades in big towns could pick, or found themselves thrust into, specialties within their crafts. Often, of course, this was the result of aptitude: not every good blacksmith could make ornamental iron; not every carpenter could build a good boat. Though many of these specialists worked for wages in group enterprises and though many of them filled spare time—their own or that of apprentices—by making staple articles for sale, as the blacksmiths made builders' nails, most of them filled orders bespoke by individual customers.

A man needed something, or he saw something of Elder Jenkins's that he thought he would like for himself, with *just* a few changes. So he

went to the proper artisan and described what he had in mind. Probably what he wanted was a familiar article and the master could show a sample, discussing and perhaps protesting his customer's personal notions. The result was a merging of tastes that sometimes failed but often resulted happily in an object, unique, or nearly so, which gave its owner the satisfaction of something peculiarly his own because he had planned it himself.

This wasn't a time when the craftsman yearned to make, or his customer to buy, anything bizarre or "different." Both stuck to well-known patterns but improved on them somewhat without hesitation. Neither had any feeling that the new article was a "reproduction" of an older one. Quite naturally the basic designs for almost everything originated in England. In American hands they were simplified and often improved, not only by less fussiness, but by refinements of line and proportion. A sense of fitness wasn't confined to the "gentry" but showed up in every social level and in every article of use however humble. All through the eighteenth century an excellent "American style" grew naturally and healthily, but somewhere around 1820 it took sick and died. No explanation of this can be offered here, nor has a satisfactory one been offered elsewhere. The appearance of factory-made goods clinched it, but the spirit had weakened before the factories got started.

This isn't to say that everything made since 1820 is bad or that all factory produce is bad. Actually, we have been making things by machinery only a short time. We have already learned to make them better than we did and we certainly shall make them still better. Which is just as well because they will be made that way for the foreseeable future. Perhaps we already have a new American style, too close to us to be detected.

The Town Blacksmiths

Nine colonists out of ten were farmers, and the villages served the farms. Even the largest towns were in many ways expanded villages existing chiefly to buy, sell, and ship farm produce. Horses and oxen moved freight to the towns and within the towns, while every man who could afford one rode or drove a horse. Many town smiths had so much work shoeing and doctoring animals that they became almost exclusively farriers. They left the making of tools, implements, and hardware, and the "ironing" of wagons and carriages to other smiths who concentrated on one or another of these things. All of them let the barbers and doctors do the tooth pulling.

If Mistress Hughes in Providence needed a long-handled cooking fork, her husband picked a smith who was especially good at such things and had him make it for her. This was a standard article and perhaps the smith had one made in advance that would serve. But there was no factory anywhere that turned out cooking forks in quantity, all alike, and no shop had a house-furnishings department where Mrs. Hughes could look for the fork she wanted. The blacksmith who made the fork was prepared to make any cooking utensil, so long as it was wrought-iron: a pot hook, a dipper, a strainer; a trivet on which to keep a pot warm near the fire; a broiler, either a plain square one or a fancy one with a rotating circular top; a toaster with a rotating rack to simplify reversing the bread before the fire. The smith couldn't make skillets, waffle irons, stew pots, and teakettles—those were cast-iron foundry jobs or coppersmith's work—but he could forge handles for any of them.

When Alderman Davis needed hardware for the dower house he put up for his daughter Sophia, he bespoke all of it from a smith: door hinges, latches, bolts; shutter hinges, shutter hooks, shutter holdbacks; cupboard hinges and latches; handrails; foot scrapers; tongs, andirons, pokers; even common nails.

Few blacksmith shops were so specialized as not to make carpenters' nails. The demand was great and filling it was profitable slack-time work as well as good practice for apprentices. Though each nail had to be pointed, cut, and headed by hand, experts could make them so fast that the earliest nail-cutting machinery made no headway. Nails came in quite a range of sizes, designated, as they still are, by "pennies," 6d., 8d., 10d., and so on, indicating, then, the cost of a hundred of that size. The nails were cut off from square rods. These the smith bought either directly from a slitting mill, about which more later, or, if there was no local mill, from an ironmonger. The rods were about five feet long; the smallest ones less than an eighth of an inch square and the largest, more than a quarter.

The nailer used such simple equipment that many men owned it and made at home the nails they needed around the place or used for money at the store: for a fire with no forced draft, the kitchen hearth would do; a small anvil with a tapered hole through its projecting end; a hammer with a wedge-shaped peen to cut rod; and a pair of tongs to use when the shortened rod became too hot to hold. Good practice kept several rods in the fire and used them in rotation so as to work always with the hottest.

Making a nail took much less time than it takes to read about it. The nailer held the cool end of the rod in his left hand and the hot end on the anvil; then, using the flat face of his hammer, he tapered an inch of the end of the rod, usually on all four sides. A novice might need a gauge to

BLACKSMITH'S WORK

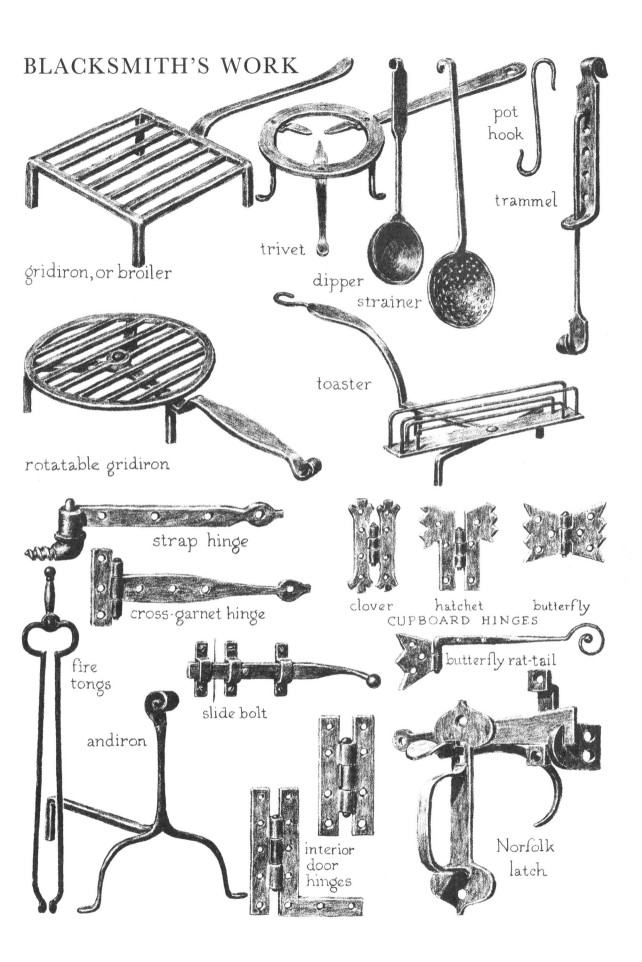

gridiron, or broiler

trivet

dipper

strainer

pot hook

trammel

toaster

rotatable gridiron

strap hinge

cross-garnet hinge

clover   hatchet   butterfly
CUPBOARD HINGES

butterfly rat-tail

fire tongs

slide bolt

andiron

interior door hinges

Norfolk latch

of a strip of metal; it had no formed head. The machine was simple. Its operator fed an iron strip as wide as the nail's length across a flat bed to a shearing blade set at slightly less than a right angle to a side guide. The nailer's foot on a pedal brought the blade down to cut off a nail and a spring raised it again. He turned the strip over sideways after each cut to make all the nails alike and to maintain their taper. The blade would cut small nails from cold iron, but for large ones the strip had to be hot. This machine was soon improved to grip the cut-off nail and bang its thick end to form a head.

keep all his nails the same length, but an expert depended on his practiced eye. Turning his hammer, he used the sharp peen to cut the rod part way through and then jammed the new point into the tapered hole in the back of his anvil. He snapped the rod off at the cut as soon as the point stuck in the hole. The blunt end of the nail, still hot, stood about a quarter of an inch above the face of the anvil, and the nailer battered it into a quite large and irregular convex head with a couple of hammer blows. The nail point protruded from the bottom of the hole, and an upward tap on it knocked the new nail out on to the floor to be picked up and counted later.

Grille in a wooden gate, Philadelphia

Hand-held nail headers to replace the anvil hole appeared late in the 1700's and are said to have speeded up production. These were no more than handles with shallow square holes in one or both ends. At this distance it seems that an unheaded straight-shanked nail would fall clear through such a hole. Soon after 1800, foot-powered machines were making cut nails at the rate of about one hundred and fifty a minute. By 1835, hand-wrought-nail making had dwindled to a trickle of home and village production, not because the machines had taken over, but because European handmade nails were cheaper than any kind of nail that could be made in this country.

The earliest cut nail was nothing more than a narrow wedge chopped crosswise from the end

Hand nail header, 19th century

Nail rod, tapered and cut

Finished handmade nail

The town smithy and its equipment were the same and its means of shaping metal were the same as those of the remotest country shop. The difference lay in special skills that the town smith acquired. A blacksmith who could make a pair of handsome gates for an estate learned to work with his iron white-hot, and hence soft, so that he could seize it with tongs and curl it into a sweetly flowing spiral with one masterly motion. Such intense heat tended to make the iron oxidize rapidly, so the smith thrust it, hot, into a mixture of sand and salt which glazed its surface and kept the air from it.

Fine ornamental iron survives in all colonial towns but the South is most famous for it, especially Charleston and New Orleans. Most but not all of New Orleans' "iron lace" is cast iron, however, replacing fine wrought iron destroyed by a great fire in 1780. Charleston has kept most if its beautiful wrought fences, gates, railings, and balconies, many of them the work of skilled slaves.

The variety of ornamental iron articles is so great that we can mention only a few of them. A fine workman had his standards, and he kept them as high when he made a simple sign bracket for a shopkeeper as when he let himself go with elaborate scrolls for a balcony railing. When large towns began to light their streets, blacksmiths made the lanterns that protected the candles from wind and rain. Taverns, meeting houses, and large homes had use for chandeliers burning up to a couple of dozen candles. The most elegant of these were brass or even silver; there were tin ones, too; but the greatest number of them were iron. Even the simplest house used iron candleholders in variety, some on tables, others, usually adjustable for height, standing on the floor.

Many barns and nearly all public buildings sported weather vanes, and those the coppersmith didn't make, the blacksmith did. Those who sold anything by weight needed scales. Brass ones were best for the light stuff of the silversmith and the apothecary, but for heavy articles only iron would do. Blacksmiths made balance scales with arms of equal length, and "steelyerds" or beam scales with one long arm on which a movable weight balanced a short hook that supported the merchandise. Such a scale had to pass official inspection for accuracy and its making demanded a high degree of skill.

We have seen that millers bore the burden of a bad reputation in the public's mind; the reverse was true of blacksmiths. They were thought of as being sturdily honest and they seem to have generally deserved the rating. If you would see this look you in the eye, examine the portrait of Pat Lyon, blacksmith, lockmaker, and builder of fire engines, which hangs in the Boston Athenaeum. Pat had made the safe locks for the bank of Pennsylvania. When its strongbox

was cleaned out one Sunday in 1798 by means of duplicate keys, Pat was accused of the job and put into the Walnut Street gaol even though he was in Delaware at the time of the robbery. They caught the real thief and recovered most of the money, but they still suspected Pat as an accomplice and his business was ruined. He became a hero when he was finally cleared, and nine years later the bank paid him nine thousand dollars damages. In 1826 Pat commissioned John Neagle to paint him, not in his Sunday best, but, uniquely, in his leather apron at his forge.

More remains to be said about blacksmiths, but that is best told along with the other trades of which they were a part.

The Locksmith

Locksmithing required the use of forge and anvil, so it was a branch of blacksmithing. Actually, most good blacksmiths could make padlocks and simple rim locks. Colonial locks seem large to us; an early padlock will weigh at least a pound.

Up to the eighteenth century, lockmaking principles hadn't changed in three hundred years or more, and they still didn't change until Linus Yale tampered with them in 1851. Even now the earlier way governs very simple locks. It is nothing more than the use of a removable key as a lever to slide an enclosed dead bolt into a keeper and out again at will. Much of the art of the

Picklock

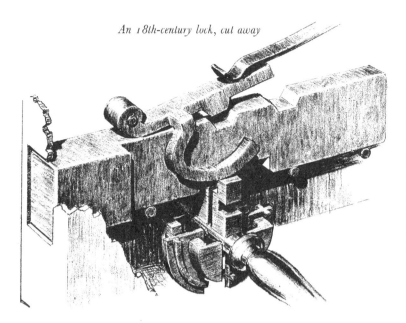

An 18th-century lock, cut away

locksmith lay in devising obstacles to prevent any key but the owner's from moving the bolt. He might try to keep an alien key from entering the lock at all, but whether he did that or not, he always tried to keep such a key from turning so as to engage the bolt. This baffled common thieves, but it was never proof against an expert who could feel his way through the obstacles with a thin picklock.

Locksmiths give the name "wards" to the obstacles. When you see a key with a groove or two on its bit or blade parallel to its stem, the keyhole it fits has wards inside to keep out all keys which lack that groove pattern. Slots or notches, cut across the thickness of the bit, fit circular wards concentric with the keyhole that will pass through the slots and notches of the right key as it turns but will stop any other key on which even one part of one notch is different.

Wrought-iron money chest, 1754

Colonial door locks were rim locks screwed to the inside face of the door at the top of the wide cross rail, rather than mortised into the door's edge as many modern locks are. The early locksmith made all of his parts by hand: forging, tempering, filing. He made the key first and built his lock around it on the iron or brass lock plate which supported the mechanism. A door lock had a latch above or below its bolt as locks have now. This is a smaller bolt, resting normally in the thrown position, but readily withdrawn by turning the knob or by the side pressure of the keeper against its beveled head as the door closes. A spring throws it again instantly when either force is released. Old locks normally had knobs on both sides of the door, but for the inside a good many people preferred ring drop handles like the one in the illustration.

The main bolt was of one piece but two parts, head and tail. A big lock's bolt might be eight inches long by an inch and a half high, its head an inch thick and its tail half as thick but taking up six inches of the total length. The tail slid on studs projecting from the lock plate.

The circular top of a keyhole accepts the stem of the key and fixes the center on which the bit of the key turns. It is placed below the bolt by about two-thirds of the bit's total depth. Thus the key, turning upward, will strike the under side of the bolt tail but for a notch there, called the talon, into which the bit passes. The key throws the bolt, or withdraws it, by pressing its bit against one end or the other of the talon. Some security was added to old locks by the pin tumbler. This lay next to the tail of the bolt and extended over it. The pin tumbler's spring forced it into a notch when the bolt reached the thrown position and it thus blocked efforts to slide the bolt back by any means other than the key. When the right key unlocked the door, it lifted the tumbler from its notch before engaging the talon. Since such locks would not operate properly upside down, they had to be made right-hand and left-hand, depending on which way the door was hinged.

The storage of money was a difficult problem. There were no storage vaults. The combination lock was still unknown. Individuals, businesses, even governments, used wooden or iron strongboxes which they hid if possible. The wrought-iron one illustrated is typical except that, having been used by the treasury of a colony, it is larger than most. It weighs twelve hundred pounds. In addition to its two padlocks, for each of which the key was held by a different official, it requires a third huge iron key which is inserted into the center of the lid to move bolts engaging three walls of the box. The hinges take care of the fourth wall and are completely concealed within the box. Instead of extending over the walls as box lids commonly do, the edges of the lid lie inside the walls. Presumably this was to make it hard to get a lever under the lid, but it did nothing to prevent a lever from bulging the walls of the box outward.

The Gunsmith

To say that every eighteenth-century American man owned a gun is so nearly true as makes no difference. A hunter could find game just outside of town and it was an important part of everybody's diet. Most shoulder guns were flintlock muskets, smoothbore muzzle-loaders, firing scatter shot effectively or solid lead balls inaccurately. More important in quality, if not in quantity, was the great "Kentucky" rifle which really came from Pennsylvania. German gunsmiths at Lancaster developed it with advice and some pressure from woodsmen who knew what they wanted. It wasn't the earliest rifle, but it was the first readily portable one, and the use of a leather patch around its bullet made it the first that could be loaded in less than five minutes. It missed fire once in a while—all flintlocks did that—but its accuracy within its 200-yard range stands comparison with modern rifles.

No tool of the time was exact enough to open a straight hole lengthwise through a four-foot gun barrel, so the gunsmith had in effect to wrap the iron around the hole. To do this he welded a quite thick strip spirally around a rod and then drove the rod out. Two feet was the practical limit on this. He couldn't get his mandrel out of a longer tube, so he made two short lengths and welded them end to end. He forged on a swage to

Boring tool

Reamer

Gun-barrel making in the early 1800's. The pair at the anvil are forging; the old man at the right is boring, and the man in the foreground is broaching the spiral rifling grooves.

compact the hot metal and at the same time to give the outside of the barrel an octagonal shape.

After he joined the two ends, the smith bored the inside, using a small square cutter of steel welded against a long iron arbor which he turned either by water power or, laboriously, with a hand-cranked machine. Before boring, the gunsmith put the barrel against a grindstone and smoothed up its eight flats. The hole always came out a little crooked and the gunsmith checked it with a tight bowstring and carefully straightened it by tapping the outside with a hammer. The bore still had to be reamed to exact size and to a high polish with the same machine that did the boring. The smith made his reamer by squaring one end of an arbor and welding a thin strip of steel against one face of the square to serve as a cutter. He pinned a polished oval of hickory to the opposite face to give his reamer a guide that wouldn't scratch the surface of the bore.

Swage for a gun barrel

Spiral grooves in the bore give the rifle ball a gyroscopic spin which makes it shoot straighter than one from a smooth-bore musket. Broaching these was a hand job done with special equipment on a long bench. The barrel was held horizontal in clamps. The cutter of the broach had four or five sawlike teeth, each minutely higher than the tooth ahead of it. This block of teeth rode one end of a hickory rod and the other end was guided by a sliding frame which the smith pulled to drag the cutter through the bore.

Mounted lengthwise in the frame and free to turn on its axis was a cylindrical jig with two spiral grooves in it. This jig slid through an index block fixed to the bench. Lugs, projecting inward from the hole in the block, rode in the spiral grooves and forced the jig to rotate as it passed them. Thus the broach, rigidly fixed to the jig, also rotated as it moved forward and scored the

Broach for rifling

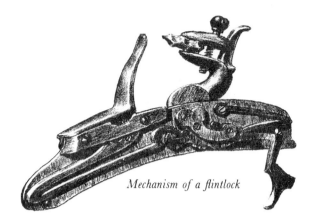

Mechanism of a flintlock

bore with a spiral groove. It took about a hundred passes to bring one groove to its full depth, the smith gradually shimming the cutter higher by slipping thin paper under it. Most barrels had eight grooves, indexed by the flats on the outside. These were muzzle-loaders and, once rifled, the breech was plugged and a touch hole was drilled in one flat, just ahead of the plug, to convey fire from the priming pan to the powder charge.

The priming pan was part of the flintlock. It held a pinch of powder under a hinged steel cover called the frizzen. Pulling the trigger tripped a spring that caused the frizzen to flip upward just in time to meet the descending flint, which struck it a glancing blow that produced a shower of sparks to ignite the priming.

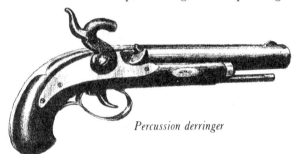

Percussion derringer

Backwoods gunsmiths could make a flintlock, sometimes filing it out of iron they smelted themselves from ore dug out of a hillside. They made springs out of old saw blades. This was doing things the hardest way, and when they could, they bought complete locks from experts in Lancaster, who also made them for urban gunsmiths. The backwoods had no monopoly on rifles, and muskets needed the same kind of lock. Gunsmiths whittled their own stocks out of walnut, maple, or persimmon wood, making them only an inch or so shorter than the total length of the gun. They filed out brass butt plates and patch-box covers, too, and also the brass ornaments they inlaid in the wood

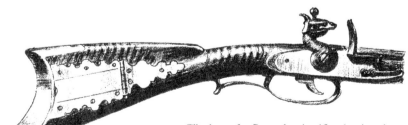

The butt of a Pennsylvania rifle, showing the flintlock and the brass patch box

Soldiers still used flintlock muskets in the Civil War, though in 1816 a Philadelphia artist named Joshua Shaw had perfected the simpler and more dependable cap lock. Shaw drilled a small steel cone and threaded it into a touchhole. A copper thimble (the cap) with a little fulminate of mercury in its base fitted on the cone. When he pulled his trigger, a hammer fell on the base of the cap and the fulminate did the rest. Many a flintlock gun was altered to fire by percussion. Percussion pistols became common in the 1830's; before that, flintlocks fired pistols.

The Whitesmith

A whitesmith is now called a tinsmith. What we call "tin" is, of course, actually tin plate—sheet iron coated with tin to prevent rusting. Early sheet iron was made in small pieces by repeatedly heating and flattening bar iron, at first under tilt hammers but, after 1800, by passing the bars between water-driven rollers. Tinners, as distinct from tinsmiths, cut the sheets to quite small sizes, the largest twelve by eighteen inches, pickled them in mild acid, scoured them with sand, and dipped them, wet, into a cast-iron pot filled with tin kept molten over a charcoal fire. A skim of tallow on the surface pre-

Tin snips

vented air from oxidizing the tin. Since tin melts at 450° F, the fire didn't have to be very hot. The tinners believed the tin penetrated the iron and formed an alloy with it, but they were wrong. No American sheet iron was tinned until 1830, and even then it had to be done with Cornish tin.

When a blacksmith at Newburyport, Massachusetts, made the first American "tinware" in 1680, his grease lamps were certainly uncoated sheet iron. The later whitesmith bought his tin-coated iron by the box at the nearest large town, cut it with bench shears to his wooden patterns, and shaped it by bending, crimping, and hammering. He worked a somewhat stubborn and restricted metal. Overheating would destroy its coating and hammering too great a bulge in it would break the coating. Sometimes he did hammer it into a dome shape for a lid, but he seldom did so without retinning it unless he knew the finished job would be painted. Simple curves and even right-angle bends, if they weren't too sharp, made no trouble.

The whitesmith stuck to boxes, cylinders, and cones, or combinations of those shapes. When he made a tin cup, he turned its lip edge over, not only to make it smooth but also to stiffen it. Any large article, like a pail, required additional stiffening in the form of an iron wire enclosed in the rolled-over edge.

Tin dipper

Plating tin, about 1830

molten solder between the lapped faces of the metal. When he put a bottom on a box or a can, he cut it slightly oversize and turned its edges up to a size that would fit exactly around the walls. Then he ran solder into the space between the wall and the little flange. He used a soft solder, probably one part lead and two parts tin, which melts at 350° F; it had no bismuth in it, as soft solder now has, because he didn't know what bismuth was. The smith applied it by setting chips of solder along the fluxed seam and then running them in with heat from a soldering iron —actually copper—which he kept hot in a small charcoal furnace. A good smith left no solder visible on his joint.

Rain gutters and downspouts made to fit a particular building and a few special articles like chandeliers and extra large lanterns constituted the tinsmith's bespoke work but by no means ended the list of the things he made. Largely his stock items were cheaper forms of articles that were also made of better materials: tin dippers,

Flatting hammer

The whitesmith used tools similar to those of workers in more ductile metals, but the simple shapes he made required far fewer special ones. In addition to the big shears anchored in a hole in his bench, he used hand snips for small cuts and nippers for trimming off tags and corners. His flattening anvil was a square block of iron set on a thick post. Bends of large diameter he usually made by tapping the metal with a mallet as he held it on a debarked log projecting horizontally from his bench. Straight and curved steel "edges" set in bench holes served as anvils for turning and rolling the edges of the tin. Hammers, punches, pincers, and files came near to completing his shaping equipment.

Tin can't be welded; its joints have to be soldered. The colonial tinsmith made a butt joint—that is, a joint uniting two flat pieces or the ends of a single piece used as the walls of a cylinder or a box—by lapping the edges or by turning the edges and hooking them together. In either case, he fluxed the joint with rosin so that the heat would not oxidize the tin, and ran

Soldering iron

strainers, and pans instead of iron ones; tin pails and cups instead of wooden or copper ones; tin lamps, lanterns, and candle holders instead of brass or pewter ones. Quite a few things—candle molds, candle boxes for handy storage, small tea and spice cans, tinderboxes, and sand shakers for sprinkling sand on letters to blot the ink— could be made of other metals but served their purpose just as well in tin. The list of tin articles is almost endless.

66

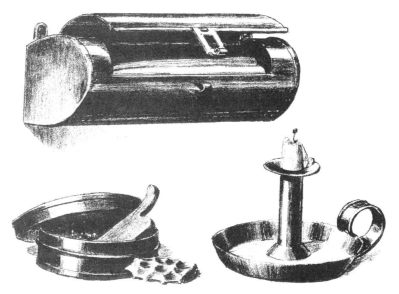

Sometime near the beginning of the eighteenth century, perhaps earlier, somebody invented the "roasting kitchen," a reflecting oven built as an arch-topped box on legs, with one open side to face the fire. A spit ran through it, a pan in the bottom caught drippings, and a door in the back gave entry for the cook's basting spoon. Some roasting kitchens were sheet brass or copper, but tin ones roasted meat as well as the best.

Square tin lanterns had three or four glass sides, usually protected by crossed wires, while some round ones had no glass whatever and allowed their faint light to escape through several hundred small holes punched through from the inside in patterns. These round ones are often wrongly called "Paul Revere" lanterns, but America's most famous horseman would have had trouble seeing one across the Charles River, and, too, his actual glass-sided lantern still exists. A drawing of it is reproduced in the front of this book. Tin sconces hung on walls reflected

A candle box, a tinderbox, and a candlestick

Roasting kitchen

their candles' light from back plates, either tall and narrow or round with crimped edges.

A tin chandelier held one or two rows of candles distributed around a rigid core with a ring in its top for hanging. When the cores were tin, they were perhaps a little too rigid to look better than quaint; turned wooden ones were better. Each candle stood in a tin socket fastened to the end of a tin arm, commonly S-shaped, and

arranged radially with its mates around the core. Most chandeliers were painted black, but some were dark green or dark red.

The Newburyport tin betty lamps were far from being the last of their kind. Such lamps are known to have been made as late as 1850 and when the last one was used is anybody's guess. The betty existed in Europe long before America was discovered. Its design is an improvement on the primitive cruse which was nothing more than a grease-filled dish with a lip for a wick to rest in and to drip grease so freely that a second dish commonly hung below the first to catch it. The betty lamp burned grease and smoked, but it didn't drip because, though it was shaped like the cruse, its wick rested, not in the lip but in a small slanting trough set a little back of the lip. The betty also had a hinged cover to limit the size of the flame, a refinement the cruse seldom had. Blacksmiths made iron betty lamps, but tin ones were easier to make and cheaper, though not as pretty.

After 1750, American whalers brought home increasing quantities of oil that gave more light with less smoke than any lamp oil ever used before. The reservoir of a whale-oil lamp could be made any size or shape that would permit a fair-size hole in its top for the burner, and of any material that could be readily shaped. Pewter, copper, brass, glass, and tin were all used, but the burners themselves were nearly always tin,

Tin betty lamp, 19th century

Sconce

67

and since tin was the cheapest material, most of the lamps were made of it.

Except in very cold weather when it needed a little warming, whale oil was thin enough to climb a wick held in a slightly tapered tube which was soldered into a disk that had its edge turned up to catch any overflow of oil. This was a "drop burner." It was dropped over the hole in the reservoir and it worked well except that oil might spill if the lamp was moved. Some

Drop burner

filled with water in front of their work lamps or their candles to focus the light.

Whale oil was expensive; the commonest kind cost a dollar and a half a gallon, and sperm oil, which gave a brighter light, cost a dollar more. West of the Appalachian Mountains it was hard to get either kind at any price; the substitute was oil squeezed from the fat of the four-footed "prairie whale." Lard oil was thick; in fact, it was nearly solid except in hot weather, so a

Tin whale-oil lamp with one bull's-eye lens; and a hand lamp with a hinged chimney

Patent lard-oil lamp and a pickwick with its wooden stand

Plug burner

American genius overcame this by adding a cork which he kept in place by soldering a smaller disk to the wick tube below it. The next step was to screw the burner into the lamp; most of the later ones were threaded. In all whale-oil burners a vertical slot in the upper part of the wick tube admitted the point of a pickwick to raise the fabric—cotton was best—as burning shortened it.

Ben Franklin found that a burner with two wicks gave more light than two lamps would give and that one with three wicks nearly equaled four lamps. By heating each other, they vaporized the oil more completely. Normally the flame of a whale-oil lamp burned unprotected with no chimney, giving a better light than a candle but not making anyone blink with its brilliance. Hand lamps, intended to be carried, did sometimes have mica chimneys like the one illustrated. Some lamps, usually pewter ones, were equipped with one or more thick convex lenses to concentrate their light for reading, and artisans often suspended spherical glass globes

Standard lard-oil burner

special burner was devised for it. The brass holder of a wide flat wick extended deep into the reservoir and, after the lamp burned low a while, the metal conducted enough heat downward to liquefy the oil. A little pre-warming by the fire hurried things up.

Around 1800 it was discovered that distilling turpentine over quicklime would remove the rosin from it and allow it to burn in a lamp with a bright white light and no smoke. Unfortunately it made a potential bomb of the lamp. If a spark reached the gas that collected in the reservoir, a fluid lamp exploded. It happened pretty frequently. Around 1826, the danger was reduced somewhat, at some cost of illumination, by diluting the turpentine with alcohol. These burning fluids are known generally as camphine, and they were used along with whale oil and lard oil until the introduction of kerosene after the Civil War. The burners for fluid lamps were quite like those for whale-oil lamps except that the wick tubes were longer and slanted away from each other; there were always two or three of them. Nobody dared to blow out a fluid lamp, so each wick tube had an extinguisher cap chained to it.

All the tin sugar boxes, money boxes, candle boxes, lamps, coffeepots, and so on were useful and cheap, but people found them ugly. Then somebody thought of ornamenting them. The first work of this sort was known as japanned tin. Artisans in Wales so decorated tin soon after 1700, and later ladies, with time on their hands,

trading pails and dippers for hides, tallow, spun yarn, rags, wood ashes, and feathers. And they learned to mind their profits and trade sharply. Success suggested longer trips, so they mounted horses and each set off with an apprentice leading a pack horse carrying panniers full of tinware. Soon the Pattersons stayed home to keep shop and hired others to do their peddling, and they added notions like needles, pins, salt, spices, buttons, and almanacs to the packs.

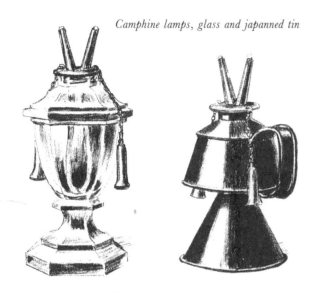

Camphine lamps, glass and japanned tin

Tole: a money box and a tea caddy

did it as a "polite accomplishment." They first gave the article several coats of dark brown asphaltum varnish and then embellished the surface by painting on bright colors. To keep from calling the product anything so common as tin, the elegant used the French word *tôle*—which meant the same thing. Tole "took on" in the colonies in the latter half of the eighteenth century and remained popular well into the nineteenth, acquiring along the way a cheaper poor relation decorated with stencils. Any tin article that might appear outside the kitchen was tole, and some of the trays, tea caddies, and so forth are handsome.

A pair of Irish brothers, William and Edgar Patterson, who were trained whitesmiths, came to Berlin near Hartford, Connecticut, in 1738, and there went to work at their trade. They bought imported tin plate in Boston. Berlin, little more than a hamlet, offered a limited market for the Patterson products, so the brothers slung sacks over their shoulders and went peddling through the countryside. They took country pay,

Other craftsmen, often tinsmiths also, began looking out over the horizon for markets. After turnpike-building began in the 1790's, they could send out wagons carrying a larger stock and the Yankee peddler was soon a familiar and welcome visitor in remote settlements. The system became well organized. In the fall the master tinsmiths sent journeymen by boat to central points—to Charleston, to Richmond, to Albany, even to Montreal. These men worked all winter making stock for the peddlers to take out in the spring. Tinware remained the core of the trade, but the peddler loaded his wagon with every portable article that people living beyond stores would need or want: hardware and horn combs; books and brushes; clothespins and cheap jewelry; seeds, shoes, spectacles, and suspenders —with springs; plug tobacco; and Terry clocks with wooden works. When he had peddled his whole "shag," his wagon was still loaded, but now with the stuff he had taken in trade. The peddler then returned to the seaport, sold his produce, his horses, and his wagon, buckled the

cash around his waist, and took ship for Connecticut where he gave the boss an accounting and was paid off. Later peddlers used specially built wagons with compartmented bodies. These they used for repeated trips.

There were cheaters, of course, but the story that the peddlers sold wooden nutmegs is Yankee humor. In general, the load on the wagon was honest. The peddler was a "slick article"—he got full value and more for what he sold—but many of his clocks are still running.

The Plumber

The plumber today is a pipe fitter who sometimes uses lead to seal a joint, and we use the term lead burner for a welder of sheet lead. But, until well into the nineteenth century, "plumber" covered any craftsman in lead except perhaps the shotmaker, whose trade was too new to have a proper craft name. Lead was scarce in early America and men cheerfully paid high prices for a pound or two to cast as bullets. England gladly sold it to the colonists, who had found none along the Atlantic seaboard. The French mined it in the Mississippi Valley quite early in the eighteenth century and may have shipped some out of New Orleans to the English colonies, but the supply never really met the demand until the opening of the Erie Canal in 1825.

Shot tower

Though artisans could buy lead in "pigs" as it was cast at the mines, much of it was recast by plumbers as sheets about thirty inches wide and seven feet long, which they sold rolled up to make handling easier. They cast their sheets on sand-covered tables. This required at least three men: two to carry hot lead from the furnace and pour it on the table, and one to gauge it flat with a kind of wide wooden hoe called a strike. The

Pouring sheet lead

strike's blade had square notches at both ends which rode long guides that limited the width of the sheet and also held the strike blade at a fixed distance above the table so as to maintain a constant thickness of the sheet. The pourers moved down the table, one on each side, at as steady a rate as possible, tilting their long ladle to pour the metal evenly. The strikeman pushed his blade behind them. Quite early in the 1800's someone devised a rolling box with a controlled slot to ride on the guides and spread the lead

70

better, but the striker still did his finishing chore.

A man who wanted to run water through something other than a wooden pipe usually chose a lead one. The quick improvements in the ways of making such pipe show how fast technology advanced once it got started. The earliest way was to bend a strip of lead lengthwise around an iron bar, weld the seam, and then pull the bar out. Pipe made that way was likely to crack. A better early way was casting in a long brass mold, hinged to open and made with a series of funnels along its top into which the plumber poured molten lead. He pulled the

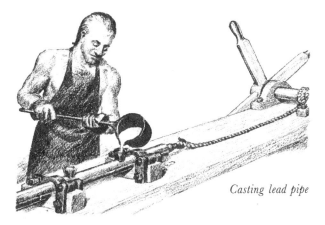

Casting lead pipe

solid iron core out with a windlass before he opened the mold—it was quite a pull. Such cast pipe had flaws and bubbles in it.

About 1800, plumbers began both to "cold-draw" and to "cold-roll" lead pipe. In either case they cast a thick-walled lead collar around one end of a polished steel bar. Drawing was pulling the collar through progressively smaller round dies that made the metal flow along the bar as a pipe, becoming thinner and longer with each die. Passing the collar between grooved rollers accomplished the same result. Hot drawing, done as early as the 1830's, was better than either. This was a continuous operation of pumping hot liquid lead into one end of a mold and pulling finished pipe out at the other. Lead sets up quickly as it cools, so the mold didn't have to be a very long one, but the speed of the draw and the volume of lead delivered by the pump had to remain constant and in the right relation to each other. Lead pipe is still made by a refinement of this method, using hydraulic pressure to force *cold* lead through a die.

71

Pouring shot

Cast-lead urns and small lead statues decorated the formal gardens of eighteenth-century estates, but all of these were cast abroad. So was the large lead statue of King George III that the Revolutionary Sons of Freedom pulled down in New York. Some small lead ornaments were undoubtedly cast here before the Revolution. Type metal was largely lead, but that is for another chapter.

A musket ball was almost half an inch in diameter. A hunter could cast his own, one at a time, and shotmakers cast them wholesale in duplicate molds, but scatter shot was another problem. Hunters sprayed many of them with a single charge at birds and other small game. Buckshot, just under a quarter of an inch in diameter with three shot weighing almost an ounce, was the largest size; of the smallest, four hundredths of an inch big, it took 4,565 shot to make an ounce. Even these little ones had to be almost perfectly spherical or they would fly off in all directions. Yet they had to be made rapidly in great quantities.

The ground floor of a shot tower

chain hoist   catching vat   testing plank   tumbling barrel   sorting chests

Porringer

Shot towers did the job and still do, but modern towers are lower and less spectacular than the old ones of which few still stand. Baltimore still has one built in 1838 and now unused. It is a tapered column of brick rising two hundred and thirty-four feet from a round base forty feet across to a crown top half that size. Inside are several platforms reached by a spiral wooden stair. Pig lead went up a central well on a chain hoist. The lower levels made small shot; the largest fell all the way from the top. The reason for the longer fall was to give the greater bulk of the large shot more time to cool and set.

Furnaces on each platform melted lead with a little arsenic added to make it "ball up" better. The ladle men poured metal into perforated copper pans held rigidly over the well. The holes in the pans were slightly smaller than the shot they made. The lead oozed from the holes and nature shaped the falling drops into balls. A vat of water at the bottom broke the fall and kept the impact of landing from distorting the shot.

Finishers ladled mixed sizes from the water and dried them, then they polished them in a tumbling barrel with "black lead" (graphite). Not all of the balls were perfectly round, but a simple system eliminated the bad ones. When the shot rolled down an inclined board, crooked ones ran off the sides while the true spheres followed the full course and fell off the lower end into a box. An odd sifter sorted the sizes. Two tall wooden boxes, looking like small chests of drawers, rocked on opposite ends of a shaft. The bottom of each drawer except the lowest was perforated to stop one size of shot. All but the largest fell through the top drawer, intermediate sizes stopped at their appropriate levels, and the smallest landed in the bottom.

The Pewterer

A little rather arty pewter is still made in this country. There is some old pewter ware in museum collections and a little is cherished sentimentally in homes. Hundreds of tons of it have vanished. The Chinese have used pewter for about two thousand years and probably use more now than any other nation. All Roman, medieval, and renaissance houses, except those of the very poor, had pewter in them. England early became the leading producer because of her tin mines—pewter is largely tin. English pewterers organized themselves as early as 1348, and in 1473 King Edward IV chartered them as the "Mistery of Pewterers" later called "The Worshipful Company of Pewterers."

With the law backing them, the Worshipful Company ran their trade with rigor. They specified metal qualities, inspected workmanship, and destroyed bad work. Members' pewter was identified by the guild's "Rose and Crown" —often stamped illegally on early American pewter—and by the member's own "touch" mark. The Pewterers Company still has the famous Touch Plate on which every member struck his mark at the time it was recorded.

No such complete record of American pewterers' marks exists, but they, too, used marks. All the known ones have been given numbers and with many of them careful detective work has connected names. We know that pewterers worked in Massachusetts as early as 1640, but only one piece of seventeenth-century pewter has been identified as "made in America." It is the handle of a spoon dug up at Jamestown and marked with a heart encircled by the words: IOSEPH COPELAND — 1675 — CHUCKA-TUCK. The town still flourishes. Some day the "restored" souvenir copies of this spoon will probably be taken for originals. Such things do happen.

The Worshipful Company managed to keep the Americans short of tin, leaving them to rework old metal which they sometimes stretched by adding a little lead or copper. Old inventories of pewter shops list quantities of scrap pewter but never any pure tin bars.

The scarcity, which kept the price of old metal high, favored the consumer. He could always get two new plates for three old ones, and some-

The Chuckatuck spoon. A restoration.

An American version of the Rose and Crown

Pewter nursing bottle

72

times four old ones bought three new ones. Pewterers lived frustrated lives because the demand for their product was huge. The value of pewter ware brought into this country between 1720 and 1767 was greater than that of all the silver, tinware, and furniture imported in the same years. Small wonder the Company kept the tin for itself.

A collection of polished pewter, used and proudly displayed, symbolized prosperity to the wives of artisans and shopkeepers. The gentry ate from silver and imported china; the very poor made out with wooden trenchers and pottery mugs. This lasted until about 1825, when the white ware of American potters invaded simple dining rooms and banished pewter to the kitchens.

Pewter never achieved a distinctive American style as silver and furniture did. Nevertheless, taking the imported along with the domestic, it served in its heyday for a wide variety of articles. It was too soft for knives and forks but it made good sad ware: spoons; plates; chargers—very large plates used as platters; bowls and porringers—bowls with pierced, flat handles; and good hollow ware which was teapots, pitchers, and tankards. Rubber was still a mere curiosity, so pewter nursing bottles had pewter nipples that screwed on. The squire might have his silver salt cellars and his silver inkstand; the tailor made out very well with pewter ones, and pewter served for the buttons of his coat and the buckles of his shoes. Even the wealthiest accepted pewter for lamps.

Pewter is an amiable metal to work. It can be readily bent, stretched, or compressed. Hammering doesn't harden it as it hardens other ductile metals, so it never needs annealing between operations. Anything that can be done to other ductile metals can be done to pewter, except that its greater softness resists detail. Any attempt to achieve the kind of sharpness that looks good on silver only spoils pewter, so it is best left plain and simple, as the old pewterers understood.

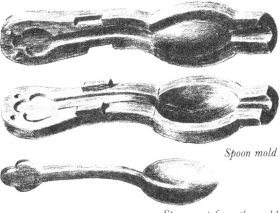

Spoon mold

Spoon cast from the mold

Pure tin is too soft to stand use, so it was always alloyed with another metal. Anciently, the metal was lead, but in England the guild demanded that the hardest pewter, called fine and used for flatware, have no lead in it. Up to the later 1600's, it had 23 per cent of copper; after that, it could have the copper replaced by 14½ per cent of antimony, which made it still harder.

Ley metal, used for casting hollow ware, had to be more ductile; it was allowed 16½ per cent of lead. A little more lead made "trifle" from which small objects like buttons and buckles were cast. Coarsest of all was black pewter, 40 per cent lead, and used only for candle molds, organ pipes, and other articles that would have no contact with food or drink. That much lead could be poisonous.

Pewter shoe buckle

The hard stuff, with copper in it, rings when it is struck and takes a bright polish: ley metal responds to the knuckle with a dull clunk and polishes to a silky sheen that has its own merits. Though much American pewter is good, it doesn't conform to the Company's standards for obvious reasons and it varies widely in quality. The final pewter alloy was britannia metal, made in England as a deliberate imitation of silver and introduced in this country about 1800. It is very hard and very white and it takes a brilliant polish. It probably shouldn't be called pewter at all.

Though pewter could be cut, bent, and soldered like tin, or raised to shape by hammering like silver, practically all American pewter

Basin mold, open

Filling a plate mold

hooks

float

Large molds, for casting sad ware that could be made as one piece, also consisted of two parts—one shaping the inside, the other the outside. The parts were hinged together and each half was provided with a long handle so the caster could hold them shut. Smoking the surface of a spoon mold made coating enough to keep the pewter from sticking to it, but the artisan had to cover the larger molds with a paste made of ocher, egg white, and vinegar. This baked on when he preheated the mold for casting and served for several pieces. A mold too cool made an imperfect cast and the first piece was often spoiled that way. The metal, too, had to be hot enough to flow freely. The pewterer knew when it was ready by the way it charred a dry stick. He held the mold, closed and edge-up with the gate at the top, on his bench, dipped metal from a pot with a ladle, and carefully poured until the gate was filled. He had to stand there holding the handles until experience told him the pewter was cool enough to be solid. He released his grip, tapped the mold on both sides to free the cast, then opened it and dropped the new piece onto a felt pad.

Though the inside of the mold was smooth, the casting came out quite rough, probably because of the coating. The first task after removing the tadge and the icicles was to fill any pits caused by air bubbles; the next, to smooth the whole surface with a two-handled float. This was much like a file except that its cutting ridges were coarse and ran straight across the tool instead of diagonally. Once smooth enough so it would not catch the "hooks," the piece was ready to be skimmed on a lathe.

ware was cast from molten metal, either in one piece or in several which were joined together later. This required molds, and molds were so costly that at least one new-fledged journeyman set up in business with only three: one for spoons, one for plates, and one for "basons," which were simple bowls for eating corn-meal mush, soup, or stew, or for use as serving dishes. Brass and copper made the best molds, but iron, soapstone, and even wood served for some things. Established masters in later years weighed their store of molds in hundreds of pounds.

A pewterer's products could be no better than his molds, which another craftsman made for him. The simplest molds, for casting such things as spoons and buttons, were two separate parts keyed to fit accurately together and, when so fitted, enclosing a space exactly the shape of the desired object. (There is a button mold on page 17.) Like all molds they were provided with a gate, or sprue, for pouring in metal. When the mold was full, a little extra metal remained in the gate and solidified into a cast of the passage as a "tadge" on the article and had to be removed. This wasn't the only unwanted projection. The running metal pushed air out and followed it into the parting line of the mold to form thin fins all around the casting. A parting line so tight that it held air would cause pockets in the metal that spoiled the piece. The pewterer cured this by filing a small trench across the face of the parting which, like the sprue, offered a cast of itself as an "icicle" on the main casting.

Skimming plates

Burnishers

The pewterer usually powered his lathe with a treadle and a cranked flywheel. The lathe rotated continuously; its construction differed from the ordinary wood turner's lathe only in the high fixed bar it had for supporting the worker's arm and in the large wooden chucks that held the work. These the craftsman shaped to accommodate particular objects: the one for a bowl had a central recess, the one for a plate was a flat disk. Both had metal rings screwed to them to which the skimmer tacked his work with spots of solder. To skim, he held the long handle of a cutting hook under his left arm and rested his right elbow on the bar of the lathe. A wood turner pressed his blade against his work, but the pewterer pulled the hook across his in a scraping action. A rounded and polished burnisher, dipped in soapsuds, followed the hook to flatten the marks of skimming and was followed in turn by rottenstone and a leather pad for polishing.

Plates would nest and the skimmer could build up a pile of them on the chuck, completing one side of each and tacking a new one on to it with solder. Then, reversing the whole pile, he skimmed and polished the backs, cutting each plate loose as he finished it. The booge or curve between the rim and the bottom of a pewter plate was sometimes hammered to compact the metal and strengthen it. This is called planishing. More will be said of that in connection with copper and silver.

The pewterer needed a whole covey of molds to make a hollow-ware article like a round-bellied teapot. He had to cast the lower half of the pot as a bowl and the upper half as an open bell shape and then join them together. He could do it with the whitesmith's soft solder, but more often he welded the halves with their own metal. He bent back their edges to make narrow flanges on both pieces; pressed face to face, these made a slight ridge around the pot. The pewterer held the halves together with wire, then fluxed the ridge with rosin, and deftly ran a hot soldering iron around it to melt it and join the pieces. A light skimming in the lathe made the joint invisible. The teapot's lid took at least two molds, one for the domed lid itself and one for the knob to lift it. The handle—unless the pot had a wooden one—and the spout were cast separately and soldered on; so was the hinge, and

Nine-inch Boardman plate

so were the feet if the pot was to have them. The flat handles of porringers, pierced to keep them cool enough to hold on to, were cast with a separate mold directly on the edge of the bowl.

Feet and knobs were cast solid, but spouts and handles were slush cast, a system used also for such things as sand shakers and nursing bottles whose inner surfaces wouldn't be visible. The slush mold's two halves shaped only the outside of the article. The caster poured hot metal into it, sluiced it around carefully, and then poured it out again. Enough stuck to the wall of the mold to form a hollow vessel.

Pewter, especially lead pewter, is easily bent, so a piece in daily use needed frequent straightening by hand. Eventually the metal tired and broke and the piece was put aside until a tinker showed up to mend it or to recast it. If his mold differed from the original shape, no one cared so long as the new article would serve the purpose of the old one. The famous tinker's dam, by the way, belongs to pewter. It served to keep hot metal from flowing where it wasn't wanted and was made of damp sand wrapped in a scrap of burlap. Some families had their own spoon molds or button molds and freely lent them to their neighbors. Spoon handles broke easily, so that, in time, all the spoons in a village could be identical.

Welding a teapot

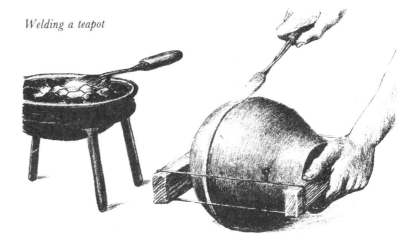

18th-century pewter teapot

Sometime in the 1820's Americans began using water-powered lathes to spin britannia metal. This was an old process, considered an inferior way of working and ruled out by the guild in England. The spinner set up his lathe using a wooden model as a chuck. This was specially turned to the exact shape of the article he was making. He centered a disk of pewter against it, holding the metal in place with a cylindrical wooden follow-block pressed against it by the screw of the tail stock. By pressing on the rotating metal with a wooden forming tool, the spinner could cause it to draw in around the model and assume its shape. Flat forms, like plates, spun easily, though rolling the edge over was tricky and needed the simultaneous use of the forming tool on the face and a back stick held against the opposite side. Drawing in high forms, like tankards, took two steps with two different chucks to keep the violent change of shape from tearing the metal. One chuck took the metal to an angle of forty-five degrees with its base, the second finished shaping it. The drawing in could never be sudden; it had to be done cautiously from the base upward. Even vase shapes, with small necks, could be spun on chucks made in removable sections, like the block for a bell-crowned hat.

Eagle touchmark of Thomas Danforth III, enlarged

Spinning

Pewter could be ornamented. In a way, the touchmark, stamped on with a cold brass die, was ornament. It was easy to engrave or chase (see silver) so soft a metal, but that kind of delicacy didn't suit it well and the marks wore off easily. Cast scrolled handles looked well; turned or cast knobs on lids looked well; and so did a simple half-round reed around the edge of a large dish. This was made separately, held on the edge with wire clips, and soldered into place.

The names of many eighteenth-century American pewterers are known, but there were no outstandingly great craftsmen among them as there were great silversmiths. The Danforth family of Connecticut is remarkable for the fact that at least twelve of its members were pewterers between 1733 and 1836; and the Boardmans of Hartford, Danforth relatives who ran America's largest pewtering business, maintained consistently high standards. After the Revolution, such men often marked their work with an eagle, but the custom died out and nineteenth-century pewter usually shows only the maker's name and town stamped on it in bold letters.

The Coppersmith

It seems to be hard to find out much about the use of copper in the American colonies during their first century. The archaeologists at Jamestown have found fragments of pans, hinges, and tubing—certainly all imported. The work of the few coppersmiths was mere tinkering and they needed a second trade to make ends meet.

The situation changed after 1709 when copper mining began in Connecticut; mines in Pennsylvania and New Jersey opened soon after that. Colonel John Schuyler's New Jersey mine *exported* 1,386 tons of copper in 1731. By 1753, his mine was two hundred feet deep and filling with water faster than hand pumps could clear it. Joseph Hornblower came to the rescue by smuggling in America's first steam engine—with spares for all parts because he knew he could never get more from England. Nobody knew enough to be of much help to Joseph, so it took him two years to set his engine up and get it pumping.

Copper ore usually has a lot of impurities in it: some valuable, like silver and lead; some dangerous or just annoying, like arsenic, antimony, sulphur, iron, and common slag. These made early processing and smelting an elaborate nuisance. Stamping mills crushed the ore in England and something similar to the bark mill did the job here. The founders added salt to the crushed ore and roasted it to burn off the sulphur and arsenic. Then they washed it to get out the lighter materials before they mixed it with charcoal dust and put it into a reverberatory smelting furnace on a bed of old slag.

Such a furnace can be understood by a glance at the diagram. Its bellows-blown fire doesn't pass through the ore as it does in a blast furnace, but is forced over a wall and over the ore through an arched chamber. The fire melted copper and a lot of other stuff to drain through the slag bed and a grate into a fire-clay crucible. Some slag could be skimmed off then through a side door. The founders drained the liquid copper slowly into a receiving basin outside the furnace where they could dip it up and pour it into hollows scooped in the sand floor. The impure copper cakes that came from these molds had to be remelted and skimmed again. If there was any silver in early copper, it stayed there and improved its host.

The founders cast their finished metal between stones—that is, between two thick slabs of clay-smeared slate—tilted to let the melt run across them and hinged together so that the upper one could be raised to get the cast out. This cast sheet was about an inch thick, five feet by seven in

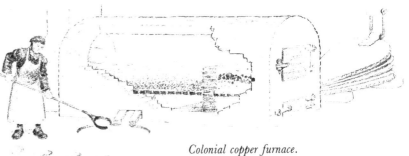

Colonial copper furnace.
This is necessarily a conjectural drawing.

size, and heavy—something over twelve hundred pounds. The workers needed tackle to lift the top slab and to move the copper over to the large levered shears they used to cut it into manageable sizes. One wonders why they didn't cast it in such sizes in the first place.

Copper shipped to England, to be made perhaps into brass, traveled in slabs. If it stayed home as coppersmith's material, the founders beat it, hot, into thinner sheets with a big tilt hammer. A cam on a waterwheel shaft slowly raised the head by pressing down on the butt of the helve; when the cam slipped off, the head came down on the anvil with a mighty thump and then rose again as the cam came around. When the hammer had halved the thickness of a sheet and doubled its area, the founders cut it in two, reheated it, and repeated the process. The thicknesses they drew elude discovery, but they hammered out the thinnest in stacks of four or five sheets together. Not until 1782 did Americans roll copper sheets, and some still flattened them with hammers well into the next century.

A native supply of metal turned coppersmithing into an active trade. Most smiths doubled as braziers, but no zinc for converting American copper into brass was found here in colonial

Copperplate works. Clockwise from
the melting pot in the far corner: the casting stones,
the shears, and the tilt hammer that reduced the thickness of the cut sheets.

Coppersmith's shop

Large heads

times. All of it came from a reluctant England, protecting a brass industry of her own which she had cosseted since the time of Elizabeth I.

A coppersmith's shop was a noisy place. It can be considered as having, roughly, three work areas: one for heavy stuff and here were the forge and the large anvils or heads; a second for the work bench where metal was cut and smaller work was shaped; and a third for the layout bench where the smith planned patterns and made them on a combination drawing table and carpenter's bench. Patterns were sketched on it and then tried out with paper. If they were for repeated use, they were made of thin wood or metal.

The small forge stood under a hood and was provided with a bellows, half the size of a blacksmith's, usually fastened to the ceiling out of the way. A long pipe led down from it to the fire. A few feet in front of the forge a heavy balk of timber, six or seven feet long, lay side on, sunk in the earth floor. Three or four square holes in its upper surface received the supports of changeable iron heads—some round, some square, some flat, some convex. Beyond the balk and parallel to it stood the "big horse," a slanting log with its heavy butt anchored to the floor. Two splayed legs supported it. These were set some thirty inches back from its higher end which was

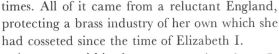

A bickern and two stakes

pierced with a square hole for heads. The device allowed the smith to get an anvil inside a large kettle.

Turning to the work bench: the bench shears, with the turned-down end of one of the long handles stuck into a hole, took up nearly half the bench's length. In front of the shears and fixed to the edge of the bench was the hatchet stake, a flat iron plate on which the smith made sharp bends. Next to it, along the front of the bench's mid-section, a row of square holes held a variety of small stakes serving as anvils for light work. Small iron "horses," some of them oddly cranked for holding interchangeable heads in tight places, also fitted the holes. Only a sampling of the varieties of stakes and horses is illustrated. The horizontal stake, a round steel bar a little over an inch thick, crossed the line of holes and projected about fourteen inches straight out from the bench to which it was strongly bolted. Bends of short radius were made over it. The special narrow vise of the coppersmith stood against the left-hand corner of the bench, bolted through the frame. It had the hundred uses of any vise and also served to hold temporary horses made for unusual jobs. A rack on the wall above the bench held a collection of hammers in a variety of shapes and weights; marking and cutting tools hung on pegs above it.

78

Once they had material, demand was great enough to keep the coppersmiths busy. Hatters, dyers, fullers, hornsmiths, and chandlers needed great kettles which they called coppers. Distillers required copper stills, the spherical retorts three or four feet in diameter which the coppersmith battered to shape on the big horse and riveted together.

Early steam engines, running on as much as twelve pounds of pressure, used copper boilers which the smiths made the same way, and copper pipe which they rolled up and soldered. Copper cannot be welded. People needed measures for liquids, from a five-gallon whisky pail like the one illustrated down to a half noggin that sized a penny tot of rum. Housewives wanted some copper pots and pans, though apparently not many, and some copper tankards though they seem to have preferred pewter. But all who could afford them wanted a copper funnel and a copper teakettle which were not only better than iron or tin ones but also prettier.

The coppersmith made all these things from sheet metal. He did little casting other than rivets, if he made his own, and knobs for lids. Much of his work was simple in shape. A tinsmith could have made the big whisky pail, but a teakettle was another matter—it bulged. The smith started making it with a flat fan-shaped sheet that he rolled into a truncated cone, nicking three or four tabs into one of its side edges and hammering them thin to make them lie close. He inserted the uncut edge under the tabs but over the metal that lay between them to make a "cramped joint." To close it, he filled the joint with a paste of borax, ground lead, and ground spelter (zinc), and dried it over his forge fire. A blowpipe used with a candle flame served to fuse this solder, harder than the tinsmith's and needing more heat to melt it. The smith filed away all lumps before he hammered the seam as flat as possible. Next he bent a series of wrinkles all around the larger end of his cone where it would be drawn in sharply to shape the upper part of the kettle; then he set about the drawing-in itself.

Resting the inner side of the cone on an L-shaped stake with a convex head, he beat the outer surface with a hammer, working from what would be the greatest diameter toward both ends and slowly bulging the metal as he ham-

Funnel and a 5-gallon whisky measure of copper. Studs, projecting inside the measure, mark each gallon.

mered. From time to time, he changed stakes for head shapes better suited to the developing curves. His hammering hardened the metal and he had to stop occasionally to anneal it to workability by heating it and quenching it in water. Iron is annealed by slow cooling, but copper and silver soften when they are cooled quickly. When he came to the large end, the smith hammered down the wrinkles he had made and kept working at them until they disappeared into the new form of the metal. Using stakes with sharply angled heads, he turned the small end inward as a flat flange to hold the bottom of the teakettle. The large end, now drawn in to a small circle, he turned straight up as a rim for the kettle's top to sit in. He rolled the free edge of this rim over into a neat welt. The smith cut tabs all the way around the disk that would make the kettle's bottom, bending every other one upward, so the turned-in flange at the bottom of the kettle body could lie between them and those he left flat. He soldered the bottom in place just as he had closed the first seam.

Now was the time to planish the kettle all over. The purpose of this was to compact and harden the metal. The smith planished on gently rounded anvils, using special hammers with flat or slightly convex faces polished so as to mark the metal as little as possible. The bottom he planished in circles, the body in horizontal rows from bottom to top. Every hammer blow had to be perpendicular to the surface to keep from marring it, and each blow overlapped the one before it and the row beside it. A fine craftsman's laps were identical every time.

Cranked horse to be held in a vise

Bumping hammers

Coppersmith's vise

Cramped joint

Drawing in

Bottom

Plenishing hammer

Riveted lug

The low dome of the lid was easily raised by hammering a disk of copper on a convex head. Since its seam would be hidden under the edge of the lid, the smith could solder on the ring that fitted into the rim he had made at the top of the body. The knob for lifting the lid he either turned from a bar of copper on a lathe or cast in the rough and finished by hand.

Two flat lugs stood up on the kettle to hold the ends of the handle, which was a fairly heavy copper wire that the smith drew himself and bent to its beautiful shape. The lugs were riveted onto the body: three holes in each, through both lug and teakettle; and three soft rivets, round heads outside, tails upset over washers on the inside. Simple loops held ordinary handles in holes made for them in the lugs, but this was a master's kettle and its handle ends curled around headed studs fixed in the lugs.

A teakettle has to have a spout and the smith took down a time-tested pattern that would outline a blank with just enough metal in the right places to make one. The blank had a notch in the middle of its larger end. This the smith pulled together and soldered. The seam would be at the bottom of the spout where it met the kettle body. Then, hammering on an iron mandrel, he rolled the spout to a straight, tapering tube that flared at its large end. The smith filled the tube with lead to keep it from flattening when he bent it with a hammer over a grooved wooden block. Once it achieved the right sweeping curve, the smith melted the lead out, finished up both ends with a file, and soldered the spout over a hole cut in the kettle body directly below one handle lug.

The blue-green verdigris that forms on copper is poisonous and would do nothing to improve a cup of tea, so it was necessary to tin the whole

Progress of a spout

inside of a teakettle or any copper pot used for cooking. The coppersmith warmed the kettle at his forge and wiped its interior with a wad of oakum dipped in molten tin. The Americans may sometimes have had to use pewter but it would serve. This was a nasty job, particularly on a vessel so nearly enclosed as a teakettle. A man could burn his hands doing it. The outside got a thorough polishing from an apprentice to pretty it up for the customer who, it's to be hoped, kept it that way.

The Silversmith

Counting them all in town and village, good and indifferent, about five hundred silversmiths worked in the colonies between 1634 and 1776. A few of them advertised themselves as goldsmiths, but this was largely swank. The English Goldsmiths Company had charge of assaying both gold and silver and its members worked in both metals. American silversmiths made a little gold jewelry and also sold some that they imported.

In the North these men did a thriving business, not only in large towns but also in country centers; one Rhode Island village almost supported four of them at the same time. The Southern tobacco planters and rice growers, selling in England, also bought silver there, so Southern silversmiths found themselves limited to repairs and to making small things like spoons,

80

ladles, and snuffboxes. The Northerners succeeded, not only because their customers liked beautiful things, but because the customers had no place to keep money when they got any. The best of the locksmiths' strongboxes offered doubtful security. Money stolen was money gone—you couldn't identify it. But you could identify a silver tray with your "cypher" engraved on it.

So, when the ship owner, the merchant, or even the craftsman accumulated enough silver coin to trouble his sleep, he had the silversmith turn it into plate. This doesn't mean that the piece was plated. Plate then was solid coin silver and what the customer got was his own metal wrought into a new shape. Little of the money was British crowns and shillings. It was Spanish dollars (pieces of eight) and pistareens (pesos); Portuguese and Brazilian crusadoes, each marked with a cross; and Dutch "dog dollars," the name jeering at the odd-looking heraldic lion stamped on the coins. Spanish dollars were pieces of eight because each was worth eight *reales* or twelve-and-a-half-cent "bits." Also, the Americans often chopped up dollars to make quarters and bits. So many of these dollars circulated that they finally became standard United States currency.

If Spanish gold doubloons (sixteen dollars) or pistoles (four dollars) turned up, or a Portuguese "half Joe" (half-Johannes or four dollars), the smith could make jewelry of them, take them as pay for his work, or sell the customer their value in silver. The smith weighed the silver coin to find out if there was enough metal in it to make what the customer wanted and also to value it. Silver money was then worth its actual weight. This was usually below standard as the result of wear and of the time-honored custom of clipping—that is, taking a little profit by scraping some silver off the edges. No American assay office existed until 1814. Assay was up to the silversmiths who kept their working metal at the sterling standard set by the London Goldsmiths Company: $92\frac{1}{2}$ per cent silver to $8\frac{1}{2}$ per cent copper. There was little cheating; no piece of colonial silver has yet tested below standard.

The customer had no choice but to trust the smith. Hence, whatever his skill, a silversmith had to have a reputation for probity. An honest

Candle cup made in New Amsterdam by Gerrit Onkelbag

man who had grown up in a community had a good start, but he did all he could to improve his standing. He joined local clubs; he undertook increasingly responsible public duties; bewigged and be-laced, he faithfully attended church, naturally the one the most important townsmen went to; and, if possible, he married the daughter of a solid citizen. As a result, silversmiths enjoyed the highest social position of any artisans and some became moderately rich.

However, not every one of them was a paragon of virtue. Young Abel Buell of Kenilworth, Connecticut, was an indifferent silversmith but a fine engraver. About 1763 he used this talent to improve some five-shilling notes into five-pound notes: paper money had been born of necessity in America in 1690. Abel was caught, jailed, branded on the forehead, and had his left ear clipped. But because he was young, he got a short sentence, the brand went on above his hairline, and the notch in his ear was a mere nick. We shall meet him again. He went his feckless way to make a notable contribution to another trade.

Earlier than this, in the village of Little Rest, Rhode Island, the really talented silversmith, Samuel Casey, hard up as the result of a disastrous fire, connived with neighbors and minted base metal into false pieces of eight. He first confessed and then, when a relative destroyed the evidence by throwing his dies into deep water, he recanted. A jury tried to acquit him but the magistrates overruled the verdict and ordered Casey hanged next morning. Casey wasn't there for the ceremony. His fellow townsmen sprung him that night and he vanished from history—a thing easy to do in colonial America.

Much old silverware was beautiful and all of it was valuable. Hence, succeeding generations held on to it even when its particular style became unfashionable and when they scrapped other fine things with what now seems like

Spanish dollar

stupidity. Some of the finest silver and some of the oldest is owned by churches, which were little troubled by fashions and which, though often poor, were seldom bankrupt.

American silver followed the English styles as fast as the silversmiths could become aware of them, usually several years after they appeared in London. Up to the restoration of Charles II in 1660, the copying was literal. The plain heavy work that pleased the English Puritans also pleased their brothers here. Except for some good Dutch work in New Amsterdam, nearly all seventeenth-century American silver was New England silver. Later, changing styles appeared there and also in towns farther south.

The baroque silverware of King Charles was heavy stuff, too, loaded with cast scrolls and

Tankard made about 1675 by Jeremiah Dummer

Queen Anne teapot by John Coney

"cut card" ornaments that made it still heavier. Cut card was sawn from thin sheet silver in the shape of elaborate formalized foliage and appliquéd with solder. This time, though the Americans followed, they didn't copy; they simplified the fancy work and used less of it, starting a preference for plainness that survived the eighteenth century and went a little beyond it.

In 1697, Queen Anne made her coins softer with purer silver to discourage English smiths from melting down money. It didn't work. To keep their work strong, the smiths made it thicker and used more cash than before. The failure of the soft silver to hold sharp ornament forced a new bareness. This was followed in America where the silversmiths did what some people think is the best American work. A plain piece had to stand or fall on its proportions and shape.

Crucible

Rococo cream pitcher by Samuel Casey

In the time of George II, about 1730, taste moved again to the fancy, this time to the free-form scrolls and shells called rococo. These could be charming in the hands of an artist who kept a tight rein on them but could be pretty fearsome when they got away from a lesser craftsman. The pendulum swung back and silverware became tall, severe, and light, with the classic revival that in this country followed the Revolution.

No American silversmith left a written account of his working methods that has been found, but most of them left tools which, listed in the inventories of their estates, give sufficient indication that they worked like the smiths of England, from whom, of course, some of them learned the trade. The first job was to get the customer's coins into workable shape by melting them into a single mass in a black lead (graphite) crucible and casting the mass as an ingot in a one-piece iron mold called a skillet. One doesn't associate silversmithing with hard manual labor, but flattening the ingot into workable sheets took strong arms and a heavy sledge.

The silversmith shaped his work by the same means the pewterer and the coppersmith used: seaming, casting, and hammering over stakes. For seaming he cut his metal by patterns and soldered it together. Silver solder, harder than that for copper, was itself mostly silver: four parts to one of brass. The smith applied borax flux as a paste and cooked it dry. Then he placed clipped-off bits of solder along the seam and melted them to run into the joint by holding the work over a charcoal fire or, for a small area, by applying flame with a blowpipe. Pickling in a weak solution of sulphuric acid removed the borax. When it has been planished, only an expert can detect a soldered seam in silver.

The worker in silver did more raising and carried it further than did either the pewterer or the coppersmith. Often he formed a cup or other vessel, bottom and all, from a single disk hammered over heads and stakes. The artisan had frequently to anneal his work. This meant holding it at a dull red heat for half a minute and then plunging it quickly into cold water. He always planished his work all over, using polished anvils along with his polished hammers.

Whole pieces were seldom cast, but the smith cast parts like feet, handles, and ornaments to be soldered on. He made wood models for parts he needed frequently and cast from them in sand flasks. Parts to be used only once he modeled in wax which he melted out of the mold before he poured the silver in. Even a highly finished model yielded a rough cast from sand and needed a lot of work with fine files.

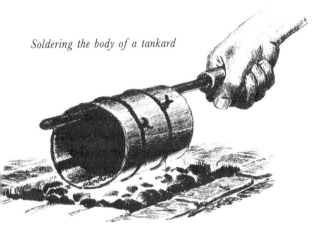

Soldering the body of a tankard

One thing the silversmith could do rapidly—he could stamp. He placed the flat blank for a teaspoon over a depression molded in a lead block and shaped the hollow bowl with one blow of a mallet on the end of a heavy iron die. The handle could be bent to shape by hand.

Often the smith reinforced and at the same time decorated his hollow ware by soldering wire on to it. This wasn't necessarily round wire, though he often used that, too; corded or twisted together, two strands of it could make an attractive fillet.

The smith drew his own wire—he needed only short lengths—and he made his own dies. For round wire, he drilled a series of diminishing tapered holes in a flat iron "draw block." He tempered the block to hardness and mounted it

83

behind chocks on his drawbench. He cut a narrow strip from the edge of a sheet of silver and tapered one end of it to enter the largest die hole and be grasped by the jaws of iron grippers. A strap wound on a drum at the far end of the bench pulled strongly on the grippers, tightening their pinch and dragging the silver strip through the die when a journeyman turned the crossed handles on the end of the drum's shaft. This rounded the metal, lengthening it, and each succeeding hole lengthened it further and decreased its diameter. But the stretching and squeezing hardened the silver, and after each draw the smith had to coil his wire and anneal it. The last hole brought the wire down to the size he wanted.

Spoon dies

For wire of special shape the silversmith filed out pairs of steel dies. Usually the upper die was flat so as to shape the face of the wire which would be soldered onto the body of the vessel; the lower die formed the visible profile which was either flat to make a simple band, or half round, or had two or three hollows to produce ridges with spaces between them. The two dies went into a swage block which had a screw at its top to press them together. The swage block fitted behind the drawbench chocks. Only slight squeeze was put on the dies for the first draw, but the squeeze was increased with each succeeding one until the wire came down to size.

Swage block

The craftsman bent his fillet to the curve of the surface it went on and cut it to fit the circumference of the piece. With the contact surfaces clean and fluxed and the fillet held in place with clips of bent iron wire, the smith distributed solder along the contact line and melted it to run in.

Swage block dies

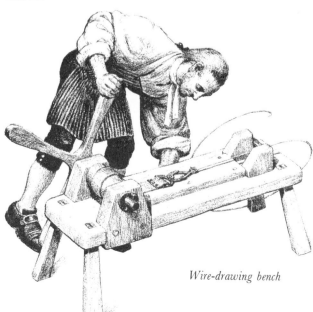

Wire-drawing bench

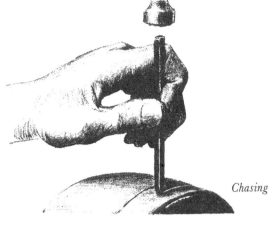

Chasing

Burin

Mention was made earlier of chasing and engraving as ways of decorating silver. Engraved ornament was especially important on later American silver. Earlier, it was chiefly a means of marking the piece for the owner, though these marks—elaborately intertwined initials or of coats of arms like that on the Coney teapot—could be ornamental. An engraver works with an angle-pointed tool called a burin, resting its mushroom-shaped handle in the palm of his hand and pushing the point away from him to cut lines in the silver. The burin removes a little metal from the line it makes.

Chasing also makes lines on silver but takes away no metal. The tracers are dull chisels of various sizes and blade shapes. They merely dent the metal when they are held vertically on it and are tapped lightly. A skilled worker can make continuous lines, straight or curved, which show no evidence of the successive blows. These blows would distort the shape of a hollow vessel if it were not filled with pitch to back up the metal and absorb the shocks.

Trencher salt

Because it was showy, many people liked the kind of embossed ornament that is called *repoussé*. Its outline was chased on the surface first; then the pitch was melted out and the embossing was bumped up from the inside with a snarling iron. This was a rod thin enough to vibrate when struck with a hammer and long enough to reach its turned-up beak to any point in the vessel. The name of the tool came from the noise it made in use. With its straight end clamped in his vise, the craftsman struck the rod between the vise and the work and the vibration transferred the force of his blow to the silver. The raised parts of the design needed some touching up with a tracer to finish them.

A long list of the articles made by colonial silversmiths would be more tiresome than useful.

Teapots, coffeepots, sugar bowls, and cream pitchers are still familiar objects. A family that owns a set of eighteenth-century trencher salts and the little round-bowled spoons to serve them is likely to put it on the table for special occasions, but a big seventeenth-century standing salt is likely to stay on the sideboard—if it isn't locked in storage. So with marrow spoons, long, slim, and usually double-ended—we just don't scoop marrow out of bones at the table any more. The half-spoon illustrated was a belated form. No colonial family could get along without porringers, silver ones if it was wealthy, pewter ones if it was not. A modern family finds little use for one, other than as an ashtray. A set of silver caudle cups can be used to serve punch but is highly unlikely to hold caudle, a kind of stirabout made with hot wine, sugar, spices and —*bread crumbs*.

Boston led in silversmithing until after the Revolutionary War, but as other centers grew in wealth, they attracted and produced fine craftsmen. Joseph Richardson and Johann de Nys of Philadelphia; Jacob Boelen, Nicholas Roosevelt, and Meyer Myers of New York—could all hold their own against the world. Many lesser men in those towns and in smaller places did excellent work. Boston had a remarkable direct succession of silversmiths—master to apprentice—all of them good and at least two of them great. Richard Storer arrived in the late 1630's from London where he had belonged to the Goldsmiths Company. He took as apprentice his half-brother, John Hull, who became wealthy and served as mint master for Massachusetts in 1652. Hull's apprentice was Jeremiah Dummer, who was a portrait painter as well as a good silversmith and who had for a brother-in-law— and probably for apprentice—John Coney, often rated as America's greatest silversmith. Coney, also a fine engraver; cut the Harvard seal and the plates for America's first paper money. One apprentice of his was a French Huguenot, Apollos De Revoire. Apollos Americanized his name, as his son and apprentice said, "on account the Bumpkins could pronounce it easier."

That son, Paul Revere, would have been famous as a silversmith if he had never ridden a horse in his life. Aside from his silversmithing,

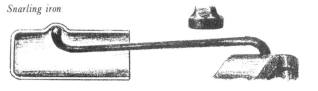

Snarling iron

84

Paul Revere was one of America's most versatile craftsmen. He was a tinsmith; he made false teeth; he engraved pictures—not always good ones; he made gunpowder; he cast bronze bells and cannon; he engraved plates for Continental money, built a press, and printed the plates on it; he made jewelry; he made hardware and sold it; he engraved seals; he carved picture frames; and sometimes he shod horses. And he really was a fine horseman, serving as a regular courier for the Committee of Safety. A sturdy, independent, irascible man, he was a lieutenant colonel of artillery in the Revolution but was, understandably, arrested for insubordination. He died at eighty-three in 1818.

The Builder

The outside appearance of a seventeenth-century house was the accidental result of its interior arrangement plus the methods used in building it. Doors and windows went in where they would be most useful, with little regard for how they would look to passers-by. In the eighteenth century educated men in England and America became obsessed with the Latin classics and began to build their houses in a style they thought of as Roman, but the designs they followed were actually invented by an Italian named Andrea Palladio in the mid-1500's. Among other rigid rules, Palladio insisted that a front door should be in the middle of a facade and that any feature on one side of it should be duplicated exactly on the other side. Large eighteenth-century colonial houses followed his dictum to the letter, arranging the rooms inside to conform to the exterior pattern. This usually meant a center hall with two identical rooms on each side of it. One man, finding it inconvenient so to plan his rooms, ended a partition against the middle of a window, but his house still faced the street in perfect symmetry. And George Washington, when he built his second addition to "Mount Vernon," put in four completely false windows to come as near to balance as the floor plan of his old farmhouse would let him.

Washington acted as his own architect and builder, though it's likely he had some design assistance from John Ariss, a professional architect who had visited England and who may have

A nearly symmetrical house of modest size built in Virginia about 1710

studied the subject there. Half a dozen Englishmen practiced architecture in the colonies, but Ariss seems to have been almost the only native professional before the Revolution. However, this reckons without the gentleman-architects who followed the trade as a graceful accomplishment: such remarkable amateurs as Peter Harrison, a Rhode Island merchant who produced a dozen fine churches and public buildings in New England; Andrew Hamilton, the Philadelphia lawyer, who not only defended the freedom of Peter Zenger's press but also designed Independence Hall; above all, Thomas Jefferson, accomplished in so many fields, who repeatedly proved his architectural abilities.

Charles Bulfinch began as such a wealthy amateur but circumstances forced him into professional practice. He graduated from Harvard in 1781 and, in 1785, made the "Grand Tour" of Europe. He used this trip to advance a boyhood interest in architecture. Excavations of Greek and Roman ruins had by then discredited Palladio's authority, and Bulfinch brought home the resulting new and more delicate interpretation of the classic, developed in England by the brothers Adam. The Federal style evolved in this country from the work of Bulfinch, Jefferson, and the Englishman, Benjamin H. Latrobe.

The architects concerned themselves with mansions and other large projects. When a simple citizen needed a house, he called in a master builder and agreed with him on size and probable cost, with perhaps some discussion of materials and appearance. The builder showed his client no drawings. He simply went ahead with construction, using Langley's *Treasury* to guide him on details. And a very good guide he had. Its full title was *The City and Country Builder's and Workman's Treasury of Designs*. Batty Langley

Marrow spoons

*Sugar bowl
by Paul Revere*

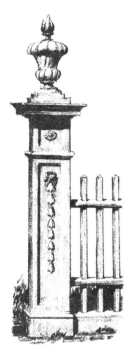

A McIntire fence post

wrote it and it was published in London in 1740. Its engravings showed hundreds of doorways, window frames, and mantels, and also entire buildings. An experienced man could pick out what he needed and reproduce it with whatever changes his customer's taste, or his own, suggested.

Langley's wasn't the only handbook; it was merely the simplest and most practical one for the general run of houses. Even the most elevated of the amateurs and professionals used James Gibbs's *Book of Architecture*, Isaac Ware's *A Complete Book of Architecture*, or one of a dozen others. *British Architect*, by Abraham Swan, was actually reprinted in Philadelphia in 1775. It was a practical builder's guide like the *Treasury*. Copies of these books exist. A person who is familiar with them can tell which book served for a given building and can note how often the native builders improved on the plates.

As in other trades, a master builder had to have served an apprenticeship and to have worked a long time as a journeyman carpenter and joiner. The most gifted masters were woodcarvers also. William Buckland, trained in England, was brought to Virginia as an indentured servant by George Mason specifically to act as carpenter and joiner for the building of "Gunston Hall." He went further than that and ornamented the interior of the house with some of the most elaborate carving to be seen in the colonies; in fact, he may have overdone it a bit. Later he set up in business for himself at Annapolis as an architect as well as a carver and "undertaker"—contractor, that is.

Samuel McIntire learned the joiner's and woodcarver's trades from his father in Salem, Massachusetts. Almost at once he showed outstanding skill at carving and a natural taste in architecture. Though he used the *Treasury* for his early work, he grasped at once the new refinements that Bulfinch brought from Europe and put them into the handsome buildings he created for his home town. Their chief glory, however, is the restrained carving with which he ornamented them both inside and out. McIntire also did some wood sculpture, but in that field he never equaled either the Philadelphian, William Rush, or the brothers, John and Simeon Skillin, who carved figureheads for Boston ships. America boasted no art schools and all these men served apprenticeships like any other artisans.

Though many, perhaps most, eighteenth-century houses, both north and south, had wooden walls and quite a few in Pennsylvania were built of stone, a great number were brick and certainly its warm color, contrasting with the white frames of windows and doors, is pleasant to look at. Country builders commonly made their own bricks on the job, hauling clay from the nearest bank. Town brickyards used much the same methods that they did.

Laborers could mix the clay with water in a pugmill knocked together for the occasion. Its only moving part was a wooden post rotated by a mule or an ox towing one end of a horizontal pole. A strongly built box surrounded the lower half of the post and clay was shoveled into its open top. Stout pegs driven into the post stirred the clay into a stiff paste and their spiral arrangement worked it downward to a slot at the bottom from which the molder took what he needed.

Any carpenter could make a brick mold. It was no more than a grid of two-inch boards partitioning six or eight brick-size spaces. It had neither bottom nor top. The molder, standing hip-deep in a pit, wet the mold and dipped it in sand so that the bricks would fall out after they were shaped. Then he used his hands to press

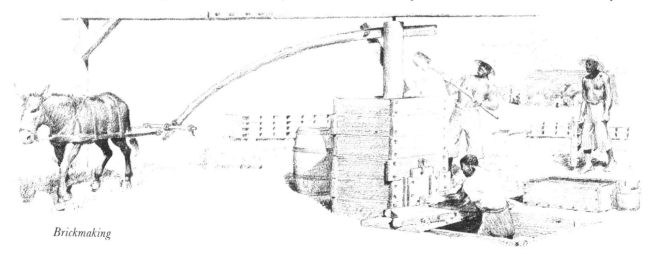

Brickmaking

clay solidly into every space. The board the mold stood on kept the bottoms of the bricks flat and a scrape with another board flattened their tops. A helper dumped the new bricks onto an improvised rack to dry for a couple of weeks.

The kiln was built with the "green" bricks themselves stacked with spaces between them to conduct heat and in such a way as to leave parallel open-ended tunnels through the pile. Only the outside walls were laid close. Wood fires in the tunnels, kept going day and night for ten days, baked the clay hard.

Bricklaying was a respected trade, complete with apprentices, journeymen, and masters. They laid their brick in a mortar of sand and lime and prided themselves on the narrow evenness of the struck (concave) joints they made. Not infrequently they "gauged" bricks—shaped them, that is—by rubbing them against a formed metal blade, so that they produced moldings when they were laid side by side. They also laid brick lintels over doors and windows that still support the walls above them with no help from metal bars. They built fireplaces, designed for heating rooms, that were so shallow that half the depth of the andirons stood out on the hearth and yet they didn't smoke at all.

The interiors of even quite simple houses provided plenty of work for a joiner, and since he had to shape by hand every piece and every molding he put in, he took a long time to finish it. Stairs had become staircases, put together almost like fine furniture. Sometimes in mansions they ascended from the middle of a large

hall to a full-width landing where they divided and returned, reaching the second floor as two sets of steps along the walls; sometimes they made the whole ascent in one great sweeping curve, a construction problem calculated to give a craftsman nightmares. The joiner had to plow out a rabbet in the underside of each tread of any staircase and fit the upper edge of the riser into it. No longer did a stringpiece hide the ends of the steps. He had to finish the exposed end of each step and often to ornament it with carving. He had to mortise two or three balusters into each tread and make the handrail that capped them. This meant shaping the rail's top, bottom, and sides with a special plane for each face: a short plane that could be pushed around the curves of the upward-turning ramps at the landings and around the spiral that often ended the rail at the bottom.

Plane for the top of a handrail

Some rooms had their walls covered entirely with framed wood panels accented by projecting baseboard, chair rail, and cornice. In others, only the fireplace wall was paneled all the way up. The panels on the other three walls went no higher than the chair rail, and above that the wall was plastered and would be painted, papered, or covered with fabric. Doors had elaborate frames and so did windows which often had paneled inside shutters made to fold away in the sides of the deep embrasures. Every room, except a center hall, had at least one fireplace and very large rooms had two. The fireplace was the central feature and the joiner had to surround it with a mantel that would set it off. He turned to his handbook for inspiration, but once in a while he scratched a rough drawing on a plank to try out the changes he would make. A few of these sketches on the backs of boards built into the structure turn up when old houses are razed.

Panel gauge

The seventeenth century left its woodwork untouched for time to color, and time made a beautiful job of it. Most eighteenth-century paneling was painted, not with pastel tints but with good strong blues, greens, yellows, browns, and reds. We shy away from anything painted to imitate something else, but our ancestors did not. They often painted woodwork to look like marble, or they stenciled borders around the edges of floors, presumably to imitate carpets.

The Cabinetmaker

All cabinetmaking involves expert joinery and it's hard to say just where the one trade leaves off and the other begins. The allotment of straight lines to joiners and curves to cabinetmakers is unconvincing; furniture can be fine with no curves whatever. "Cabinetmaker" is the newer word but no definite date can be set for the beginning of its use for furniture makers. As late as 1728, Christopher Townsend still called himself a "shop joiner." In London, in 1740, Batty Langley started off his *Treasury* with a blast at the incompetency of the "Spurious Indocile Chips, expelled by Joiners," who called themselves cabinetmakers.

An illiterate could be a joiner, doing his work carefully and well exactly as his master had showed him how to do it, but he would be unlikely to acquire the taste and originality that would make him a cabinetmaker. The men of that trade had to know some mechanics and geometry, and even some architecture. They made money—the Philadelphia Quaker, William Savery, left $46,000—and they stood only a little below the silversmiths socially. Many of them were officers in the Revolutionary army; Marinus Willet of New York was a colonel.

Furniture styles, like those of other things, followed England with a considerable time lag. Anne became queen in 1702, but the sturdy furniture named for her was hardly known in America before 1725. Along with Queen Anne came the idea of providing chairs for everybody. Before that, a chair was a kind of throne for the master of the house and the rest of the family usually sat on stools. In urban centers, after about twenty-five years, the Queen Anne style began to weaken under the onslaught of Thomas Chippendale. An Englishman, perhaps the greatest cabinetmaker who ever lived, he was great enough to be copied on this side of the water early in his career and to cause his book, *The Gentleman and Cabinetmaker's Directory*, to be rushed to this country when it appeared in 1754. It showed furniture designed in the playful and graceful rococo style, some of it fancier than any Chippendale himself ever made. From its appearance until after the end of the Revolutionary War in 1783 the *Directory* was the American

Philadelphia Chippendale armchair

cabinetmaker's bible, though he interpreted its plates in his own way instead of copying them literally and seldom followed the author's wilder flights of fancy.

Chippendale had his least effect in Newport, Rhode Island, where a handsome furniture style, almost entirely native, appeared from the hands of an astonishing family of Quakers, fourteen of them named Townsend and five named Goddard. John Goddard, the most famous one—though perhaps not a better craftsman than Job Townsend—had been the master of a small vessel before he married a Townsend girl and learned her family's trade. At first he made cheap furniture to sell southward along the coast, but in the 1760's he joined the family in making blockfront—he called them "sweled front"—chests and desks that are considered the best of all colonial cabinetwork. The Townsend-Goddards liked to ornament their work with carved scallop shells, but its distinguishing mark is the two flat-faced bulges down the faces of the drawers. They hewed the drawer fronts from solid mahogany more than three inches thick.

Furniture of all grades, cheap as well as costly, had, of course, to be made entirely by hand. Much of the cheap stuff came from wood butchers, but good men didn't hold themselves above making it or anything else—even chicken coops. Their bills frequently included coffins and sometimes their services as funeral director. A coffin item names the person who was measured

*American
Queen Anne chair*

for it and occasionally specifies "with nails." Only haste and emergency would force a cabinetmaker to use a nail.

Some common furniture was pretty. It had iron hardware instead of brass and was nearly always painted. It was made of pine, chestnut, or, in the South, tulip wood—which is called poplar but is actually magnolia. These woods also served for the hidden parts of good stuff. Maple made a lot of everyday furniture in the North and, when its grain was curly, it was valued for fine pieces, too. American black walnut is one of the finest cabinet woods in the world. English eighteenth-century craftsmen preferred its appearance and workability to their own walnut. Americans not only made a lot of handsome furniture from it, they also wasted it prodigally on such things as fence posts and barn floors. Our wild black cherry yielded beautiful wood and seems to have been specially liked in Connecticut. Honduras mahogany turned up in the colonies in the 1720's and naturally found favor, but it was Chippendale who made it *the* wood for furniture on both sides of the Atlantic. For a long time after his influence began, American artisans in towns made little of their good furniture from native woods, though country workmen continued to do so.

Obviously, it isn't the wood that gives quality to furniture, and it isn't the polished surface. It is, first, good proportions and precise shaping of visible parts like moldings and legs; next, it is the perfect fitting of invisible joinings and the use of the right kind of joint for each purpose. The result is neatness, strength, and rigidity. The basic joint was the same mortise and tenon, often with a dowel as a treenail, that served a carpenter to frame a house or a barn, but a cabinetmaker had special ways of using it. He glued it together with hot animal glue, but unless tenon fitted mortise perfectly, the glue would not hold. The craftsman usually couldn't cut a mortise clear through; he had to make it blind to keep the end of the tenon from showing on the outside. For a similar reason he often couldn't hold it with a pin. But by widening the bottom of a mortise to a keystone shape and slotting the tenon for a wedge to spread it as it was driven in, he could lock the two together so that something had to break to separate them. When he

could use a dowel, he drove it into a "drawbore." He bored the hole across the mortise just slightly farther in than the one through the tenon. Forcing the pin through both pulled the shoulder of the tenoned piece tight against the mortised piece.

Well-made furniture drawers are still held together with the interlocking splayed fingers called "dovetails." Colonial dovetails were commonly narrower than modern ones and spaced wider. There was also a sliding dovetail, in which a long keystone-shaped tongue slid into an exactly matching groove. Glued and clamped, this would hold two boards edge to edge or end to side in a joint no shrinkage would open. It could also hold the legs on a tripod table, resisting both downward pressure and outward thrust.

In good modern furniture factories, cabriole legs are shaped by incredible machines which feel their way over the surface of a hand-carved model and cut thirty or forty exact duplicates of it simultaneously. Such a leg is all complex curves with flat surfaces only where it attaches to the body of the piece. This makes it a difficult object for a hand worker to hew from a solid billet. The colonial craftsman had to depend on his eye and on measurements taken from the flat surface of his workbench. He roughed the leg out with a drawknife, pared it down with a spokeshave and a scraper, and carved its ball-and-claw foot with chisels and gouges. It took him a lot more time to make one such leg than it takes the machine to make forty.

The cabinetmaker had few tools that a joiner did not also have, but he used his tools with infinitely more care. He had some saws smaller than the joiner's, with finer teeth, and he had such things as gooseneck chisels for making the bottom of a mortise absolutely flat, and corner

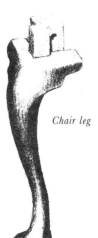

Chair leg

Big-wheel lathe

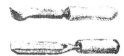

Gooseneck chisel; corner chisel

Brace and spoon bit

chisels to make its sides clean and square. His brace for turning boring bits was, like the joiner's, all wood except the metal pin that the knob turned on and the thumbscrew or the spring catch that held the bit in place. But, rather than a spiral auger that would satisfy a joiner, the cabinetmaker would use a spoon bit which looked rather like a gouge and which cut very slowly but never split the wood it was boring. A spiral auger, by the way, had then only a smooth point at its bottom with no screw thread to draw it into the work. The user started it in a hole made with a small crosshandled gimlet which he called a wimble.

Naturally, the cabinetmaker used as many molding planes as the joiner did. He had little need for very wide ones, but he did use a type with a straight towing handle on its forward end so that an apprentice could help in running it cleanly through hard wood like maple. He also used an ingenious "moving fillister" plane with an adjustable fence to control the distance from an edge that the blade cut a groove.

Most cabinet shops had their own lathes, but some are known to have "sent out" such things as round legs and chair stretchers to be made by a professional turner. These men used the great-wheel lathe, so called because it was driven from a wooden wheel six or seven feet in diameter, cranked by an apprentice or by a hired "turn-

wheel"—usually an old man or a cripple unable to do other work. A rope belted the drive wheel to a small pulley which spun the headstock at about seven hundred revolutions a minute.

A furniture leg or a baluster, set up between the lathe centers, rotated around its long axis toward the worker. The old turner used the same kind of long chisels of various shapes that are still used for lathe work. He held such a chisel with both hands horizontally on a steady rest and brought the blade to bear against the spinning wood very slowly, so that it wouldn't catch suddenly in the "stuff" and cause splitting or throw the tool out the window. These risks lessened when the flats had been removed and the work surface reduced to roundness. If the turner had no previously made piece to copy, he worked from a full-size drawing, carefully measuring the length of each member and checking its diameter with calipers. Specialists turned bowls and dishes from solid blocks, generally working freehand. Instead of holding the stuff in a chuck, they usually put it between centers, leaving a core of wood inside to be cut away after the turning was done.

We still use a lot of turned wood but not as much as our ancestors did. Hourglasses and foot warmers had their wooden ends supported by turned spindles. An eighteenth-century potato masher was entirely the product of turning.

90

Seat cutter for Windsor chairs

Spinning wheels stood on turned legs, and the legs, stretchers, and arm supports of the famous Windsor chair were lathe turnings.

A stiff English version of this chair existed. It had a flat splat in the middle of its back. There's a story, proved by no written evidence, that King George I had a copy made of a chair that he had sat in at a Windsor tavern. The design wasn't in any of the pattern books, but it somehow reached Philadelphia where an unknown turner began making Windsor chairs out of American woods. The chief of these was hickory, tough and springy, which allowed the back spindles to be more slender than the English oak ones and gave the new chair a resilient lightness lacking in the original. The Americans hewed the seat of a Windsor chair out of green wood, boring holes in it to receive the seasoned legs and spindles. As it dried, the seat shrank and gripped the parts inserted into it tighter and tighter.

Because they were cheap, and because their hollowed-out seats and sloping backs made them comfortable, "Philadelphia chairs" became known all through the colonies, and turners became chairmakers. Some in New England changed the design, substituting a shaped horizontal strip for the original hooped back to make the comb-backed Windsor. A few of these were made as writing chairs with greatly widened right arms. Other makers lengthened the seat of the original form to make a settee, or made the comb back into a rocking bench with a cradle at one end to serve an obvious dual purpose. Windsor chairs were almost invariably painted, more often barn-red than any other color.

In 1796, George Washington shipped two dozen Windsors for the piazza at "Mount Vernon" from Philadelphia, and an obliging sea captain landed them at the plantation wharf for him. Though few cabinetmakers made Windsors, they are included here because of their excellence at their best. They were made well into the nineteenth century, along with some offshoots which couldn't deny their ancestry. One was the "Sheraton" or, as some call it, the "bamboo" Windsor, with its leg turnings reduced to mere swellings with grooves around them. The Boston rocker was a late version, and so was the bent-armed varnished chair that schoolteachers sat in at least as late as 1920.

91

Windsor chairs: hoop-back, comb-back, and "Sheraton"

The Revolutionary War made a seven-year break in communications with England, so the colonies heard little of the "Pompeian" architecture and furniture designs of Robert Adam. The Yankees continued to follow Chippendale while he became unfashionable in England. After 1783, the new United States learned about Adam's successors, George Hepplewhite and Thomas Sheraton, both of whom published pattern books. American versions of the furniture appeared quickly. Baltimore cabinetmakers earned some reputation for inlaid Hepplewhite, but the master of these Federal styles was a crusty Scot in New York named Duncan Phyfe.

Both kinds were lighter in construction than any fine furniture that preceded them and the best of both used ornament only sparingly: the Hepplewhite tended to inlay, the Sheraton to delicate carving. Hepplewhite legs were square and tapered and his chair backs were often shield-shaped; Sheraton legs were turned and frequently reeded and his chair backs had square lines.

Hepplewhite

Sheraton sideboard

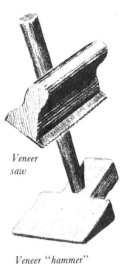

Veneer saw

Veneer "hammer"

The unadorned fronts of Federal chests and sideboards led cabinetmakers to decorate them with matched veneers. They sawed thin slices from strongly grained mahogany and glued them on, side by side, with opposite faces showing, so that the grain appeared as a symmetrical pattern. Modern veneer is pared down to a thirty-second of an inch, but a sash saw couldn't cut thinner than an eighth. A curious fine-toothed saw, mounted sideways on a block, served to cut the slices to size; a toothing plane, with a notched blade, ridged the backs to give the glue a better grip; and a wooden "veneer hammer," which never struck a blow, squeezed out excess glue with the top of its head pressed against the face of the veneer.

Most cabinetmakers upholstered the armchairs and sofas they made right in their own shops, but big towns had a few specializing upholsterers, most of whom employed woodworkers to make chair frames in *their* shops. Some of these, as well as some cabinetmakers, made Venetian blinds exactly like those used now.

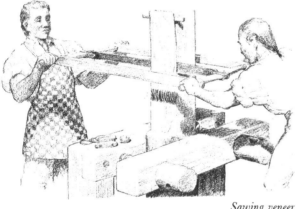

Sawing veneer

All cabinet shops did finishing, of course; rubbing was the first job an apprentice learned. Many masters held that the only proper finish for mahogany was boiled linseed oil, put on hot or sometimes thinned with turpentine. The oil soaked in and dried, then it was rubbed, and rubbed again after more coats of oil, before beeswax-and-turpentine was applied, and rubbed still further. Walnut, cherry, and maple received repeated coats of copal varnish or of shellac, and again the apprentice rubbed endlessly between coats, this time with pumice and oil, to get them as smooth as an apricot.

"Butcher" furniture

American Empire and Hitchcock

Napoleon surrounded himself with a lot of florid grandeur, part of which was a heavy style of furniture called Empire. It was based on the current French interpretation of the classic and was laden with architectural ornament, some of it executed in applied brass. The excitement over the emperor made the style popular here. The style is commonly associated with Duncan Phyfe. He made it lighter and simpler than the French version but never as handsome as his earlier furniture.

The steam-driven band saw, introduced in the 1820's, was thin enough to run as a belt around two pulleys and narrow enough to cut tight curves. It could readily shape any kind of curlicue, even from thick black-walnut timber. This seems to have killed American taste. People were enchanted by monstrosities and would buy no furniture that wasn't machine-made. They had never seen such extravagant ornamentation or such low prices. With bitterness in his heart, Duncan Phyfe called it "butcher" furniture, but he could fine no buyers for anything better, so he had to make it or quit business.

One of the early factories, Lambert Hitchcock's in Connecticut, used water power to make simple cottage chairs which, however different they may seem from what Napoleon had in mind, were actually derived from the Empire style. Hitchcock started his factory in 1826 and made chairs by thousands until 1843. He sold various styles, but the differences between one and another were not great. Most of them were painted shiny black and were decorated by female factory hands who dabbed metal powder on them through stencils while the base paint was still tacky (sticky).

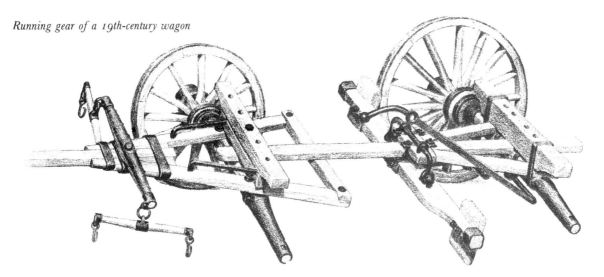

The Wainwright and the Coachmaker

Many a country blacksmith could build a satisfactory wagon or cart, but in towns some men devoted their whole time to the wainwright's trade. Roads extended—even if they didn't improve—after the first quarter of the eighteenth century, and a few men began to build lighter passenger vehicles for use on them.

A farm wagon or a town dray in the colonies in the 1700's wasn't essentially different from a Roman wagon in the second century; the only real improvement, the one-piece iron tire, may not have reached America until after the Revolutionary War. The dimensions of a wagon resulted from ages of unconscious experiment and from the limitations of man and horse. Wheels were large for easy rolling on rough ground. Modern farm wagons, pulled by tractors, often have small rubber-tired wheels that will turn under the body as the old wagon wheels would not. The hitch was placed at a height that would give the draft animals their best pulling advantage. The height of the body from the ground was limited by the height to which a man could lift.

The working parts of a wagon's running gear are its wheels, the axles on which they turn, and the axletrees that connect the axles and, hence, the wheels in pairs. A long pole, called the perch, positions the axles fore and aft. It is fixed rigidly to the rear axle and is braced to it by the two angled hounds; hooping wings they used to call them. The forward end of the perch rests on the front axle but is secured to it only by the iron

king bolt which passes vertically through both and on which the front truck can swivel freely for turning corners.

Set across the hounds and the perch above the rear axle and firmly "ironed" to them is a timber called the "bolster" to which the floor of the wagon body is bolted. There is also a bolster at the front, but the front wheels of a wagon are smaller than the rear ones, so, in order to reach the level of the rear, the front bolster rests on an additional timber (the transom) placed above the tip of the perch. The transom is part of the front truck and swivels with it on the king pin. The bolster does not; it is fixed to the body.

The hounds of the front truck angle ahead to hold the butt of the tongue or pole by which the draft animals pull, hold back, and steer. Oxen use their yoke to pull the tip of the pole, while horses use collars and long traces to transfer their pull to the double trees held on the pole by a single bolt near the wagon. Horses hold back by "sitting" in a heavy leather breeching connected by the harness with the pole's tip. The forward hounds perform a second job of steadying the front of the wagon on turns. Behind the axletree their splayed ends are connected by the crosswise swaybar which bears against the under side of the perch.

Colonial America's great achievement in wagons was the Conestoga. The Palatine Germans in Lancaster County, Pennsylvania, devised it about 1750 to haul their produce down to the seaports. They adapted their recollections of the big stage wagons of Europe to the more rugged conditions of this country. They also de-

*The back of a
Conestoga wagon*

Hub

*Wooden axle
with clout
and linchpin*

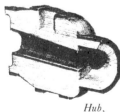

*Hub,
split to show box*

veloped a special breed of large horses used in teams of six to pull the Conestogas over fiendish trails that eventually became roads.

The running gear of a Conestoga was like that of a farm wagon except that it was stronger. The Germans made the wheels very high for easier running and to ford deep streams without wetting the cargo. The remarkable feature of the wagon was its body, but if you hear that it would serve as a boat, don't believe it. Both ends of the body floor curved upward to keep the cargo from shifting on steep hills; its sides and ends flared out from the floor for the same reason, and also to gain carrying capacity. The "waggoner" rode the left-hand horse nearest the vehicle; on the later Conestogas, his helper rode the "lazy" board projecting from the side of the wagon where he could reach the long iron handle of the brake. The early ones had no brakes; on a downgrade the helper simply chained a wheel to keep it from turning.

Most of the supply wagons that Benjamin Franklin hired for General Braddock in 1755 were Conestogas; Conestogas hauled flour to Valley Forge; they hauled freight between the new states; they hauled it to Pittsburgh to drift westward in flatboats on the Ohio; they preceded the prairie schooner on the plains; and a few of them made the terrible journey to Oregon.

Wagon wheels were hard to construct. Only a master wheelwright could do it and often he had a blacksmith to help him. Many blacksmiths were also wheelwrights. A wooden wagon wheel had a more or less barrel-shaped hub from which a dozen or fourteen or even sixteen spokes radiated to the wooden rim, which was shod on its outer face with iron. A hole through the hub was lined with a tapered cast-iron tube (the "box") which served as a bearing for the axle.

In early days, the axle was simply the rounded end of the wooden axletree, shod on its under side with a trough-shaped iron strip, called the "clout," to take the rub where the weight rested. Later, the wood was entirely sheathed, and still later, in the early part of the nineteenth century, the axle arm was a solid forging made with an extension for bolting it to the axletree. Ultimately the two axle arms were forged on the ends of a single bar. None of these axles projected straight out from the wagon. They all toed in; they had "gather," that is, they bent forward a very little so that rolling on the road would tend to make their wheels stay on and reduce friction on the wide tires. They also had to bend down somewhat to allow for the dish of the wheel. A wooden wheel isn't flat. Looked at from its edge, its spokes are seen to form a shallow cone with its apex toward the wagon. This counters the side thrust of a load when the vehicle tilts, a force that will turn a too-flat wheel wrong side out and will splinter a completely flat one. The spokes below the hub carry the weight. As each one reaches bottom, it has to stand vertical to endure the stress, and to make that possible, the bent-down axle tilts the top of the dished wheel slightly outward.

The hub of a Conestoga wheel could measure a foot in diameter by eighteen inches long. Often it was made of black gum, the contorted grain of which makes it unsplittable. The wheelwright cut rectangular, evenly spaced mortises around the midriff of the hub and shaped a tenon on the inner end of a particular spoke to fit each mortise and fit it very tightly. To set the spokes in place, the wheelwright rested the hub ends on the sills of a narrow wheel pit and clamped them there with the number one mortise on top. He started the tenon of the matching spoke by tapping it lightly. Then, gauging his distance, he raised a long-handled maul and, leaping into the air as he swung it full circle, he brought it down on the outer end of the spoke. So tight was the fit that it took two or three such blows to drive the shoulder flush against the hub.

The rim of the wheel whose hub measurements have just been given is roughly four and a half inches square and is made up of seven curved sections (fellies) with their butted ends doweled together. The fellies were not bent. A thin wood

Traveller

Even when the hoop-tiring of wheels was commonplace, through the first quarter of the present century, watching the operation was interesting and exciting. Most people now living were born too late to see it. Continuous tires probably originated in France. An illustration in Diderot's *Encyclopédie*, VII, published in 1769, shows workmen putting one on. Even as late as 1884, tires had not wholly replaced strakes in rural England.

In order to cut an iron strip the right length for a tire, the smith measured the wooden rim with a traveller. This was a six-inch wheel mounted in a handled fork. He trundled it carefully around the circumference, marking his start on both wheel and traveller, counting turns, and chalking any fraction of a turn on the traveller at the end. He then ran the traveller the same number of turns on the flat iron strip. For a five-foot wagon wheel he cut the metal, with cold chisel and sledge, three-quarters of an inch *shorter* than the circumference.

Many a tire must have been bent by the slow hammering of hot iron, but a hand-cranked machine which would bend the iron cold was invented around 1825. One end of the strip had to be bent slightly with a hammer to start it. Three rollers did the bending. Two of them set some sixteen inches apart—the distance was adjustable—supported the tire on its outside. The third, usually the driver, pressed against the tire's inner surface between the other two. It took three men to butt the ends of the tire and secure them together with a bent nail through two holes.

tongue

knock

SPOKE

shoulder

foot

pattern was used to mark their curves on the side of a dressed block of oak and they were hewn to shape with ax and adz. The wheelwright mortised each felly to receive the tongues of two spokes. He didn't shape the tongues until after he had driven the spokes into the hub so as to avoid damaging them with his maul. The tongues went all the way through the rim. Early ones were square and were slotted for wedges driven in from the face of the rim to lock them and make them help to hold the wheel together. Later, when a continuous iron tire did the holding, tongues became round and did without wedges.

Early wheelwrights shod their rims with "strakes" (curved strips of iron), each as long as a felly, nailed onto the wooden rim. Each strake bridged over the joint between two fellies, the wheelwright having pulled the joint hard together with a large threaded clamp called a samson. Its operation can be better understood from a drawing than from description. A blacksmith made the strakes and nailed them on red-hot, with the lower half of the wheel submerged in a water-filled shoeing hole. As soon as he drove the nails for a strake—with one left standing for the samson to catch on—he spun the wheel to carry the hot metal under water and quench it. Cooling, it shrank and drew its two fellies tightly together.

95

Samson in use

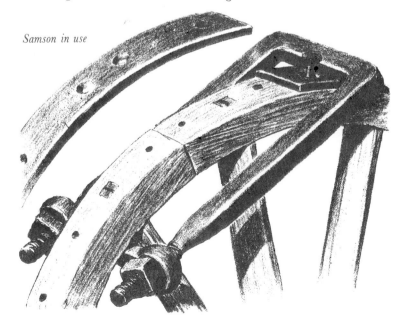

Hanging the tire over the forge on a chain, they heated both sides of the joint, nail and all, swung it over to the anvil and welded it. The master checked the inside circumference with his traveller. Usually it was right, but if it was wrong by as little as a quarter of an inch, he scrapped it and made a new tire. Nails, the same kind as for strakes, would be put through the tire and holes had to be punched for them with the metal hot.

Since the tire was smaller than the wheel, it had to be expanded with heat to get it over the rim. The smiths built a ring of fire on the ground and placed the hoop on it. It took about half an hour to reach the necessary dull red. During this time they put the wheel, face down, on a circular stone platform pierced in its center for the nose of the hub. Apprentices filled sprinkling cans, one for each man, and distributed them, along with three heavy sledges, around the work area.

The master and two journeymen lifted the tire with forge tongs and rested it on the rim, being careful to keep the nail holes between the felly joints. Even expanded it was too tight a fit to slip on. One side would go part way down, the other stood on the edge. The whole circle

Chaise

smoked and in places the wood flamed. The man on the low side held his advantage by pressing on the tire with his sledge; the other two swung theirs and drove the hoop down into place. As soon as the lower edge hit the stone, everybody grabbed a water can and doused the wheel. Steam replaced smoke with a great hissing and a stench of charred wood. The tire contracted violently and the wheel snapped and creaked as the squeeze tightened its joints and increased the amount of its dish. Sprinkling cooled the metal only partially. When the smiths hung the wheel on a temporary axle and spun it around in the shoeing hole, the water in the hole boiled, and the additional contraction squeezed putty out of cracks, even in the hub.

The ironing of the wheel wasn't finished until the blacksmiths had shrunk four iron bands on its hub: two narrow ones on the largest diameter against the bases of the spokes; a wider one of somewhat smaller diameter on the inner end; and a still wider and a still smaller one on the outside end. This last one had an inch-wide slot in its outer edge, matched to a slot in the wood, to allow the removal of the linchpin that kept the wheel on its axle. After that, the job was turned back to the wheelwright for final painting.

For the first few years of use, the tire nails served no purpose, but when the wood began to wear away *under* the tire and the grip that had been so powerful loosened, they came into their own. With very long wear both wooden rim and iron tire became rounded.

Almost from the start, farmers in the northern and middle colonies widened the trails to the nearest villages to get their products to market and themselves to church. In the southern tidewater settlements where most travel was by water, some points were more handily reached overland, even though the road was no more than a trace marked by ax cuts on trees. There is a paved highway in that area that is still called The Notch Road. By 1725, widened trails radiated from towns and villages everywhere and passenger vehicles suited to withstand their colossal holes and stumps became possible. By then, half a dozen centers were large enough for carriages to be useful within their limits.

Chaises (chairs) and gigs with but two high wheels set far apart could most readily cope with the surface difficulties, but even they upset frequently. There was no fundamental difference between chaises and gigs. The owner of the gig in front of the shop at the head of Chapter 3 may well have called it a "cheer."

A two-wheeled vehicle, called a *chaise à cheval*, with its body hung on long shafts halfway between its wheels and its horse, carried Frenchmen as early as 1664. It was an adaptation of the *chaise à porteurs* or sedan chair. The English copied it and modified it by moving its weight closer to its wheels. The Americans improved it further by enlarging its wheels and suspending the back of its body from hickory springs bolted to the tops of the shafts. One like this was the original of the "Wonderful One-hoss Shay."

Speaking of sedan chairs: Negro slaves, and sometimes Indians, carried elegant American ladies in them on calling and shopping trips in towns. And Benjamin Franklin went about Philadelphia in one when age enfeebled him and a wheeled vehicle was painfully rough.

Boston chaisemakers exported their product to other colonies before 1735. In the mid-1700's postriders began to carry mail from colony to colony with some regularity, and the routes they used soon became crude roads "graded" by the wheels of stage wagons carrying freight and passengers and by those of private vehicles. The new invention of S-shaped steel springs from which to suspend bodies made travel barely endurable in closed coaches and chariots (short-bodied coaches for two passengers), and wealthy men began to import them and to have them built in this country.

Nicholas Bailey built coaches in Philadelphia as early as 1740. Adino Paddock of Boston, who began as a chaise builder, was making both chariots and coaches by 1758 and was selling them southward. Paddock was one of the artisans who was able to advance himself to wealth and a higher social level. He held a number of civic offices, became a colonel of the "Ancient and Honourable Artillery Company," and had the privilege of keeping a cow on Boston Common. Perhaps because he was doing well and feared the effects of change, he didn't join his fellow craftsmen when they took fire for Independence but, along with many other honest men, remained loyal to the king. The revolutionaries

made their disapproval of this so harshly clear that Paddock took ship with General Howe for Halifax and his property was confiscated.

Both coach and chariot were heavy vehicles. Their running gear was like that of a wagon, except that the perch was often bent downward to allow the body to be reasonably close to the ground. The enclosed body was framed of ash joined with mortise and tenon, the spaces in the frame were filled in with thin panels of poplar, and the frame was rabbeted to receive them. The coachmaker needed skill because both frame and panels curved. Some of his woodworking tools had special shapes to cope with this.

Sedan chair

Only one original chariot and two eighteenth-century coaches survive in this country: the John Brown chariot in the Rhode Island Historical Society; the Beekman coach in the New York Historical Society; and the Powel coach at "Mount Vernon." The Beekman coach, long thought to be French, is English and dates from the early 1770's; the Brown chariot, 1782, and the Powel coach, 1798, were built in Philadelphia.

A large coachmaker's shop employed quite a range of workers: wheelwright, blacksmith, woodworker, trimmer and upholsterer, painter. The ironwork on a coach was elaborate and highly finished, the body work was as exacting as cabinetmaking, the whole interior of the body was lined with fabric, and the seats were cushioned. Both running gear and body got eight or ten coats of paint, each rubbed down, and then several coats of varnish, each of which was also rubbed down.

Coachmaker's compass plane

Small wonder that Elkanah and William Deane, who ran the largest coachmaking shop in New York about 1770, charged one hundred and sixty-five pounds for a plain coach and two hundred pounds for a fancy one. The brothers built a coach for the Earl of Dunmore, probably an "elegant" one, since he was so pleased with it that he persuaded Elkanah to move to Williamsburg when his Lordship went there in 1772 as governor of Virginia. Why Deane would leave an apparently prosperous business to set up in a small center is a mystery, but he did so and prospered there for the three years he had left to live.

The Bookbinder

Folio

Real bookbinding is done today much as it was done in the fifteenth century, but very few modern books are really bound. All but a minute number of hard-cover books are now cased in covers made separately and held in place by nothing more than glue. The leaves of a properly bound book are sewn onto cords which are tied firmly into its binding boards. Through the whole colonial period and for more than thirty years after the Revolution, all American books were hand bound, some well, some shoddily.

Quarto

John Saunders started binding books in Boston in 1637, a year before the first print shop opened. He may have helped to set up the first press; it's possible that he knew more about its operation than did the printer, who was a locksmith by trade. The reason Saunders could start business before he had books to bind was that he, like his successors, did much rebinding of old volumes. Like them, too, he probably ruled and bound "accompt" books and kept a stock of writing paper, pen quills, ink, sealing wax, wafers (small disks of dried gelatin used to seal folded letters in pre-envelope times), and bandboxes that he made himself and covered with decorated paper. The first bandboxes held men's bands or collars; the word was extended later to cover boxes for hats.

Octavo

Most binding was bespoke. A man bought the printed sheets of a book and had them bound to his taste to match his library or whatever way his binder's skill, tools, and materials permitted. But even the seventeenth century did some edition binding. John Ratcliff came to Boston in 1661 especially to bind the edition of John Eliot's Indian Bible. This was the first Bible printed in North America but few people ever learned to read it. Large eighteenth-century print shops employed binders. They did a lot of cheap work, using thin sheets of wood called scabbord which could be made here when pasteboard couldn't be and covering them with paper and sheepskin back strips. Plain blue paper, probably domestic, was commonest, but Dutch gilt, stamped all over with animals or small scenes in gold, was popular and so was marbled paper. This last was made by floating colors on gum-thickened water and lifting their swirled pattern by dipping a sheet of paper facedown upon them. Most marbled paper came from France and it was much favored as end papers to line the binding boards of good books.

The bookbinder did more than cover a new book. He had to "forward" it, also. Forwarding is work done to the pages before the cover is put on. The printer's flat sheets had pages printed on both sides: two to a side for a folio, four for a quarto, eight for an octavo. The pages of a folio all stood the same way up on both sides and a single fold made the big sheet ready to bind. Those of the other sizes were arranged so they would be right side up, with their page numbers in the right order, when the quarto was folded twice or the octavo, three times. An apprentice folded them and creased them with a bone blade. Regardless of the number of pages on it, the binder called each folded sheet a signature. His next task was to gather the signatures in their right order. The printer helped by identifying the first page of each one, usually with a letter at the bottom. You can find it in old books.

To hold the signatures together, the binder sewed them to a series of five cords, fewer in cheap books, strung on a sewing frame. The frame stood on the edge of a table. (The setup can be seen in the illustration.) The cords are stretched between the top bar and five wooden keys that are held down by the weight of the signatures. The cords of a well-bound book stayed outside the folded backs of the signatures. For cheap bindings with flat spines, the binder sawed shallow trenches across the backs for the cords to lie in, and the cuts showed inside the book. The cords of such books were sometimes rawhide.

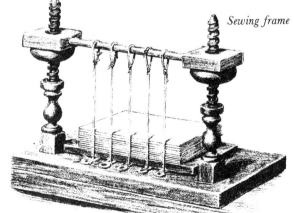

Sewing frame

Sewing key

98

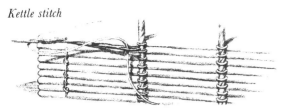

Kettle stitch

Starting with the lowest signature, the binder ran a needle threaded with linen into the edge of the fold about half an inch from the head. The sheets of the book lay piled on the base of the frame with their folded spines facing the binder. The top of the book, called the head, was at his left. Each stitch passed through all the leaves of the signature to its middle. The binder brought his needle out against the upper side of the first cord, went over it, and back into the fold on its lower side. He continued this around each cord and brought his needle out beyond the last one, half an inch from the bottom (the tail). He went into the next signature at this same point and worked back the other way, tying his thread to the loose end at the head. At the tail of his third signature and before he started on the fourth, he caught a kettle stitch (catch-up stitch) around the short hitch that connected the first two. He then repeated this kettle stitch on both ends until the whole book was sewn.

The binder placed the sewn book with its back flat and square between two stiff boards and clamped it, front edge up, in his horizontal trimming press. Two strips on the upper surface of this press guided his plow as its sharp tip trimmed the leaves to evenness. After each three or four passes, he gave a turn to the plow's long wooden screws and moved the cutter forward a little. Finally it met the board on the far side, where it projected slightly above the surface of the press.

Plow and trimming press, both cut away

A good book needed a round back, so the binder turned it over, put an angled backing board on each side and clamped it in a laying press with the spine standing a little above the boards. He then carefully backed the spine by hammering it to roundness, bending each signature away from the middle. A flat back can cave in and cause the front edge of the leaves to bulge forward.

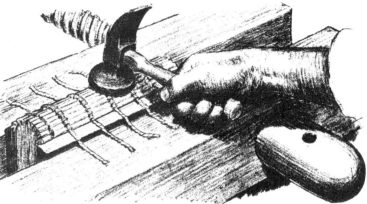

Backing

One purpose of the hard cover is to protect the edges of the leaves, so the craftsman cut the two pasteboard blanks for it a little oversize and used the cords to fasten them on. He made a row of holes down the back edge of each board, one hole directly opposite each cord, and notched to the edge of the board, so the cord could reach the hole without making a hump on the cover. A second hole for each cord went alongside the first one. The binder threaded a cord into its first hole from the outside and brought it back out through the second hole. There he spread its frayed end flat on the board and glued it down. Repeating this on both ends of each cord tied every part of the book into a unit which years of use would not separate.

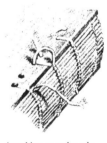

Attaching pasteboards

The remaining work was ornamental. First came the head and tail bands at the ends of the spine: small strips of leather covered with two colors of bright silk thread overcast and anchored in the kettle stitches; only the edges of the bands would show. Then the thin leather cover—imported morocco for the best, calf next best and most used (sheep not good enough for fine work)—was cut three quarters of an inch larger than the boards. The binder thinned its edges with a skiving knife and "drew it on" wet with paste on the inside. He pressed his leather close over the

Headband

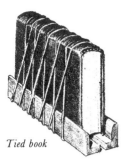

Tied book

Stamping a title

Pallets

hammered spine, working it against the cords and stretching it a little over them, so that they showed as neat projecting welts called bands. The front and back he smoothed flat, turning the leather over the edges "in the neatest manner," as he advertised, and pasting the overlap to the inside of the board. The end papers he cut to the size of two pages and pasted one half against the inside face of each cover, hiding the edges of the leather. Then he stood the front edge on shaped blocks and tied the book up with string—blocks and all—to let the paste dry.

The work now needed a few days between boards in the big standing press to dry out thoroughly and flatten. But even the simplest binding required a title on its spine to identify it on a shelf and to indicate its top. Almost universally eighteenth-century binders stamped titles in gold on small rectangles of thin dark leather, black, red, green, or blue. They glued this patch on the spine to fill the space between the top band and the next below it. Quite often the binder went further and ornamented the leather with tooling, on the spine only or on both it and the front cover. He did this, as binders still do, with heated brass tools pressed hard on the leather. The tools had two forms: the pallet, its handle perpendicular to its flat face which was engraved with a raised letter or with one or more straight lines or with various curlicues, and the roll. This was a disk rotatable at the end of a long handle on which it was mounted much as a wheelwright's traveller was. The edge of the roll yielded either filigree borders or merely straight lines. In the latter case, it was known as a fillet and was notched to permit making neat corners. It took great skill to press a border into a cover with rolls, to run each course perfectly straight by gauging against the left thumbnail, and stop and start at the right points. Old books show that skilled workers sometimes slipped.

When colonial binders used gold in their tooling, they almost always confined it to the spine where it would make a display in a bookcase, and where it could be applied with pallets. It was hard enough to put on with those. The pattern had to be applied "blind" first, using only the hot tool, then precisely painted with glair (egg white and water), then covered with clips of gold leaf and stamped over again with the same hot

Tooling

tool and in exactly the same place. The glair and the pressure made the gold stick. Any that lay beyond the pattern would brush off.

Tooling on very early American books was simple: lines across the spine on both sides of each band and a fillet around the margins of the cover. The fillet lines crossed at the corners to avoid the stopping problem. This was all left blind. After 1700, front covers acquired double panels in their centers and a little filigree, still blind, and spines took on panels outlined in gold between the bands, with a gold rosette sometimes stamped in the center of each. In 1782, Robert Aitken of Philadelphia printed the two volumes of the first complete American Bible in English. He bound some copies of it himself, handsomely. His own copy survives, covered in soft green morocco with a neat gold border on the covers and with the panels of the spine enriched with gold flowers and leaves.

It wasn't unusual for printers to bind books. William Parks, who printed in Annapolis and Williamsburg around 1730, was a binder. James Franklin in Boston, his brother Benjamin in Philadelphia, and William Goddard in Baltimore and New York, were all printers and they could all bind books.

From 1800 to 1840 American publishing boomed. Printing was still handwork, but the printers met the demand by multiplying presses and men. Binding, too, was still handwork and it caused a bottleneck. At first the books were sold in bare boards, but sometime in the 1820's the cloth-covered case binding, made as a unit in

Fillet and roll

advance and simply glued to the spine, solved the problem. Its making and application were still handwork but both could be done by semi-skilled labor. In an effort to relieve the supposed commonplace appearance of cloth, the publishers resorted to the arming press which, by squeezing a book-size plate on a cover, embossed its whole surface with an elaborate pattern.

Some books were still bound in leather in the early 1800's, but, because skins had begun to be tanned with mineral salts instead of tanbark and sumac, they didn't hold up well. Books bound then are usually in worse shape now than much older ones are.

The Weaver

The first weavers who worked professionally in this country were a group of twenty Yorkshire families that John Pierson set up as a cloth "factory" at Rowley, Massachusetts, in 1638. It was to process their work that he started his fulling mill. They spun and wove wool from Spain. England would export no raw wool, and the few sheep then in the colony yielded far less than enough for household use. The Yorkshiremen also wove cotton brought all the way from India.

There is ample proof that some women, working at home, became highly skilled weavers and had equipment for producing quite intricate patterns. The simplicity of their looms held most home weavers down to the plain, over-and-under weaving called tabby. Done in wool, this made warm, sturdy cloth of the homespun kind, likely to be a little stiff for clothing. By using pre-dyed yarn, the simplest looms could weave linen in stripes, checks, and plaids.

A colonial home loom differed not at all from European looms of the fourteenth century and apparently very little from Roman ones. A local carpenter made its frame, big as a four-poster bed, exactly as he would frame a house or a barn, with mortise-and-tenon joints, only he often drove a wedge in to hold the tenon instead of pinning it with a treenail. This made the frame stiff and also allowed it to be taken apart quickly. The builder had to make every part of the loom absolutely square; a crooked loom weaves a crooked web.

Any loom must: (1) hold the parallel warp threads stretched from front to back at a convenient working height; (2) allow them to be moved toward the weaver as the web grows; (3) provide the weaver with a means of raising part of the warp threads to form a "shed" with the rest through which to pass the shuttle carrying the weft yarn; and (4) provide a device for compacting each new weft yarn against those already woven.

Considering these points in order and in the forms they took on the old barn looms:

1) The warp was fed from the warp beam (actually a roller across the back of the loom) and led forward to a smooth timber, the breast beam, above which the weaver leaned to work. The parallel threads passed over the rounded edge of the breast beam, then down and back to attach to the cloth beam (another roller) just out of the way of the weaver's feet.

2) As work progressed, the weaver used a crank at one side to turn the cloth beam from time to time and roll up the finished fabric. Both cloth beam and warp beam had ratchets—sometimes only wrapped ropes and weights—which the weaver could release or set to hold the warp at proper tension. The weaver always slacked the tension when work was interrupted to avoid a break across the cloth.

3) The weaver worked on a rather high, backless bench hung across the front of the loom. About halfway between the bench and the warp beam, the warp threads passed through the harnesses. A simple household loom had but two of these hanging parallel from the ends of two ropes which passed over a roller lying across the top of the loom. In their old form, each harness was no more than two sticks, one above the warp and one below it, connected by the "heddles" stretched vertically between them. The heddles were string—they are metal or plastic now—and each had an eye tied into its middle through which one warp thread passed. The warps carried by the heddles of the front harness lay between the heddles of the rear harness and vice versa. A short rope hitched to the middle of the lower stick of each harness was tied to one of the two treadles extending from the back of the loom to a point within reach of the weaver's feet. Tramping on one treadle pulled its harness

Simple two-harness loom

the loom. A second, lighter, member crossed above the warps, and fixed between it and the shuttle race was the sley or reed. This was a comblike affair through which all the warp threads passed. It was the reeds of the sley that bumped the cloth when the weaver swung the batten. These are now metal but originally they were actual slivers of reed.

The loom used by colonial experts differed from the simple one in having at least four harnesses and sometimes as many as twelve. By shedding selected warp threads instead of merely alternate ones, and thus letting some weft threads pass over several warps at once, this loom could weave patterns. These could be small surface variations in one color, or quite large repeats in a color different from that of the background. Such were the "overshot" coverlets in wide variety which are prized examples of old weaving. They were woven on cotton warp with two woolen wefts, each of a different weight and of different colors. The lighter yarn matched the warp, and the tie-up of the harnesses allowed the two to weave as a tabby background at the same time that the heavier yarn wove the overshot pattern of contrasting color. Professional weavers made the bulk of these coverlets in the early nineteenth century.

A harness had to come straight down, so the cord from the treadle had to be tied to the middle of the lower harness stick. Since four or more treadles couldn't all be in the middle, multiple-

downward, and the ropes over the roller pulled the other upward at the same time, each carrying its own warp threads with it. For tabby-weaving, these were every other thread, so a shed was opened with—say—the odd threads up and the even threads down. The weaver threw the shuttle, trailing a weft behind it, through the shed, tramped on the other treadle to bring the odds down and the evens up, and thus enclosed the new weft. This tramping created a new and different shed through which he threw the shuttle back.

The smooth boat-shaped shuttle was whittled out of a close-grained wood like box, dogwood, or holly. A narrow cavity in the shuttle held the weft, wound on a "quill"—usually a section of hollow reed—that rotated freely on a wire sprung between the ends of the recess. The yarn ran out through a hole in the shuttle's side.

Quill, shuttle, and shuttle wire

4) After each shuttle pass, the weaver pulled the heavy batten toward him to compact his web. It bumped when it hit, and one may guess that the characteristic sound of a colonial village was a steady thumping from house after house. The batten's weight came from a crosswise timber, the shuttle race, hanging below the warp on two long wooden bars pivoted at the top of

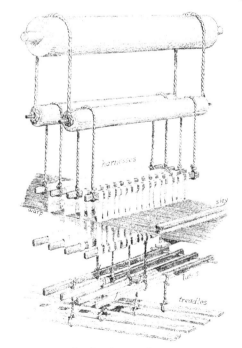

The arrangement of a four-harness loom

Warping

harness looms used lams to equalize the pull. Lams were slats hinged to the side of the loom, one lying under each harness. It was easy to tie the middle of a harness down to its lam, and the proper treadle could be hitched to the lam wherever the two crossed.

The weaver's most exacting job was warping. Skeins of warp yarn went on a swift to be wound from it on to long spools as the woman in the drawing on page 37 is doing. Rows of the spools stood on vertical wires in a frame on the wall. The weaver drew threads from them in bouts of forty which he measured to the full length of the projected web around pegs set in a long warping board or driven into the wall of his workroom. He tied each bout together at both ends and looped it into a loose chain for handling. With the threads spread evenly, he fastened an end of each bout to the warping beam and undid the chains as he rolled the whole business on to the beam at even tension. The exact methods for doing this are beyond the scope of this book—and of its author. A quite coarse linen will have thirty warp threads to the inch, or nine hundred to a thirty-inch-wide web. These had to be drawn in through the correct heddles according to the "draught" of the pattern. If, at the end, the weaver found one warp end threaded wrong, he had to take it and every strand beyond it out of the heddles and put them in correctly. In front of the harnesses the weaver sleyed each warp through the reed and secured its end to the cloth beam. The whole operation took him and three helpers two days or more.

Except to an expert weaver, a draft, as we now spell it, gives no more idea of a pattern than does written music to the tone-deaf. Drafts resemble

music. There's an old joke about a weaver setting up a loom from a couple of bars of Mendelssohn's "Spring Song." Actually a draft diagrams not the pattern but the loom. The old one, slicked up here for clarity, used each horizontal line to represent one harness and each tick on a line to mark a warp threaded into that harness. This whole pattern, used for a kind of tweed, covers less than an inch and repeats continuously. The zeros at the left under the harness lines show to which treadles each is tied, and the numbers on the vertical spaces give the order in which the treadles are to be tramped.

Competent weavers read drafts as easily as English and can "weave" them with a pen on squared paper to judge their appearance. Further, they can write one from a sample or even from a photograph. Modern draft writers use the spaces between horizontal lines for the harnesses and fill them in solid to mark warps, as you may see from "Sweetbriar Beauty." "Sweetbriar Beauty" is one of the simpler coverlet patterns. Their variations are extensive and their names fanciful: "Blazing Star," "Whig Rose," "Star of Bethlehem," "Queen's Fancy," for example. Some patterns have different names in different states. A few are very old and came from Europe, but the American weavers invented dozens that Europe never saw.

Chained warp

String heddle

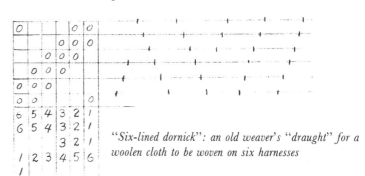

"Six-lined dornick": an old weaver's "draught" for a woolen cloth to be woven on six harnesses

Modern weaver's draft for "Sweetbriar Beauty,"
four-harness overshot coverlet

Though weavers made cloth from their own materials to sell in the open market, customers bespoke much of their work and the weaver wove with yarn that the customers spun. This was especially true of coverlets. The Pennsylvania Museum owns a pattern book of bed-cover designs by Weaver John Landes. These are not drafts but were obviously drawn to show to customers.

Four spinning wheels had to work full time to keep one weaver in yarn. But since most spinners could work only between household chores, the real figure came nearer to eight or ten wheels per loom. A weaver often quit work to ride his nag through the country hunting yarn. In 1767, when English weaver James Hargreaves's little daughter, Jenny, upset the spinning wheel, he noticed that it ran for a moment with its spindle standing vertical. This gave him the idea for a machine that eventually spun cotton on eighty spindles at once. The jenny solved the English weft shortage, but it couldn't manage the steady tension needed for drawing out the harder-twisted warp. Thomas High thought of stretching the yarn between pairs of rollers, one pair turning faster than the other. Richard Arkwright unethically seized the idea for his water frame, the first machine to use water power for spinning. Weft and warp: the yarn supply problem vanished in England and the weavers prospered. But the hand spinners did not.

Botched copies of jennies, tried out in America, didn't work well. The British government prevented the removal from the island of any

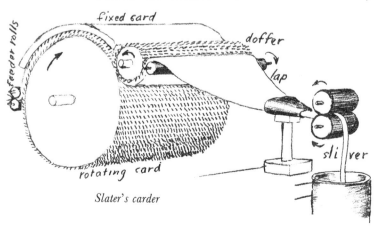

Slater's carder

cotton-spinning machinery or any model or drawing of one. A young Englishman, Samuel Slater, broke through the fence in a remarkable way. He apprenticed himself to one of Arkwright's many cotton-spinning partners and deliberately memorized every detail of the methods and the machines. Then he sailed secretly for America in 1789.

He signed a contract with a wealthy Quaker merchant, Moses Brown, who controlled a cotton mill full of nearly useless jennies at Pawtucket, Rhode Island. Slater scrapped the lot. He chalked outlines of machine parts on timber and Sylvanus Brown cut them out for him. He made sketches of iron parts and Oziel Wilkinson and his sons forged them while Slater successfully courted Oziel's daughter, Hannah. When the work was done, water power ran machines for carding (combing and condensing into a thick strand), drawing (stretching with rollers), roving (more stretching and slight twisting), and final spinning on an Arkwright frame. Soon Slater was spinning cotton warp so good that his new wife and her sisters respun some on their home wheels into America's first cotton sewing thread. The mill made more than the hand weavers could use and in two years had a ton of spun yarn on hand. Slater got a note from Moses Brown: "Thee must shut down thy [water] gates or thee will spin all my farms into cotton yarn."

Slater's cotton came from the West Indies. The Southern states were growing some, but the slow hand removal of seeds held down production. Then, in 1793, young Eli Whitney went to South Carolina as a tutor, and in less than two weeks he built a crank-run machine that removed more cotton seeds in an hour than a hand could pick out in three days. This, of course, was the cotton gin, which the whole South copied freely without permission. The price of slaves jumped and everybody planted cotton. More spinning mills sprang up in New England, but all they spun still had to be woven by hand.

Over in England, the Reverend Edmund Cartwright learned that the spinning mills there were turning out more yarn than the weavers could use. So, without ever having seen a weaver work, he built a power loom. Assuming that weaving was hard work, he made his first springs so powerful that a strong man could hardly turn

104

the machine's crank, but when he did turn it, the loom wove. Cartwright was granted a patent in 1785.

Francis Cabot Lowell visited England in 1811 and succeeded in seeing all the kinds of cotton machinery except the power loom. Nevertheless, with the brilliant help of Paul Moody, he built a completely able power loom from scratch. The revolving eccentric cone that drove his machine was later adopted for all looms.

By the late 1830's, water power was weaving plain woolen cloth in this country. Two looms, watched by a single operator, produced twenty to thirty yards a day, but home-operated spinning wheels still spun much of the wool yarn for them. This was about to end. Even then machines in England were successfully spinning prime wool yarn.

The first imported Jacquard loom started its complex work in Philadelphia in 1826. It deserves some sort of credit as the first automation. Its punched cards could control every individual warp thread, and so could weave any kind of pattern, including bedcovers with realistic flowers on them and with borders of eagles and uplifting mottoes. Though these charmed people, just as the butcher furniture did, the Jacquard didn't quickly oust the hand weavers. One of them, Weaver Rose, unkempt and snuff-sprinkled but a master who had learned the

trade by long apprenticeship, still worked in the early years of the twentieth century. Back in 1898 Alice Morse Earle predicted that the craft would die with him. She was wrong. Partly through him weaving continued as a handicraft, and it is said that there are more hand looms in this country now than there ever were in the colonies. Perhaps there are, but few of them work as hard as those did.

The Shoemaker

In the seventeenth century you could still call a shoemaker a cordwainer and be understood; you wouldn't be safe doing so much after 1700. The guild of shoemakers in England is still The Cordwainers Company, but the word now gets almost no other use. No doubt America's first English shoemaker, Thomas Beard, was officially a cordwainer. He brought his tools and materials to Plymouth in the *Mayflower*, but not on her first trip; he arrived in 1629. The community gave him fifty acres of land and paid him fifty pounds a year for his work, very high wages.

Thomas Dekker called shoemaking "the gentle craft," and so it was. It required little violent exertion; a shoemaker did almost all of his work seated on his bench and hunched over. The procedures were routine to an expert, so he could allow his mind to rove elsewhere. It was work that bred philosophy—and tuberculosis.

The shoemaker needed light, so he had a big window in his shop. But it lighted only a small room; he required little more space than would hold his bench, his lasting jack, and a pail of water for soaking sole leather. He bothered with no sales room or counter. You opened the door under the big wooden boot and there he was, busy, but full of opinions and free to discuss them. Men liked to drop in and smoke a pipe by the shoemaker's fire while they tested their ideas against his.

Almost any farmer could make casual repairs on his family's shoes, but very few men could make a complete shoe or boot. True, frontiersmen, far distant from shoemakers, managed to assemble "shoepacks" that, but for their high tops, looked like crude versions of modern loafers. But any wearer of shoepacks would have

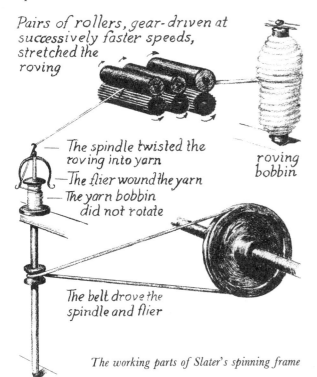

Pairs of rollers, gear-driven at successively faster speeds, stretched the roving

roving bobbin

— The spindle twisted the roving into yarn

— The flier wound the yarn

— The yarn bobbin did not rotate

The belt drove the spindle and flier

The working parts of Slater's spinning frame

Work shoe

*Man's shoe
and woman's, 1760*

Child's shoe, 1732

been glad to trade them for a pair of boots. The shoemaker was secure. He always had work to do; he could even make a living in the South. There he made rough shoes for plantation slaves which probably fitted their wearers as well as the planter's London-made shoes fitted him.

Throughout the eighteenth century, in the middle colonies much shoemaking was bespoke work made from the customer's own leather, but some was sale work that the craftsman made to standard sizes. The keeping of marked leather for its owner was a monumental nuisance that the shoemakers endured until, in the early 1800's, they hit on the idea of charging a fourth less for sale work than for bespoke work.

Any footgear that reached above the ankle-bones was a boot in early times, so all shoes were low shoes. Farmers who could afford them used cowhide boots in the fields, but their price was too high for most, so the majority wore coarse shoes with inch-thick soles made of three layers of leather, the two extra soles held on with big-headed hobnails. Gentlemen, who usually could afford boots, wore them most of the time even in large towns. They protected the leg on horseback and a man going more than a hundred yards almost always rode a horse. Riding boots could be quite low, light, and elegantly finished, or—like the jackboots which were made, probably in England, for long journeys—very high and almost as heavy as farm boots.

When knee breeches went out after 1800, light, low boots became fashionable for men on all occasions, but, earlier, buckled calfskin shoes served for church and social functions. Women wore fairly heavy leather shoes for every day, but grand ladies affected silk, satin, and brocade shoes for parties. When the "classic" French styles became popular around 1790, ladies went into very light fabric slippers without heels and boasted of making their own. They shortly returned to more practical footwear, and the shoemakers made them slippers with tops of prunella, a tightly woven woolen stuff.

The craftsman deliberately cut a child's shoes a couple of sizes too large and the youngster had

Jackboots and light riding boots

to wrap his feet in woolen cloth to fill them out until he grew into them. Shoes were too expensive to be replaced every few months. Iron heel-pieces and hobnailed soles extended their lives as far as possible and some even had wooden soles. Outgrown completely, they passed on to the next younger child. The eminently practical trick of covering juvenile toes with sheet copper didn't appear until Civil War times, but the shoes of eighteenth-century children were often ornamented with patches of red or purple leather. The practice of mating shoes as rights and lefts started in England in 1785 and appeared here shortly after that. Years later, when all adult shoes were so made, children's shoes remained unmated and the wearers had to switch them daily to equalize wear.

Probably the colonial shoemaker's most violent exercise was whittling the wooden lasts on which he made his customers' shoes. He measured the foot at several points, followed its contours as well as he could and marked it with the patron's name. When he slipped up or when the foot changed shape slightly, he could build up the tight places with glued-on leather. The traveling cat whipper might hold a last on his knees, but a man in his own shop preferred a lasting jack which held the wooden mold on a solid base.

The shoemaker shaped uppers by thin wooden patterns, not special ones for each last, but sets on a small–medium–large basis for which he made allowances by eye. His upper-cutting knife had a short rather broad blade and a sharp point. He could make the upper of an ordinary shoe with but two pieces of leather: one, the vamp, covering the toe and instep and ending in the wide tongue; the other, the counter, covering the heel and sides and ending in two straps. The shoemaker didn't supply buckles or attach them to shoes—he merely punched the proper holes in the straps for them. A shoe buckle had two sets of tongues: one set to hold it on to the outside strap, the other to tighten the inside strap in the usual way. For shoes tied with latchets, both straps had matching holes in them through which the wearer passed the leather string. The best shoes had their counters made in two pieces, with a seam up the back to shape the leather over the heel, as is now done. All colonial shoes had to be much longer than the foot that wore them

107

because the shoemakers hadn't learned to "cramp" the leather over the toe but brought it straight out to meet the tip of the sole.

The thick leather for the tap (sole) soaked all day in water and was wrapped in cloth overnight to mull so it would be soft enough to work. In the morning, the craftsman cut it to rough shape on his board with a half-moon knife that had a crosswise handle like a spade. Seated on his bench with his lapstone on his knees, he thoroughly beat the tap with a broad-faced hammer to give it the contour of the sole. A flattish water-smoothed rock made a lapstone.

With his last upside down on the lasting jack, the shoemaker stretched the upper over it with special pincers and tacked the leather to the wood temporarily. His pattern allowed a little extra material around the bottom of the foot. This he turned outward to receive the sole instead of inward to a welt, as is done on modern shoes. He coated the projecting flange with glue from his paste horn to hold the tap in place while he sewed it.

The stitches that would hold the sole passed through it and through the edge of the upper. If they lay on the surface of the sole, they would quickly wear through, so the shoemaker cut a shallow "feather" (channel) for them to lie in near the sole's edge. He ran a marking wheel around the feather and used his awl to punch a hole for each stitch where the wheel's teeth dented the leather. He sewed with waxed linen or hemp and, instead of a needle, attached a hog bristle to the thread with wax. This combination he spoke of as a wax end. It would pass through a small hole more readily than would a threaded needle. The sewer used two wax ends at the same time, passing both of them through each hole in opposite directions. This was "whipping the cat," and though its connection with the scathing term "cat whipper" seems obvious, the reason for it doesn't.

Sole knife

Shoemaker's hammer

Marking wheel

Awls

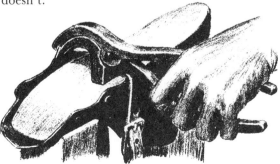

Stretching the vamp on the last

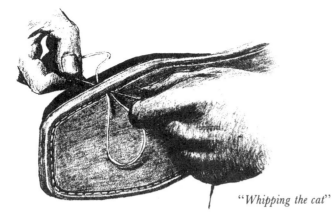

"Whipping the cat"

When he had sewn the sole, the shoemaker cut several heel-shaped lifts from sole leather and fastened them on with small nails. Then he finished trimming the sole and the upper edge with a hook-bladed knife and so could remove the last. The wooden form fitted the new shoe so tightly that he needed a special cross-handled hook to pull it out. He burnished the heel and the edge of the sole with a smooth, curved iron heated over a tin lamp. The uppers of dress shoes he blacked and waxed, work shoes he merely smeared with tallow.

The toe of a boot last was exactly like that for a shoe, but the heel and leg part was made as a separate form. Since this was necessarily rigid and since the top of a boot leg narrowed above the calf, the form had to be made in three long sections in order to be removable. The pieces were held together with a bolt through the top from front to back. Removing the bolt and the tapered middle section loosened the other two sections so that they came out readily, and the toe piece could then be hooked out.

Shoe pegs

A man named Philip Kerkland started a shoe "factory" at Lynn, Massachusetts, in 1636; another is recorded on the Eastern Shore of Virginia in 1640. In early eighteenth-century New England such enterprises employed as many as forty men, each making complete shoes, from cutting the uppers to nailing the heel taps.

Ships brought hides from South America, from New Orleans, and eventually from California. The hide ships took out diversified trade goods, with barrels of shoes as an important item. A barrel held as many as two hundred shoes tied together in pairs. By 1790, a pair of men's shoes cost three dollars, while in the early 1800's, a pair of three-dollar shoes brought eleven dollars in California. Long before that, however, methods changed in the shoe business.

In 1750, an enterprising Welshman named Thomas Adams Dagys turned up in New England. Before he started business, he studied shoes, dissecting European examples, noting their shortcomings, and designing new patterns that were simpler and stronger. Then Dagys introduced a brand-new idea that started the industrialization of America. He broke down the making of a shoe into parts and gave each worker only one job to do on it. His shop was small and only leather cutting and packing for shipment were done in it. Dagys farmed his cut leather out to local people to be sewn by hand as piece work in their homes. Women "bound" uppers together, men who were not journeyman shoemakers put on soles, even children learned to paste in linings. The whole township became a shoe factory and presently other townships became other shoe factories. Everybody made shoes. Even sailors and fishermen took them along to work on at sea.

The slowest and most arduous part of shoemaking was the sewing of the sole. Inevitably Yankee ingenuity found a quicker, if not a better, way of putting it on with square, blunt-pointed wooden pegs. At first these came in "cards" (blocks) about four inches square, the points shaped with a notched plane-blade run in two directions and the pegs separated by saw cuts that stopped just short of the bottom. Later, a machine split the pegs off and they were sold by the quart.

The pegger made holes through the sole with his awl and through a narrow welt sewn to the upper. He held a mouthful of pegs, "spitting" one at a time, placing its point in an awl hole, and striking it one blow with his hammer. The next change, in 1833, was a machine to peg shoes. Then, in 1851, John Nichols, a shoemaker out of work, bought one of Elias Howe's new sewing machines with the idea of sewing pants to support his family. He made a new needle for it and sewed leather uppers with it. Where a woman could bind only four pairs of uppers a day by hand, a man with a machine could bind fifteen pairs a day.

Boot last, burnisher, and lamp

The Limner

Except for the few, painting pictures hasn't generally been a good way to make money. In colonial America the few were fewer, and the rank and file had a thin time indeed. Painting was, as the best of all the limners put it, "no more than any other useful trade . . . like that of a carpenter or shew maker." A man who could paint passable "faces" (portraits) could just manage to live by hunting patrons from town to town and through the countryside.

Daguerre made the first practical camera in France in 1837. None was seen in this country until years later. Painted or drawn portraits or silhouettes scissored out of black paper were the only ways of preserving likenesses. So the limners who could paint faces did better than the rest of their kind. Once in a while one of them would pick up a job of decorating the wall of a room with romantic scenery or of portraying the farmstead of a house-proud squire—minutely, to the last cow and fence and the family carriage—to be framed in a panel over the parlor mantel. But even so fortunate a knight of the brush—he called it a pencill—had to fill in with sign painting, frame gilding, the silvering of mirrors, and any little varnish job that needed doing.

If he was lucky, the limner rode a skinny nag, carrying his paints and brushes in saddlebags. His brushes he made himself from mink and squirrel hair tied in carefully arranged bunches and cemented into quills to which he attached handles. He bought his colors, as dry powders, in small animal bladders—mouse, rat, rabbit—and ground them with oil in a mortar. The later men, who rode in light wagons, could carry samples to show to prospective sitters, but the man on foot or on horseback had seldom even a reputation to help along his sales talk. He couldn't carry so much as a blank canvas. When he got a commission, he had a local joiner plane a wood panel to paint on or build him a rectangular frame on which to stretch tow linen or any other fabric at hand. One of the finest of early American portraits is painted on blue-striped bed ticking.

Most of the early portraits are unrelentingly wooden, with strong emphasis on exact details of jewelry and lace. But the crudest have charm and quite frequently they record character with

startling clarity. This is true even of some of the later mass-production portraits for which the limner completed all but the face before he ever saw the sitter, whom he thus provided with far grander clothes than his subject was likely to own. Considering the difficulties of learning the trade, the old work is astonishingly good. No art schools existed and no limner needed an apprentice even if he could afford to feed one.

Most remarkable of all is one man, John Singleton Copley, who taught himself to paint portraits that, by today's standards, are better than those of most of the famous Englishmen painting at the time. Copley was highly successful. But he was a Loyalist, so he left Boston for London in 1776. He succeeded there, too, but his work became fancy and he lost the strong simplicity of his American work.

Benjamin West went to London so young that he wasn't really an American painter at all, but he remained an American at heart. He became president of the Royal Academy and a personal friend of King George III who kept him busy—and prosperous—for thirty years. West wasn't as good a painter as he thought he was or as others thought him to be, but he was a fine old fellow and his house in London became home and school for young American artists. Charles Willson Peale, John Trumbull, Gilbert Stuart, and Robert Fulton all had help and instruction from Benjamin West.

A painting of any kind, and especially a large historical one, was much more a popular wonder in early times than any picture can hope to be today. A single big canvas like Trumbull's "George Washington Crossing the Delaware," exhibited in a hall or even in a tent, would draw crowds to see it at sixpence a head. Historical painters depended on such showings for part of their income.

Engraving wasn't considered limning, but it required similar talents. Though it was a town trade, there was seldom enough work in any one town to keep a man busy full time. So some engravers like Abel Buell also made silver, and some silversmiths like Paul Revere did engraving to be printed. Much of Revere's work was political broadsides, like his famous rendering of the "Boston Massacre." Buell engraved maps, excellent ones, and plates for printing paper

"Pencills," palette, and mahl stick

Rat, mouse, and rabbit

money. Copper plates had to be flattened and polished by hand, so their size was limited. One of Buell's maps covers two of them, printed side by side.

The proud owner of a library might feel that he needed a personal bookplate, something classic, with a goddess on it in her shift, and a scrap of Latin. Only an engraving was acceptable for this. Trade cards, too, had to be engraved if they were to confer status. These were advertisements issued by tradesmen and craftsmen and they were not actual cards but small sheets of paper. They carried some kind of image related to the business, as a beaver or a hat or both for a hatter, or perhaps a miniature of the shop's sign. They gave the owner's name and address and listed the goods he sold. The whole was surrounded by a fancy border, the more elaborate the better. A craftsman sometimes pasted his trade card on large articles as a label. Otherwise he simply distributed the cards where they would do the most good. Often he rendered his bills on the backs of them.

Illustrations for books were either woodcuts or engravings, with the latter much the better. The first known American copperplate is a portrait of Increase Mather by Thomas Emmes for the frontispiece of a 1701 edition of Mather's *Blessed Hope*. There was no way to print music except from copperplates, and, in 1752, Thomas Badger of Charleston, South Carolina, engraved and printed the "choicest tunes," the only American sheet music before the introduction of lithography in the nineteenth century. Illustrations gradually grew more ambitious. With war only a year away, an English architectural book was reissued in Philadelphia with sixty good plates in it engraved by Thomas Norman; and in the 1790's, the first American edition of the Encyclopaedia Britannica contained five hundred and forty-three plates, the work of at least seven men.

The print engraver worked with a burin exactly like the one used to ornament silverware. He used it to plow little V-shaped ditches as lines in the highly polished surface of his flat plate. He then warmed the finished plate and daubed it with thick sticky ink made with boiled linseed oil. The ink covered the surface and also filled up the lines. The craftsman wiped the surface

clean with rags and polished it cleaner with a chalked palm, but he was careful to leave the ink in the lines. His press was something like an old-fashioned clothes wringer. It had two iron rollers, one above and one below. A flat bed lay between them. The plate, with a sheet of damp paper over it and a sheet of soft dry paper and two felt blankets over that, lay on the press bed. When the printer applied great effort to four radiating handles and turned the top roller, bed and plate together moved between the rollers. The pressure forced the paper down into the lines so that it took up the ink from them.

An ordinary printing press which transferred ink to paper from a flat surface wouldn't print copperplate engravings. For such presses, another kind of artist made woodcuts. He drew his design on a smooth block of hard wood which was exactly as thick as type was high. He then used a knife and small gouges to lower the surface of all the wood not covered by his drawing. Only the high parts of the block were inked, and paper pressed down on it came off with an approximation of the drawing. The results improved when it was discovered that the *end* of a block of close-grained wood, like box, could have lines engraved in it with a burin. These printed as white lines, however; only the wood left between them came out black.

Except for a few political cartoons, woodcuts in colonial newspapers appeared exclusively in the advertisements. Announcements of packet sailings were often headed by a cut of a ship; coach schedules appeared under a ragged-looking vehicle drawn by a single hobby horse. Two horses presented technical difficulties.

Some details of the press are guesswork

5.

GROUP WORK

The Shipwrights

MANY of the trades included in this chapter could be and were carried on in small centers by one man with a helper or two, but in larger places the same trades employed many workers. Other enterprises, especially those which combined many trades as shipbuilding did, had to be group efforts and had always been. One man could build a boat, but one man's life wasn't long enough to complete a ship single-handed, even if he learned all the skills he would need. One ship, built in 1740, required work from twenty-three different crafts.

The first English colonists all settled on the shores of bays and rivers. Fish were essential as food and were important as a trade item when salted. It took boats of some size to catch fish at sea. Trade between colony and colony and between the colonies and the West Indies started early. The Massachusetts Bay settlers built a small ship of thirty tons, *The Blessing of the Bay*, at Malden in 1631. Ten years later Richard Hollingsworth's shipyard at Salem, Massachusetts, built "a prodigious ship of 200 Tons," more than half again the tonnage of the *Mayflower*. Soon shipbuilding became the leading industry of Boston and Salem and of other towns all down the coast. Hamlets sleep now along the Chesapeake Bay that once throve as shipbuilding

centers. They faded, not because demand slackened, but because they used up all the nearby white-oak timber.

The greatest asset of the American shipwrights was American trees. In a century or so of overseas expansion, England had depleted hers and the Royal Navy could hardly wait for the settlers to land before it began branding the "Broad Arrow" on oaks for hulls and tall pines for masts to be held for the Crown. But even a navy could use only a fraction of American trees, so English merchants could have ships built in this country cheaper than at home. By 1774, a third of England's merchantmen had been built here and almost a century later American yards still built clipper ships for the Empire trade.

There are tales of early ships being built in the woods and hauled to the water on rollers by many oxen. Perhaps—but seldom. Ships were built on slips or ways at the water's edge. They are now most often built in drydocks, and even in the eighteenth century, France and England had these gated basins which can be flooded when a hull is finished so that it floats where it stands and can be quietly towed out to the fitting dock. An eighteenth-century slip was a series of squared timbers called stocks fixed side by side on a wood foundation, a foot or so apart, in a long row sloping upward from the edge of the water at about four degrees. The new ship's keel

The Broad Arrow

was laid down the middle of the line of stocks, stern toward the water and as close to it as was consistent with dry working space. Temporary treenails held the keel in place until the hull was ready for launching.

Up to the 1700's, an English shipwright began work by making a complete scale model, fully rigged. He built his ship from it exactly. His eighteenth-century successor made "draughts of the lines" on paper and from them cut full-size patterns of the timbers out of thin wood. These he often took into the forest and tested against standing trees, searching for natural growth that would yield the curves he needed. The Americans held to the model idea but used it for the hull only and, since the two sides were mates, they made only half of it. You may see such half-models in museums, built up of alternate layers of pine and walnut, varnished and fastened to a board. The varnish and the board mean that the model's usefulness is past because it can no longer be taken apart for measuring the layers as the master shipwright measured them.

Most craft of all sizes, in both the seventeenth and eighteenth centuries, had fat bodies, flattish bottoms, round "apple" bows, and narrow, elevated quarter-decks aft. They carried a maximum of cargo at a minimum of speed. Most sails were square and set athwart the deck. But the Americans began early to rig their smaller vessels with handier and more effective fore-and-aft sails set parallel to the keel. Boats so rigged became known as schooners. In the last quarter of the eighteenth century, Chesapeake Bay shipwrights began building small schooners with a different kind of hull copied from a sloop used in Bermuda, which may, in turn, have been copied from a French fishing boat. The type

Stocks, keel, sternpost, and stem

came to be known as the "Baltimore Clipper" and some of its features survived in the famous clipper ships of the mid-1800's. The original clippers had narrow hulls, sharp bows, V-shaped bottoms, and thin keels that became quite deep as they ran aft. Such hulls had little cargo space, but they could sail faster and carry more canvas for their size than any boat before them. Because they could run away from all hostile ships, clippers made the best privateers. In spite of their small capacity, but because of their speed, they carried three-quarters of all American cargoes around 1812. They also served as revenue cutters and as slavers.

Some very old half-models are sliced downward, instead of horizontally, to show vertical cross sections through the vessel. These gave the successive shapes of the frames (ribs) which, as can be seen from the diagram, were built up of sections in two layers, with overlapping joints, pinned together. This was the only way that the necessary curves and the necessary strength could be combined in so large a timber.

Keels were built up, too, but somewhat differently. A squared timber, free of big knots, large enough and long enough for the keel of a ship, was impossible to get even from the huge trees of virgin forests. So the shipwrights joined shorter pieces with long scarfs and bolted them together. Since galvanized iron was unknown, colonial shipwrights used copper and bronze bolts which sea water wouldn't destroy. The stem was scarfed into the forward end of the keel and the sternpost into its after end. Both stood erect "out of winding"—true with the center line of the keel—and were propped in place until they could be supported by the structure.

The cutaway illustration will explain the construction of a wooden ship better than words can do it. The closely spaced frames rested on the keel and the keelson rested on the frames. All three were firmly bolted together. As each frame went in, it was braced from the outside with a

Knee pattern against a tree

Half model

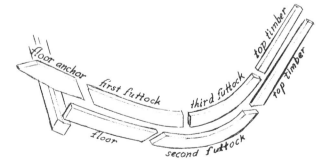

The parts of a frame. The ends of the short sections are butted and the two halves are pinned together side against side.

couple of temporary shores. The lower ends of these stood on planks (sholes) and were "trigged" in place with treenails. The inside faces of the frames were completely covered by the ceiling and their outside faces were solidly planked over with four-inch stuff. Carpenters bored holes and drove treenails clear through planks, frames, and ceiling, standing on staging (scaffolding) to do the work. The stringer supported the middles of the deck beams and was braced by the stanchions. The knees supported the ends of the deck beams. A ship with two decks had a second stringer and a second set of stanchions and knees.

The skill of a ship's carpenter surpassed that of his landsman brother. It had to—lives depended on his work. Most parts of a hull were curved, some parts in two directions. The carpenter had to make these fit together with little more than his eye and his experience to guide him. Further, he had constantly to watch the grain of his wood in relation to the stresses it would have to bear. The grain had to bend with a curve or at least lie parallel to a chord of it. If it "ran out," a curved timber would split under stress along the grain. That's why the shipwright sought natural curved growths for sharply bent members like knees, and it's why he built up the ribs with short pieces. Curved parts of small thickness which took no great strain he could soften with steam in a tight box and bend into shape. Planking, ceiling, and decking were bent that way.

Even ornamental trim involved curves and odd angles. The paneling of the captain's cabin at the stern had to be fitted to a room with a curved and sloping floor and ceiling and with walls that sloped and even bulged a little. Ship joiners became so used to off-square panels that when they worked ashore they sometimes raked panels on perfectly square walls.

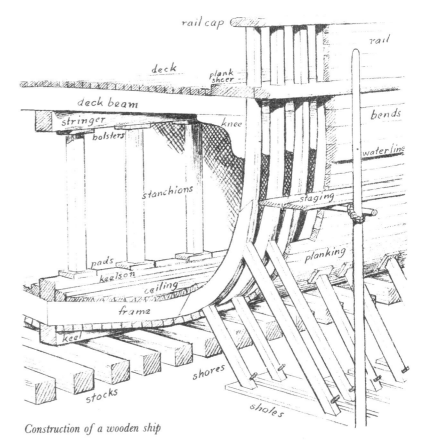

Construction of a wooden ship

Behind the carpenters came the calkers to stuff all the seams with oakum, pressing it in with wheels and driving it tight with flat irons struck with banded wooden mallets that had long heads and short handles. Oakum is hemp fibers from old rope untwisted and picked apart; picking it was the work of pensioners in almshouses. After the calker had packed the seams, his helper payed them with hot pitch. Calking didn't end with the planking or even with the deck; every crevice that could possibly leak water had to be stopped, including the scarf joints in the keel. Even so, all wooden ships leaked, and pumping the bilge was a daily chore.

When the last treenail was driven and every seam was tight, when the whole bottom was thoroughly tarred and, if it was to be done,

Scarf joint for a heavy timber: The hammer is a bolt set.

Mallet, calking irons, and wheel

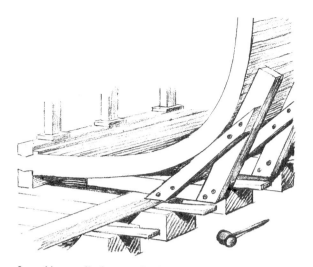

Launching cradle for a craft of moderate size

Poll-headed adz

sheathed with copper, the shipwrights laid rails, called bulge ways, for launching. These were timbers placed across the stocks parallel to the keel and well out from it; they extended into the water. The carpenters then built a cradle, under the ship and resting on the top surfaces of the ways, which they greased with tallow and soft soap. To keep the craft from going overboard before its time, two short timbers called dog shoes or triggers angled against the cradle and held it back. These were carefully shaped and so placed as to allow a blow from above to knock them down out of the way. Weights, suspended above each trigger, dropped to accomplish this. The shipwrights removed the treenails that held the keel to the stocks, but the weight of the hull still rested on it. Now many men, working in unison with mauls, drove wedges under the bulge ways to raise them, the cradle, and the hull, until the keel came clear of the stocks.

A launching was a ceremony then as it is now, but instead of a lady christening the ship, the oldest sailor present did the office. Notables gathered, however, and a clergyman blessed the ship. Then, at a signal, two men swung axes, cut the ropes, and dropped the weights on the dog shoes. For a moment there was stillness. Nothing happened at all. Then—a creaking and a slight motion of the whole great bulk. The cradle was sliding. The spectators held their breaths, and the master, who feared for accidents, held his. Speed picked up; the rails smoked from friction; then they flamed. The crowd yelled. And, with a rush, the new ship slid down the ways, plunged into the water, and floated free of the cradle. Its

impact created a big wave which, in narrow rivers, sometimes backwashed and drenched the spectators.

Henry W. Longfellow described the launch of a fully rigged ship—and apologized for doing so. Normally the riggers didn't take over until the ship was in the water and their complex work took nearly as long as did building the hull. Their first job was to bring the ship broadside to the shore so that they could use the shipyard's big windlass to careen her over on her side for stepping the masts. These were the trunks of white pines, two feet thick or thicker, and forty feet long. No equipment of the time could lift their whole weight and lower it through the deck and down to the step on the keelson. It was labor enough to raise one end and inch it through the partners horizontally.

Once the masts were in and guyed by the shrouds, they could be used as derricks for hoisting up topmasts and topgallants. As each went into place, the riggers guyed it with its standing rigging of shrouds, forestays, and backstays. Russian hemp, which wouldn't stretch much, served for these. Then they went on to raising spars and providing them with the running rigging that would control them. Manila hemp, or local hemp, would do for this. The resulting maze of stays, braces, bowlines, halyards, and downhauls, perfectly simple to a seaman, is a mad cat's cradle to a landsman. Rigging was slow, careful, and tarry work. The end of every line had to be served (bound) with marline (twine) to keep it from fraying. Wherever a line would chafe, it had to be protected. A line too short had to have a splice to lengthen it without increasing its thickness so much that it would bind in a block (pulley).

There is a town on the east coast of this country with a very wide street leading away from its harbor. At its foot there was once a "rope-walk," a building a thousand feet long, with a narrow road on each side of it. When the town grew and the rope-walk vanished, the city fathers simply extended the road for the full width inland.

In the long building, a roper spun hemp, backing slowly away from a revolving hook turned by an apprentice manning a crank. The roper wrapped a bundle of hackled hemp around his waist and fed fibers from it to the twisting, length-

Spinning hemp yarn and laying rope

ening yarn. Next to him, two men twisted two yarns into a strand of marline. One of them turned a crank that rotated two whirl hooks in a direction opposite to the twist of the yarn so that the strand would not unwind. The second man formed his strand by guiding the yarns through two spiral grooves cut into a bullet-shaped wooden block called a "top." Beyond this pair, another team used three whirl hooks, again reversing the direction of rotation, to lay three strands or, for large sizes, three groups of strands into a rope. Their top had three grooves in it, of course. The strands reached from the hooks to a swivel (a loper) at the far end of the rope-walk and the man guiding the top backed from it toward the hooks as he worked. Still farther over and once more reversing the twist, several men labored to lay three ropes into a ponderous cable that would stay a mainmast or hold a ship to its anchor.

The gear for handling sails was the business of the rigger, but he did nothing with the sails themselves. They would be "bent on" by the ship's crew when it took over. Meanwhile they had to be made in a sail loft large enough to spread the mainsail out flat on the floor. There the sailmaker cut his linen or hemp canvas, length after length of it, which he seamed together with strong twine. His skill lay in cutting the sail so that it would "belly" just enough under the pressure of wind. The sailmaker's needle was four inches long and he pushed it through the cloth by pressing against its head with the dimpled brass stud on his leather "palm." He called it a pa'm.

He made a strong hem all the way around the sail and whipped the bolt rope onto it. Into the corners of the bolt rope and on the leaches and across the foot, he spliced rope cringles to which the various controlling lines would be fastened. Across the hem at the head of the sail he punched holes which became grommets when he reinforced their edges with twine, much as a buttonhole is bound with thread. These were for the lash lines that would hold the sail on to its spar. Across all the larger sails he sewed from one to four strips of canvas to strengthen other rows of grommets that would hold the reef points. These would be tied up to the spar to shorten the sail when the wind blew too hard. Without counting any of the extra or temporary ones, the sailmaker made a round dozen sails for a three-masted ship.

Two kinds of blacksmiths specialized in nautical ironing. We may call them the light-work smiths and the heavy-work smiths, though the terms are made up for the occasion. The light-work men used the normal equipment of their horse-shoeing fellows. They made the thousand and one special fittings that a ship needed. For instance, every wooden block for the lines that handled the sails—it took about two dozen for the foresail alone—had to have an iron axle, an iron band around it from top to bottom, and a swiveled eye by which it was fastened in place. Often two blocks were banded together, one above the other. Iron bands around masts and spars for holding this and that had to be individually forged; so did the gudgeons and pintles on which the rudder swung; so did all chains.

The man we have called the heavy-work

yarn

marline

rope

cable

Sailmaker's "palm"

blacksmith might also be called the forger—with no reflection on his honesty. His principal product was anchors and he needed a husky crew to help him make them. The anchor of an ordinary merchantman, say the brig illustrated on page 11, could weigh four thousand pounds. That of the frigate *Constellation* weighs five tons. A powered tilt hammer had to shape such a mass of metal, and to move it from hearth to anvil required swinging derricks. In order to weld two parts of the anchor, the smith had to heat both simultaneously on separate hearths, each equipped with bellows, and then bring the parts together under the hammer. That took two derricks and fast work.

Rushlight holder

The Chandlers

Like tanners, chandlers were not welcome neighbors. Theirs was a greasy, smelly trade. They made candles and, since the materials, equipment, and parts of the processes, were similar, they also made soap. Josiah Franklin, Benjamin's father, though a dyer in England, became a "tallow-chandler and sope-boiler" in Boston to maintain his family. In the eighteenth century, the word "chandler" was still struggling with "grocer" in designating a storekeeper, so the distinctions—ship chandler (which survives), wax chandler, and tallow chandler—were in common use. An association of candlemakers who did not make soap called themselves "candlers" in the 1760's, but no one followed this lead. A candler is only an egg tester now.

The use of lamps to solve the lighting problem was mentioned earlier. It was as often solved by burning fat or wax soaked into, or surrounding, some kind of wick. The homemade rushlight was the crudest of these solutions. The pith of the soft rush (*Juncus effusus*), with a strip of "bark" left on to stiffen it, was dipped once into melted fat, cooled, and then burned in a special clamp. Such a rushlight was about two feet long and would burn almost an hour. The flame consumed the pith completely, leaving no ash to need snuffing. But the rushlight did smoke objectionably and moving it up in its holder as it consumed itself was a nuisance. Dipped candles and molded candles, whether wax or tallow, made less trouble in the house.

Out-of-doors a candle in a lantern gave a meager light, so "persons of substance" who walked abroad in the dark had link boys with flaming torches to precede them. Sometimes the torch was no more than a splinter of resinous pine, yielding a more pleasant odor than a flambeau, a huge candle made with four hemp wicks, or than a true link which was a short length of rope soaked in pitch or rosin. Chandlers made flambeaux and links.

Before 1750 the chandlers made their best candles from beeswax, or from bayberry wax which they obtained by boiling the berries of the beach shrub *Myrica carolinensis*. After mid-century they began to get some spermaceti, better than either of these, of which more shortly. Cheap candles are now made of paraffin, a petroleum product unknown to our forefathers; their cheap candles were tallow right up to the early years of the twentieth century. Tallow for candles was hard animal fat, chiefly from beeves and sheep. A bull yielded enough of it to make twenty-six dozen candles. When the Yankee ships brought hides from the Spanish colonies to the shoemakers, they also brought the tallow from the same animals to the chandlers.

Whether he was making tallow candles or soap, the chandler didn't merely melt his fat, he tried (rendered) it by boiling, so that the fibrous material in it rose to the surface where it could be skimmed off. The trying pots were huge coppers battered out by a coppersmith. If the chandler was dipping candles, he ladled the hot fat into a rectangular vat and allowed it to cool

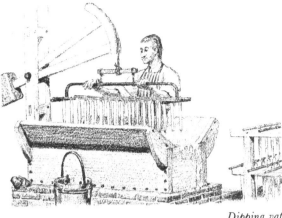

Dipping vat

somewhat. Very hot tallow would leave a thin deposit on a dipped wick or, worse, would melt off the accumulation of earlier dippings. If the tallow became too cool and began to make lumpy deposits, the dippers built up the fire under the vat or added tallow from the hot pot.

The earliest settlers used linen wicks, or dipped the same kind of pith they used for rushlights, because they had no other materials. But loose-spun cotton made the best candlewicks. After Samuel Slater, the cotton mills spun candlewick and sold it in balls. An apprentice cut wicks about twenty inches long on a simple measuring cutter equipped with a sharp blade. If they were for dipping, he hung them a hand's breadth apart over three foot-long rods (broaches) which lay side by side across a wooden frame. He twisted the two hanging strands into a single wick. There was a trick in this. The boy first tightened the twist the spinner had put in the yarn and then twisted the strands together in the opposite direction. Like a rope, they would then "hold their lay."

A professional dipper took several broaches at a time from the frame and placed them on the "rake" suspended over the tallow vat. With this device, it was possible for him to dip all the wicks on the broaches simultaneously and evenly. After each immersion, the broaches went back to their frame to allow the new tallow to cool before they were dipped again for another layer. One man and a helper could dip five hundred pounds of candles in a day. As the candles grew, they developed a slightly irregular tapered shape. When each candle had accumulated enough tallow to weight about a quarter of a pound, all were removed from the broaches and

117

packed in barrels. The loop of wick by which each candle had hung remained on its base.

The chandler prepared tallow for molding the same way as for dipping, but wax didn't have to be boiled. Simple melting and skimming would do. The process of molding was the same for all materials. Such town chandlers as Josiah Franklin had racks of pewter molds that made two hundred candles at a pouring. The molds hung upside down, showing from the top as holes in the shallow pan that covered the rack.

When the apprentice set up wicks for molding, he doubled and twisted them as before, but he had to poke each loop down through the mold and fish it out of a small hole in the bottom. He tied the free ends together over a metal broach at the top of the rack. A later method reversed this and hooked the loop of the wick upward through the hole in the bottom of the mold. The molder used a special large ladle to fill the molds with hot wax or tallow. His apprentice scraped up what was spilled in the pan before it could harden and join the candles together at their bases. In cold weather the molds had to be warmed to keep the wax from congealing before it reached the bottom. In any weather a filled mold was submerged in cold water to harden the candles and, after some time, in hot water to free them from the metal so that they could be withdrawn. Pewter was the best mold metal because it conducted heat so quickly.

When American whaling ships began to bring in cachalots or sperm whales, it was discovered that a fatty solid would precipitate from the head oil of the animals. This was spermaceti and it was the best candle material ever found. Candles made from it gave a brighter light than any had ever given and they never dripped. There was,

Iron grease pot for dipping rushes

Poking stick for stringing molds

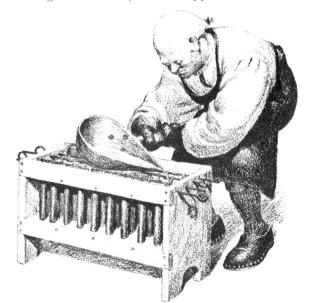

Scraper for spilled tallow

Soap kettle

*A dipped candle
and a molded
candle*

Lye hopper

in fact nothing to drip; the flame burned without melting the usual pool of liquefied wax. So good were these candles that, when a standard was needed to measure the illumination produced by gas light, the output of a spermaceti candle, seven-eighths of an inch thick, became "one candlepower."

A candlemaker could sell at high prices all the candles of this kind that his supply of sperm oil would let him make. Obediah Brown, of the enterprising Rhode Island Browns, started the first spermaceti candle works in 1753 and made three hundred barrels of them in his first year. He and his brother, Nicholas, became the leading spirits of the United Company of Spermaceti Candlers which rationed the limited supply of oil—and they got the largest share. The association kept its trade secrets closely. Nantucket, which perhaps caught more cachalots than Narragansett, couldn't find out how to make the candles until 1772.

Candles remained an important light source until well after the Civil War. A way of extracting much of the grease from tallow by pressing it between hot plates was found in the early nineteenth century. The residue was stearin, and candles made from it gave a clearer light with less smoke. About the same time, it was discovered that a braided wick would curl out of the flame as it was consumed and thus snuff itself automatically.

The chandler could use lard and even common whale oil, as well as tallow, to make coarse yellow soap. For fancy white soap, he used vegetable oils such as olive oil, palm oil, and nut oil that was pressed from hazelnut and walnut kernels. Whether for plain or fancy, he had to combine the fats with an alkali to form the new substance. His alkali was potash of varying purity, produced from black salt which was the main product of the American frontier. Even as late as 1836, potash so produced was one of the principal exports of the United States.

Great excesses of wood resulted from the clearing of new land. The pioneers burned it to get rid of it, but they didn't waste it entirely. They wet its ashes down in hoppers and collected the seepage of "black ley" (lye) that resulted. They evaporated the water from this by boiling it in cast-iron pots and chipped the resulting deposit off the insides of the vessels. Every spring they sent their year's accumulation of "black salt" eastward on pack horses and traded it for powder and shot. Black salt was potash. It was black only because of the carbon from the ash that was mixed with it. Specialists in tidewater towns "scorched" the crude stuff in ovens and burned most of the carbon out. It was then commercially usable for making cheap glass and yellow soap. Dissolved in water, recrystallized, and baked again, it became a fine white powder known as "pearl ash." In this form, it was an ingredient of white soap and of the best crown glass and was also used as a mordant for some adjective dyes.

In preparation for making yellow soap, the chandlers mixed three solutions of potash and water. The weakest would barely float an egg on its side, with most of the shell submerged; the next stronger floated the egg, still on its side, with half of the shell above the surface; the strongest floated the egg end-up. The soapmakers stirred their boiling fat constantly and, with great care, added the solutions progressively, beginning with the weakest and watching the effects closely. The smell that came from their cauldrons would sicken a goat. Soapy stuff formed and rose to the top and the workers skimmed it off into a second pot for more boiling with a little powdered rosin added. When this batch reached the consistency of honey, the chandlers drew their fire and let the pot cool overnight. The soap was now "paste," and it was reheated, with salt added, and stirred for two or three hours before it was cooled again to let the salt expel the free

118

water and harden the batch. Before it was quite cold, the soapmakers ladled it into large rectangular hardening molds. When the mass became strong enough to stand alone, they dumped it out and sliced it into bars about the size and shape of bricks by pulling brass wires through it, side on. The bars were dusted with slacked lime to keep them from sticking together when they were packed in wooden boxes. They were sold by weight and with no wrappers.

White soap got exactly the same treatment except that the rosin was omitted. The chief difference lay in the quality of the materials. However, such soap was cast in bar-size molds which yielded a raised impression of a crown on each bar. When a prejudice against the Crown appeared about 1776, the chandlers replaced it with an eagle.

The Potters

Archaeologists have found the dump at Jamestown where a competent potter tossed his spoiled pieces soon after 1625. The earliest American potter known by name was Philip Drinker who worked in Massachusetts in 1635. Pottery was more important to the colonials than it is to us. Large towns supported considerable works with several kilns and a number of potters, and almost every village had its one-man "pot house" operating at least part time. Mrs. Laura Woodside Watkins has listed the names of three hundred potters who worked before 1800 in New England alone. An enterprise set up in New Jersey in 1684 to make "white and chiney ware" failed because its promoter didn't learn beforehand that there was "noe clay in the Country that would make white ware." Actually there was, but he missed it. The Corselius pottery started in New York in 1730. William Crolius married a Corselius daughter and their descendants still made pottery in the late 1800's.

All very early American pottery was "redware," shaped from plain brick clay that was colored naturally by iron oxide. It varied from pink to an almost fiery red. It was soft and leaky. After about 1725, some potters began to make better stuff but some still made redware well after 1800.

Redware: the canteen went to the fields around the shoulder of a harvester

Clay is earth leached from ancient rocks and is largely aluminum silicate. Its fine particles, each only five thousandths of a millimeter in size, make it tend to stick together and also make it easy to shape when it is wet. Kaolin is white, but most clay is colored by some mineral impurity: red, yellow, tan, gray, or blue. The proportions of their elements make some clays produce harder pottery than others and hardness can also be improved by what the potter adds to his clay.

The colonial potter found the stuff he dug was full of unwanted junk such as pebbles and the remains of old leaves and roots. His first job was to clean it. If he wasn't too particular, he could use a device like the one illustrated to push it through an iron sieve. He would then mix it like brick clay in a pug mill. If he wanted it really clean for good pots, he mixed it with a lot of water, skimmed off the floating vegetable impurities, and decanted the clay soup, leaving the pebbles behind in the tub. Allowed to stand, the clay would settle and the potter could draw off most of the excess water.

Pure clay will crack when it is heated, so the potters "tempered" it by mixing in a sixth part or even a fifth part of clean sand while the clay was still quite soupy. For the later and harder stoneware, they added powdered flint as well as

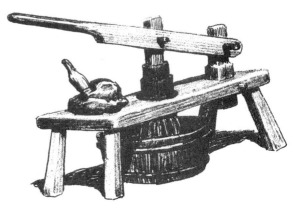

Kick wheel

sand. It seems almost impossible to powder flint, but it could be done by heating the stone red-hot and throwing it into cold water before going to work on it with a sledgehammer or a stamping mill.

There was still too much water in the clay mix and it had to be got rid of by evaporation, often hastened by heat. When the mass had thickened, it was gathered into lumps and stored for weeks in a damp cellar to cure. Just what happened to it isn't clear. Old writers speak of fermentation and decay, but there seems to have been nothing to ferment and nothing to decay. Take it as cured. But the clay still had air bubbles in it. A strong-armed apprentice beat it thoroughly with a club and then "wedged" and "slapped" it—that is, he cut slices off it with a wire and slapped them back together again. Then he kneaded it.

At this point the clay was quite wet and soft. It would yield instantly to pressure, yet it was stiff enough to hold any shape imposed on it. It could be shaped by pressing into plaster or metal molds; such things as spouts and handles were made that way and stuck on later with thin clay called slip. It could also be modeled into almost

Pennsylvania German sgraffito

any shape the craftsman was skillful enough to give it. But most plates, bowls, pans, crocks, mugs, cups, and jugs were round and the potter could "throw" them on his wheel.

The potter's wheel is a circular table revolving on a vertical shaft. The colonials sometimes belted the shaft to a crank-turned pulley and sometimes a water wheel turned it. But more often it was a kick wheel, operated by the potter's own feet nudging a flywheel at the bottom of the shaft. In any case, the object was to spin the mass of clay around its own center and thus assure that the vessel being formed would be perfectly round.

To see skill shape clay on a wheel is to watch a small miracle. The wet lump seems to take on a life of its own as it flows upward under the potter's hands and swells and shrinks at his will into the wanted form. The colonial potter didn't seek novelty, but stuck to standard articles and made each piece as nearly like others of its kind as he could. He would fill one drying board after another with paint pots all alike. Colonial paint didn't come in cans; painters mixed it themselves in jars.

When a board was filled, assistants set it on pegs driven in the wall and left the clay to dry. After a day or so, when it was hard but still damp, the potter stuck handles on if the piece required them. Slip decoration, if any, also went on with the clay still damp. Slip for this purpose was a fluid mix of white clay and water. Most often the potter applied it by dribbling it from a small "slip cup" (pitcher) in flowing patterns, much as some modern artists dribble paint. Another way, much favored by the Pennsylvania Germans who were good at it, was to dip the whole article in white slip and, when it had set up, to scratch patterns through it, the lines revealing the red of the body. This is called sgraffito. The pottery stood on the shelf until it became bone-dry—green, as they called it—it was then ready for firing.

The kiln was circular and was built of common brick. For redware it had a domed top; for harder stuff the top was conical, though no text seems to explain why. If, as with redware, the pottery must be glazed in a second firing, the pieces stood in saggers (seggers, the old potters called them) which were stacked in the kiln.

Slip cup

Saggers were themselves pottery; they had circular bottoms and fairly high perforated sides. Their purpose was to equalize the heat and to keep direct flame from the ware. The potters closed the kiln and gradually built up a hot fire of small wood, maintaining it for twenty-five hours. After that time, they allowed the kiln to cool as slowly as possible to avoid cracking and didn't open it until it was nearly cold. Accidents happened anyway and a potter expected to lose about a fourth of his production from breakage in the kiln.

Redware as it came from firing was no harder than a modern flowerpot and it was just as porous. To make it useful, the potters glazed it, on the inside only for cooking pots but all over for most things. Even glazed, most utensils "sweated" the liquids left standing in them. The glaze was red or white lead (oxide) and sand, ground together between the stones of a hand mill and watered to about the consistency of house paint. For an all-over glaze the potter dipped the piece and often missed a few spots where his fingers gripped it. For inside only, he poured some glaze in, sluiced it around, and poured it out again. He let the glaze dry and refired the pots to vitrify it. The heat turned the lead oxide to glass.

Lead glaze after firing was as colorless and transparent as varnish, but the potters could color it brown by adding manganese before firing, or green by adding copper oxide. The worst thing about lead glaze was that it *was* lead—and therefore poisonous. It could poison the potter who got it on his hands or the user who ate acid foods that had stood in a glazed vessel. Because it avoided this and because it was watertight and stronger, stoneware gradually supplanted redware.

Up to the firing point, the method of making stoneware was the same as has been described, but it required special clay, usually gray or tan, with a lot of silica in it. This clay needed longer and hotter firing to harden it, but it became very hard indeed after forty hours of heat. No saggers could be used to protect stoneware in the kiln because of the way it was glazed at its first firing. Just as the fire reached its hottest point, the potter opened the kiln and threw in some common salt which vaporized in the heat and combined with the silica in the clay. Saggers would interfere with the salt vapor reaching the pots.

Many potters decorated stoneware by cutting the outlines of a flower, a bird, or a fish in the damp clay and filling them in with slip colored blue with cobalt. Later they got careless. They skipped the outlines and merely splashed on some cobalt slip with a brush.

In its heyday, redware appeared at meals, along with pewter, as plates, cups, and so forth. Stoneware was made into such things, too, but less often because, just as it was coming into its widest use a few years before the Revolutionary War, the colonists became interested in white ware or Queensware. This wasn't porcelain or "chiney," but good white pottery, salt-glazed like the stoneware. At first it came from England but American potters quickly learned to make it. Even in the backwoods of western North Carolina, Brother Gottfried Aust of the Moravian colony made "a good product not very different from Queensware" in 1774.

Stoneware and whiteware

Pipe-head mold

Brother Aust also made clay pipe "heads" to be used with hollow reed stems. His brass and lead molds were made in two halves. He pressed them full of clay and then reamed out the bowls and the holes for the stems. He shipped most of them north for sale.

The Block Printers

The term here covers two separate but related trades, the equipment and methods of which were almost alike: the printing of woven fabrics and the printing of wallpapers. Americans imported printed cotton calicos and printed paper wall hangings from at least as early as 1700. Both began to be made here after the mid-1700's and both required teamwork. One "paper stainer" in Philadelphia employed thirty helpers.

Early European wallpaper makers printed the same wood block endlessly all over a small sheet. The blocks were usually square and the designs on them were geometric. The first papers sold in this country were either of this kind, or they were small floral designs printed in rows with every other row inverted. John Rugar of New York is recorded as having produced several patterns of paper hangings in 1765. He may have made one or the other of these, but he could have been more advanced. The householder bought the wallpaper sheets in quires from a stationer and stuck them on to his wall himself, or he hired an upholsterer to do it for him.

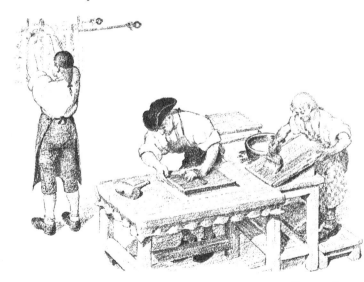
Paper stainers

In France, early in the eighteenth century, Jean Papillon succeeded with a design that joined onto itself when duplicated and thus yielded a continuous "repeat." Some of his blocks were three feet square. He printed only one key color and very beautifully added others with stencils. His repeating patterns suggested the ideas of continuous rolls of paper, and these were created by pasting sheets together. Such rolls were advertised in New England in 1730. The British paper stainers imitated Papillon and also imitated and improved the French flock papers which were supposed to look like cut velvet. The makers of these printed the designs with glue and sprinkled them, while they were still wet, with chopped, dyed wool. Of course the wool stuck.

Around the middle of the century, Chinese scenes on paper began to reach Europe and soon American ships in the China trade brought them directly here. Some of these murals were entirely hand-painted, but most were woodcut outlines filled in by hand with color. They came in wide strips twelve feet long and, mounted side by side, the strips revealed a detailed landscape. Most American ceilings were low so as to conserve heat, so thrifty Yankees often cut the strips in half and hung the bottom of the landscape in the front parlor and the top of it in the back one. France and England made scenic papers around 1800 but, though some Americans painted scenery on walls, they didn't try to make it portable.

This country's wallpaper makers were held down at first by the scarcity of rags which were the only known raw material for paper, but they made it increasingly as a growing population wore out its shirts and shifts. After John Rugar, Plunket Fleeson, upholsterer, advertised locally printed wallpaper in Philadelphia in 1769. In the same town, in 1786, Joseph Dickinson made paper with "pin grounds that fly marks will not be perceptible upon; also dark grounds which the smoke will not considerably affect in twenty years."

It seems that the oldest surviving American wallpaper that can be dated with certainty is some made by William Poyntell in 1794. Poyntell advertised in a Philadelphia newspaper that he made flock patterns and plain patterns "cheaper than whitewashing." One of his plain patterns is sketched here. He printed it from wood blocks repeated on big thirty-by-forty-inch sheets. The sheets could be mounted vertically one above another, but the paperhanger had to stagger them horizontally to make the repeat work sideways. In effect, modern rolls match the same way. The French achieved continuous paper strips in the last years of the eighteenth century and, by 1817, the trick was being tried on the Brandywine in Delaware.

The "gentlemen adventurers" brought printed cotton cloth to England from India, probably before 1600. The English soon learned to print cloth themselves. The American colonists knew about this—a few had some of it—and the eighteenth century had hardly begun before women here were stamping linen and cotton of their own weaving with little wood blocks their husbands and brothers hacked out for them. These have been called "a successful imitation of rich flowered brocades," which seems a little optimistic. Like the early wallpaper, their fabric was covered with an unconnected repetition of one simple block.

In 1716 Francis Dewing announced in Boston that he "cuts neatly in wood and printeth callicoes." However, Francis is a faint spark in the far distance. The first established calico printer definitely known in this country was John Hewson who came to Philadelphia, under Benjamin Franklin's wing, in 1774. Though trained in England, he proved himself an American by carrying a musket in the Continental Army. The British captured him at the Battle of Monmouth and when he escaped they put the extraordinary price of fifty guineas on his head. This high reward was due to Hewson's known skill and to Britain's determination to protect her monopoly on printed cloth. In 1779, Hewson reopened his works, vilifying the British in print for destroying his stock and equipment. Martha Washington wore his "very neat gown patterns," and her husband proudly called attention to them.

In Hewson's time, calico printers—and wallpaper printers, as well—used blocks made of three layers of wood held together with dovetail strips and glue. The top layer was often close-grained sycamore; the lower ones were pine,

A sketch of the pattern of one of Poyntell's wallpapers. The dotted square shows the area of his block.

with the grain of the middle one running crosswise. This was to prevent warping and to stand the blows the block would get. The artisan drew his design on the top surface. Then he wet the wood and kept it wet so that it wouldn't splinter as he cut away the background and left the lines of the pattern standing about an eighth of an inch above the new surface. A line needed support, so the knife cuts slanted away from each side of it. Two more opposed cuts left the line cresting a ridge between two V-shaped troughs. Beyond each of these, the cutter made parallel U-shaped ditches with a small gouge that he called a veiner. Thus he created barriers on both sides of each line to protect it from accidental tool slips when he cleared the open areas with gouge, chisel, and mallet. He removed the barriers after he finished all other cutting.

Line, with temporary barriers

Wood cut on the plank side, as this was, doesn't print a dot or a fine line very well. So the cutters who came along after 1800 "coppered" these. Instead of leaving a small cone of wood to yield a dot, they left nothing at that point, but drilled the lowered background and drove a copper pin in the hole. The "pin ground" of Dickinson's flyspeck-hiding wallpaper was undoubtedly coppered. Strips of copper, set in narrow slots, made fine lines. When all the metal was in and standing a little above the surface of the wooden part of the pattern, the craftsman turned his block face-down on a stone slab and ground the copper off even with the rest.

Design cut on wood block

Design cut on wood block

Coppered and felted block

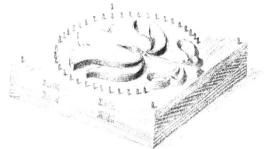

Large blocks of solid color came out mottled if printed from bare wood. Hewson licked this by gluing flock (the same chopped wool that went on wallpaper) to the big areas to make them hold more color. His successors coppered the outline of such an area and hammered a piece of thick felt down on it. The copper strip cut the felt to the right shape and a sharp knife took off any fuzz at the edges. The felt soaked up color and printed perfectly.

The last things added to any block were its four pitch pins. These were brass and were left standing just a bit higher than the printing surface, high enough to make little dents in the cloth. A pin stood near each corner of the block, its position precisely measured, so that the four marked out perfect ninety-degree angles.

The calico printer needed a level solid surface on which to print. At its best, this was a stone slab covering a heavily timbered table a little wider than the widest fabric he printed and some eight feet long. A woolen blanket, stretched tight over the stone, was protected by a coarse cotton cloth called the back gray. This was fed from a roll at one end of the table and taken up on a roller at the other end. The printers moved it forward so as to work always on a dry surface.

Printing mallet

The cloth to be printed came from a second roll at the feed end. After processing, it was hung over horizontal supports to dry.

Wallpaper was printed with a mixture of powdered pigment and glue called distemper. Since this color didn't penetrate the paper, the stainer's back gray didn't have to be moved. Dyes, thickened with gum to a creamy consistency, served for fabrics. For these, a way was needed to get enough color, yet not too much, onto the printing block—just as an inking pad now serves a rubber stamp. The solution, no doubt a good one, looks needlessly complex. It was called the color sieve and it had three nested parts, all of them square. The smallest was larger than the printing block. The swimming tub was on the bottom, a wooden box three-quarters full of flour paste or leftover thickened dye. On this unlovely surface floated the drum, a frame with a bottom made of waterproofed cloth. Inside the drum sat the sieve proper, another frame bottomed with plain woolen cloth. The printer used a wide brush to charge this cloth with dye before each impression. The tub of paste gave resilience; the drum kept the paste from diluting the dye; the sieve spread the dye evenly on the block.

The printer is ready to start. He pulls a length of fabric down the table and pins it flat. Near its cut end, he strikes a starting line straight across it exactly square with the selvage. The width of his block must divide evenly into the width of the material: for stuff a yard wide, the block may be two, three, six, nine, twelve, or eighteen inches. An apprentice slathers a brushful of dye across the sieve; the master presses the block on it twice, north-south, east-west, and lifts it to the table. Carefully he sets it face-down near one edge of the cloth; it must not move once it has touched. The two bottom pitch pins sit exactly on the starting line. He picks up a short mallet,

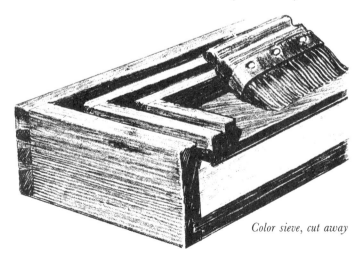

Color sieve, cut away

headed with lead and padded at the bottom of its handle with leather. He strikes the block two hard blows—not with the head of the mallet but with the butt of its handle. He repeats the impressions all across the line, setting the two left-hand pins on the dents made by the right-hand ones; then he proceeds to the next range, placing the bottom pitch pins on the dents of the first row's top ones. When he has covered the whole table, helpers lift the fabric and move it forward to the drying racks while others roll up the back gray to a fresh surface.

The paper stainer didn't use a color sieve. He could spread his distemper on a cloth stretched over a slanted board, and he apparently struck his block with the head of a mallet. A billhead of the Boston stainer, Ebenezer Clough, dated 1795, shows a man doing it that way.

The patterns of early fabrics are overwhelmingly floral. Sometimes the printers formalized the flowers and covered the whole surface closely with small ones, and sometimes they "sprigged" the surface with small flowers scattered widely. Larger flowers, but not often very large, might be repeated with quite free arabesques of stems and leaves like those on William Poyntell's wallpaper. Even the popular stripes were flowered; plain stripes could be woven and hence looked commonplace. Additional colors had to be printed separately, each with a special block. Though they were registered on the first block's pitch-pin dents, they seldom hit exactly where they were supposed to be.

European fabric printers often inked their blocks with a colorless chemical resist and then dipped the cloth in a dye vat. The resist prevented the dye from taking, and when the cloth

Fabric printers

was washed, the pattern came out white against a colored background. Often the dye was blue and "blue resist" was so widely used in this country that it has been commonly accepted and labeled as early American work. Perhaps it was, but a panel of experts, meeting at the Cooper Union in New York, could present no positive evidence of blue resist's being made here.

Just as so many other crafts turned to machines in the early 1800's, so did calico printing. A water-powered roller continuously imprinted a whole width of fabric with the pattern cut on it. Wooden rollers seem to have been tried, but they quickly gave way to copper ones with the designs engraved on them. The rollers printed, not dye, but a mordant such as iron acetate which, just the opposite of the resist, would fix dye. The machine flooded the roller with mordant to fill up the engraved lines and a "doctor blade" scraped the excess from the surface before the roller met the cloth. Dyeing and then washing revealed the pattern where the mordant set the dye, dark this time against a light ground. Fabrics printed this way sometimes had colors added to them with hand-printed blocks.

The Letterpress Printers

In 1638, the locksmith-printer, Stephen Daye, set up his press in the cellar of the president of Harvard College. Two years later, he printed America's first book in English, *The Whole Booke of Psalmes*, in bad verse. Daye wasn't the first American printer: the Spanish had a press in Mexico in the 1550's and another at Lima, Peru, in 1584.

Pattern of a striped calico

In 1660, Samuel Green of Boston printed John Eliot's Bible in the Algonquian language and started a dynasty of printing Greens that spread through the colonies and flourished for nearly two hundred years.

Only minor colonial printers were mere jobbers. Most printers were also publishers and even editors. They issued newspapers and some books and they also acted as postmasters. The first newspaper, issued in 1690, was quickly suppressed in Boston. The second, *The Boston News Letter* printed by B. Green, appeared in 1704, and after that almost every shop with more than one press put out one. All of them were read to tatters. Their readers' descendants need determination to wade through the four small pages. The two outside pages of local advertising are the most interesting feature. Much of the news was reprinted from foreign exchanges several months old. The papers carried literary efforts, often in blank verse, by local worthies who signed them with such classical pen names as "Plato" or "Augustus." These pieces hinted early at colonial dissatisfaction with England. They grew steadily more explicit and less bombastic, culminating in the thunder of Tom Paine. The postriders carried newspapers from town to town; the South read what was printed in New England and vice versa. The newspapers unified the colonies.

A colonial news editor's difficulties are suggested by a sentence from *The Maryland Gazette* for January 14, 1768, Anne Catherine Green, printer: "As the Northern Post is not yet arrived, and the Southern One brought no Mail; and our Rivers, at the same time being frozen up, by which we are prevented from receiving any Articles of Intelligence from the different parts of the Province, we hope we shall stand excused for this Single Half Sheet."

Poor Richard's Almanack was but the best of many. Farmers needed almanacs to be sure of not planting corn on the wrong phase of the moon. Sailors and fishermen needed to know the hours of tides. For the general public, the almanac gave weather predictions for the whole year, a gazette of courts, and schedules of postriders, public coaches, established freight wagons, packet boats, and long-haul ferries. Any leftover space was devoted to jingles, jokes, and home remedies.

Colonial books ran to religious commentary and translations from the Latin and Greek, though a few histories of individual colonies appeared. The printers also issued schoolbooks, legal and medical handbooks, and "ready reckoners" which gave the values of coins from colony to colony.

Most of any printer's daily bread came from his job work. Some of it was official. New laws and the frequent proclamations of governors had by decree to be printed and displayed. Much of it was private: broadsides, at tuppence each and covering a whole sheet of paper, to be posted and distributed by hand for advertising or for political propaganda; smaller handbills with the same circulation and objects; legal forms, from promissory-note blanks for a penny to apprentice indentures which sold in pairs for a shilling. Lottery tickets were a standby. Towns raised money for public works with lotteries: the first monument to George Washington was paid for that way.

The colonies produced at least one great man who was a printer and a good one—Benjamin Franklin. His was the largest colonial printing house, but the colonies produced no great printers as such. Neither the conditions these men struggled under nor the public they served encouraged technical excellence. Most of them were good men and bold men, fearlessly defending their own rights and the rights of the colonists. Some of them suffered for their courage, not only at the hands of authority but also from the violence of mobs. William Bradford started printing in Philadelphia in 1685. He left for New York at the insistence of the Quakers in 1693, but his needs had launched the first American paper mill. Baltimore's Whig mobs twice wrecked the shop of William Goddard whose ironies they took for Tory sympathies. John Peter Zenger, perhaps inadvertently, struck the great blow for press freedom when he printed the truth about a New York official and was jailed for libel. The aged and feeble lawyer Andrew Hamilton journeyed all the way from Philadelphia to defend Zenger successfully.

The number of women active in colonial printing is remarkable. Stephen Daye's press was actually owned by Mistress Jose Glover. Like her, most of the women in printing were widows who "kept the business going" and depended on trusted journeymen for the actual work. However, Mary Goddard was her brother's partner and was an expert compositor, and Ben's sister-in-law, Anne Franklin, and her two daughters were all three good compositors. Way back before 1700, Dinah Nuthead ran her late husband William's business. Dinah couldn't read, but it's entirely likely that she could pull a press handle.

American printers had special American burdens. Paper was hard to get. Most of it came from abroad and when a ship was late, the press waited. It isn't surprising the printers gave very practical encouragement to the starting of paper mills and were glad to collect at their shops the papermakers' indispensable rags. They imported type at high prices. A printer's stock of type was often worth more than all else he owned. Franklin paid the great English type founder, William Caslon, more than fifty-seven pounds for a font of brevier, this size; we now call it eight-point. The fonts were small. As soon as a page was printed, its letters were distributed and the press often waited until they had been set up again. This constant use wore out the letters quickly, but the printer had to go on using them, worn or not. Printing from stereotypes was the only way to save type, but the journeymen resisted their use. A stereotype, as it was known in the eighteenth century, was a cast made by pouring plaster of Paris on a set-up type page, and then casting the page as a unit by pouring hot type metal in the resulting mold.

The crudeness of much early American printing isn't wholly due to sloppy provincial work and worn letters. Up to 1740 or later, the new type that came from England was badly made. Caslon issued his famous specimen sheet in 1734, but the fine type it represented took some time to get into general use over here, and not every printer bought from Caslon. A type designer can now make a large drawing of each letter and "trace" it in metal and in minute size with a machine called a pantograph, but in the eight-

Typefounder, early 1800's

eenth century he had to shape a model for each letter by hand, at its actual size, on the flat end of a steel punch. The punch was barely larger than the letter to be cut on it and was about an inch and three-quarters long, "long enough to hold on to, but too short to bend." The type cutter aided his work by annealing the steel to soften it and by first cutting counterpunches to form the insides of closed letters like B, D, O, P, and so on. He hardened his counterpunch and, hitting its butt with a heavy hammer, struck it into the face of the still soft punch. Then with sharp gravers, small chisels, and files, he lowered the face of the punch to leave the letter standing on it. At that point, it was exactly like the type letter that would result from it, a raised mirror image of the ultimate printed one.

Type was cast with hot metal and a mold was needed. To make it, the artisan struck his hardened punch into one side of a small copper bar, indenting the letter. The result was a matrix. A complete font required a separate matrix for each capital, each small capital, each lower-case letter, each punctuation mark, and each numeral. All the matrices were of identical size so as to slip into the hand-held mold in which type was cast.

Fonts duplicated each letter according to the ratio of its use. A modern eighty-pound font will have six and a half pounds of lower-case *e*'s but only five ounces of *x*'s. In such large foundries as that of Binny and Ronaldson, started in Philadelphia in 1796, a man might cast only *e*'s full time.

The caster, wearing leather cuffs, stood by a small charcoal-heated crucible full of molten type metal—five parts lead and one part antimony.

counterpunch

punch

matrix

One size of William Caslon's hand-cut type.
Reproduced from his specimen sheet.

Pica Roman.

Melium, novis rebus ſtudentem, manu ſua occidit. Fuit, fuit iſta quondam in hac repub. virtus, ut viri fortes acrioribus ſuppliciis civem pernicioſum, quam acerbiſſimum hoſtem coërcerent. Habemus enim ſe-natuſconſultum in te, Catilina, vehemens, & grave: non deeſt reip. conſilium, neque autoritas hujus or-dinis: nos, nos, dico aperte, conſules deſumus. De-ABCDEFGHIJKLMNOPQRSTVUWX

Ladle

Type mold

Cast type

He held the two-part mold, with a matrix in it, closed in his left hand while his right hand filled its mouth with a small ladle. Instantly he "shook" the mold with an abrupt upward motion to drive the metal down into the matrix before it set, which it did so quickly that he could at once open the mold and throw the new type out on his bench. He kept up a fast pace—an expert could cast fifty letters a minute. As soon as they hit the table, an apprentice snapped off the "jets" (sprues) that the mold gate left on the bottom of the type body. "Dressers," often women, cleaned up the bodies on grindstones that lay flat and were turned by water power. Other workers threw out bad letters and cut the groove on the bottom of the body that gave the type "feet." The nick on the body, which told a compositor's fingers how to keep the type right side up, could be cast in the mold. Packers at the foundry set up identical letters in blocks and tied packthread around them.

Antonio de Espinosa cast type in imported matrices in Mexico in the mid-1500's. Desperate Yankee printers sometimes managed to produce a few essential letters by using old type as a punch and lead as a matrix. Abel Buell, he of the nicked ear and the branded hairline, cut punches for the first colonial font in 1768. The one surviving proof of it shows just about every crudity that type could have. Abel did better the following year with a second font. On the strength of it, he borrowed a hundred pounds from the Province of Connecticut which was encouraging anything that would reduce dependence on England. Abel then left town and his wife had to run his silversmithing business and pay off the debt. In 1781, with war on and foreign type unobtainable, Abel cut another and still better font to supply the shops of three despairing Greens.

Jacob Bay set up as type founder in Philadelphia in 1774. He cut punches for a number of good fonts and made all his own apparatus for casting them. The *Pennsylvania Mercury* appeared the next year set in Bay's type and needlessly apologized for the "rustic manufacture" of its letters.

Print shops came in three sizes: small, with but one press; medium, with two presses; and large, with three or more. Each press had its complement of servitors: compositors, pressmen, a stone man, paper men (or women) who cut and folded, and "devils" (apprentices) who ran errands, swept floors, and absorbed ink. Print-shop equipment changed little in the whole colonial period. Samuel Green's inventory of 1662 is almost identical with the list Franklin ordered for his nephew's one-press shop at New Haven in 1753.

Today, monotype and linotype machines cast letters and set them up directly from a keyboard like a typewriter's, and we have gone even further and can now print from photographs of letters with no actual type whatever. This book is printed that way. All colonial type was hand set, one letter at a time, by compositors working at the type case. A case is an irregularly partitioned shallow tray. The colonial frame, or stand, for the cases was built of wood, sturdily, because the storage racks in its lower part might hold five hundred pounds of cased type. Cases in use rested on top of the frame. The one holding capitals stood high and tilted rather steeply at the back because capitals get less frequent use than small letters whose case lay, lower and more nearly flat, at the front. The case positions gave the printers' names to the two kinds of letters: upper case and lower case.

Compositor

A compositor knew the case without looking as a typist knows the keys of the machine. He picked out letters from it and set them side by side lengthwise in a composing stick, a small three-sided tray with one end adjustable to the type measure (length) of the line being set up. The compositor viewed the letters in the stick upside down and backwards and could read that way as fast as he could read in the usual way. He had more to do than merely to place the types next to one another in their right order; he had to drop in spacers—quadrats or quads, made like type but too low to print—to keep words apart; he had to put in punctuation marks; and he had to "justify" each line by adding or subtracting space in it so that the right-hand edge would be as straight as the left. He sometimes had to "lead" the lines, that is, to put strips of lead between them to separate them for better readability, though much colonial work was set solid to save paper. For the same reason, colonial books usually have narrow margins.

When he filled his stick—it was only two inches wide—the compositor slid the accumulated type carefully on to a page-size tray called a galley. When he had filled a galley, he or an apprentice pulled a proof of it by inking the type and hammering a piece of paper down on it with a rawhide mallet. The master printer or someone he trusted read the proof and marked the errors in it. The compositor lifted out the bad letters with tweezers and put in the right ones so the master could pass a final corrected proof.

Approved galleys went to the stoneman. He put the type on his level imposing stone and made it up as a form with one or more other pages, depending on how the printed sheet would be folded. (Folding is described in the section about the bookbinder.) Assuming this was the first form of a quarto and was to be printed on both sides with a two-page form on each end of each sheet—the press couldn't print all four pages at once—the stoneman placed pages one and eight side by side, with an inner-margin gap between them. Folding would put the pages in their right order. He framed the two blocks of type with a rectangular iron chase and filled up all the spaces around and between them with wooden blocks known as "furniture." He then locked up the form by driving opposed wedges

129

in pairs around the edges between the chase and the furniture. Once locked, the form could be lifted without falling apart and placed on the bed of the press.

The Old Wooden Presses, as used by Stephen Daye in 1639, by Franklin in 1776, and by Isaiah Thomas in Worcester in 1812, were hardly more different than three eggs from the same nest. The press was constructed of heavy timbers with only its working parts, and not all of those, made of metal. Its base was commonly spiked to the floor and its top was braced to the ceiling. This kind of press still creaked and groaned here and there up to 1850 or later, long after iron presses appeared.

The bodies of type letters are all the same height, just under an inch. The letters stand in relief and thickish ink is spread on their surfaces. The job of the press is to bring sheets of paper successively to the same position in relation to the type; to apply enough pressure to transfer the ink, equally for all letters, to the sheets; to release the pressure and allow the sheets to be recovered clean except for the ink they pick up from the type. All this is now done automatically at many impressions per minute, with but one man watching the machine. With the hand press, two journeymen working together could turn out only 1,920 impressions in a ten-hour day. This was eight "tokens"—a token was half a ream or ten quires 240 sheets—printed on one end of one side only. A full sheet, printed on both sides, went through the press four times.

The two pressmen were known as "companions"—First and Second. Each did an allotted part of preparing for work. First, who was the leader, made ready the form on the press bed. He pulled proofs to see where low spots failed to print clearly, and he increased the

Composing stick

Form

Imposing stone

Wooden press

pressure there by cutting the weak areas out of a proof and pasting them in the right places on the heavy sheet called the tympan that backed up the paper in the press. This was, and is, skilled work, demanding many trials. Second's chief job was to mix ink with lampblack and "varnish," as printers called linseed oil boiled with rosin. Second also saw to damping the paper just enough to be soft but with no free water on its surface. The companions evened up the laborious work of "pulling the Devil's tail" by trading jobs after every three tokens.

If First acted as puller, Second would be "beater." The beater inked the type. He first rubbed out ink on a stone slab—that is, he spread it thinly over the surface with a square-ended blade like a putty knife—then he took up an ink ball or often two of them, one in each hand. An ink ball was a large leather-covered dabber, stuffed with hair, padded with wool, and attached to a handle. The beater rocked the ball on the stone to charge it with ink and then "beat" it on the type.

While he was doing this, the puller, who kept his hands clean, placed a sheet of damp paper on the tympan. This membrane, often parchment, was stretched on a light frame hinged to the outer end of the press carriage. Small pieces of card-board which First pasted to the tympan acted as guides to position the sheet exactly. The puller lowered the "frisket" over the sheet to hold it in place while it was being turned down over the type, printed, and recovered. The frisket was paper stretched on another and still lighter frame which was hinged to the farther edge of the tympan. Holes cut in the frisket exposed the printing paper only where it would receive the type impression.

With tympan, paper, and frisket down over the form, the puller placed a small wool blanket on them and ran the carriage in by turning a crank called the rounce handle. The handle rotated a small drum under the carriage. A leather strap, making one turn around the drum and having its ends nailed to the ends of the carriage, slid the form under the platen (the thick wooden block on which the press screw bore) to be printed and then out again after the paper had been impressed on the inked type.

With the carriage in, the puller seized the press handle with both hands and pulled it toward him, leaning back to gain the advantage of his weight. The handle turned a large screw to move the heavy platen downward and squeeze the paper against the type. Hand-press platens delivered so much squeeze that they impressed the type *into* the paper. This gives old printing a lively look that the run of modern work doesn't have.

The puller dropped the newly printed sheet on the "heap" which it was the beater's job to peruse, that is, inspect and count. All printers' wages depended on production. Pressmen got the equivalent of about thirty cents a token, which came to a bit over fourteen dollars for a six-day week. Compositors made about eight dollars a week on the basis of twenty-five cents a thousand ems. The square body of the letter *m* served as a unit of measurement; a journeyman compositor set some fifty-four hundred ems of type in a nine-hour day.

Clumsy as it looked, the wooden press was accurate in the hands of men who knew its quirks. But the accuracy had to be built into it and American craftsmen couldn't manage to do that for a long time. It is said that the precise machining of the big press screw baffled them. Christopher Sower, Sr., the German Bible printer, built his own presses in 1750. He was the man to do it—he practiced sixteen trades—but he sold no presses to other printers. Nineteen years later, Amos Doolittle of New Haven built an "elegant" mahogany press for William Goddard, then in Philadelphia. Before the turn of the century, John Hamilton was making presses, for seventy-five dollars each, in Elizabethtown, New Jersey; and Adam Ramage was introducing improvements in Philadelphia. About 1807, John Clymer built the first iron press, though it was little more than the old press with a new material used for its frame.

In 1786 Lexington, Kentucky, gave John Bradford some free real estate to help him in starting a print shop. Bradford's press and type traveled to Pittsburgh by wagon, floated down the Ohio River on a flatboat to Maysville, Kentucky, and came from there to Lexington on packhorses. The type, as he said, "fell into pi," but he managed to print the first issue of the *Kentucke Gazette* by August 11, 1787.

Casting pig iron

6.

MANUFACTORIES

HERE are some of the enterprises that employed many hands to work continuously on one product. A few of them are omitted, either because their work, like lumbering in the woods, was so simple as to make explanation silly or because enough of their methods has been explained earlier. The merchant miller, for instance, who bought grain and sold flour—often for export— did his grinding just as the local custom miller did, though he ran several sets of stones and his mill was equipped, after Oliver Evans's time, with ingenious lifts and conveyers for moving material.

The Papermakers

Printer William Bradford, seeking supplies, persuaded William Rittenhouse to start the first colonial paper mill in 1690 on Wissahickon Creek near Philadelphia. Rittenhouse had learned papermaking in Germany where he was born. His first mill was a log building straddling the stream, with an undershot wheel beneath it. Wheel and building washed away together in 1700, but their replacements operated for many years.

As late as 1736, the four paper mills in the colonies were all in Pennsylvania, three near Philadelphia, the fourth at the religious colony in Ephrata. After that, mills sprang up rapidly in other colonies, but never enough of them to supply American demand until long after the Revolution. They made white paper for writing and printing—Rittenhouse asked twenty shillings a ream for it—and brown paper for wrapping things that absolutely had to be wrapped. Brown paper cost two shillings a ream.

It takes quantities of water to make paper. Had the Americans made it on primeval streams in the forests, the clear water would have made their white paper really white, but they built mills on streams that ran through cleared land and the mud that washed off the farms is generally visible in their product. However, they made good rag paper with no harsh chemicals in it, and books printed on it will survive long after the wood pulp of this one is brittle tatters.

All American paper was made from linen and cotton rags until after 1867. The best of it, such as that for printing money, still is. Actually, no matter what the source, the ultimate material is cellulose fiber. We now get most of this from chewed-up wood, just as the Orientals always have, but the cellulose fibers from rags are longer and stronger. You'll have gathered that colonial rags were scarce. The newspapers after 1750 are filled with advertisements for them, imploring, cajoling, offering rewards. Paper production was of public importance, editors urged the saving of rags. Legislators took a hand, ordering that the dead be buried in wool only. All sorts of substitutes were tried: straw, corn husks, pine cones, seaweed, Spanish moss, and wood. None of these worked because nobody knew enough about chemistry to break down their structure.

Rags needed no chemistry. Boys in the paper mill cut them to bits on fixed scythe blades, wet them, and left them in piles for a month to rot a little. Then they went to the stamper. This worked much as a fulling mill did: a series of heavy wooden pestles lifted and dropped by cams on the shaft of a water wheel. The pestles were of three kinds, used successively. The first set was shod with coarse iron teeth, the second had finer teeth, and the third was plain wood with a flat surface. The pestles fell into mortars hollowed either in stone blocks or in oak logs, in which case they were lined with lead. Water flowed into the mortars serving the iron-shod pestles and escaped through horsehair strainers near the upper edges. By the time the pulp reached the last mortar, it was too fine for any strainer, so no extra water was added to it.

Small American paper mills used stampers until after 1800, but in 1775 Abijah Burbank installed two "hollanders" to do the pulping job in his mill in Massachusetts. As its name suggests, the hollander was invented by the Dutch.

Mechanism of a rag stamper

It worked better with a windmill than pestles did; actually it worked better with a water mill, too. In its colonial form a hollander was an oval tub, about eight feet by four, with round ends. A wooden drum, armed with some twenty iron knives, rotated at the middle of one side. It reached halfway across the tub and only its lower half was submerged. The radius of the drum was long enough to allow its blades to rub against a stone or iron bedplate fixed on the bottom of the tub, and thus to chew up the rags. The bedplate lay embedded in a shaped block called the "backfall." This followed the curve of the drum upward for a short distance and then fell away steeply, creating turbulence to mix the pulp or "stuff," as papermakers call it.

The moving knives acted as paddles to circulate the pulp in the tub. A hollander could keep one molding team supplied with material.

Mechanism of a hollander: the drum had a cover to reduce splash.

Molding paper

Paper mold and deckle, cut away

Every mill, whether it used hollanders or stampers, kept a reserve supply of pulp in a large tank known as the stuff chest, from which apprentices fed the molding vats with tub barrows and buckets. The apprentices also had the job of frequently stirring the vats with long-handled paddles. In later years an agitator ("hog") turned slowly in the bottom of the vat to do this.

The moldman formed sheets of paper individually at the vat, a watertight box almost filled with stuff. The moldman faced it, standing on a three-inch-high platform to keep his feet as dry as possible. This was seldom very dry in the sloppy vat room. A small fire in the "pot" (stove) submerged in the vat kept the stuff warm but did little for the temperature of the room.

A paper mold was a rectangular sieve made by stretching brass wires on an oak frame. A number of wedge-shaped ribs crossed it the short way, edge up and doweled into its long sides. Along the crest of each rib and "sewed" to it with fine wire ran a fairly heavy brass wire, known as the chain line from the way it marked the finished paper. Chain lines and ribs ordinarily stood less than an inch apart. Smaller brass wires, the laid

lines, some thirty of them to the inch, ran the long way of the mold. Every wire marked every sheet by thinning the soft pulp lying over it. Papermakers took advantage of this to identify their work with watermarks. They bent wire to the shape of letters or of some simple design, which they fastened to the web of the mold. Paper showing chain-and-laid lines is known as "laid" paper. Just before the Revolution, a few makers began to cover molds with woven wire cloth like window screening to make "wove" paper which shows little or no impression of the wires except for the watermark.

The webbed area of the mold was a little larger than the paper it would make. To limit the size of the sheet and to release the sheet readily, the vatman slipped an empty frame on the mold. This was the deckle. One deckle served for both of the two molds the vatman needed to keep up with his assistant, the coucher. With the deckle in place, the vatman dipped a mold into the stuff edge on, turned it face up, and lifted it. As it came up, he shook it, right and left and back and forth, to cross the fibers and make the paper strong. These motions were apt to have

134

disastrous effects after years of work. Some men "lost their stroke" temporarily or permanently, others shook uncontrollably. Small wonder that papermakers earned their reputation as tosspots.

As the mold cleared the surface, much of the water in the pulp drained out. The vatman at once took the deckle off, breaking rather than cutting the edges of the soft sheet and leaving them clear of the mold frame. He stood the mold slanting to drain against the horn, fixed in a plank that bridged the vat. Then he at once picked up the second mold, slapped the deckle on, and dipped again. As he dipped, the coucher took the filled mold from the horn and couched its sheet by quickly inverting the mold and dropping the new paper on a pile of alternate felts and sheets. He covered the new sheet with a felt, placed the empty mold where his companion could get it, and reached for the next filled mold. It was a fast, continuous operation. The two men alternated the work the way the printer's pressmen did.

The felts absorbed water. They were not actual felt, though that probably was used in very early times. Colonial felts were woven loosely of wool, with a loose-spun weft on a hard-twisted warp. It took 145 of them to "felt a post," that is, a pile of 144 sheets or six quires. The coucher kept count. An apprentice moved the completed post to the bed of an enormous screw press, placed a thick beveled plank on top of it, and added press

blocks, ten inches square and three feet long, on top of the plank. Thrusting a club into a hole in the big press screw—William Rittenhouse's nephew carved one eighteen inches thick—he ran the screw down enough to bear on the post. Then he blew a horn and every man in the place dropped what he was doing to take "aholt" of a twenty-foot lever to turn the screw and "press the post." They squeezed more water out of the pile and reduced it from two feet high down to six inches.

Large paper mills where one press served several vats often used a samson post, which, by lending great mechanical advantage, did a better job with fewer men. It reached from floor to ceiling, was mounted at both ends on bearings, and had four handles by which men could turn it. As they did so, the samson wrapped around itself a heavy rope hitched to the outer end of the long press lever.

The sheets of paper came from the press still wet but strong enough to hold together when the lay boy lifted them off the felts and stacked them on an inclined board. He took the felts back to the coucher and delivered the paper to the dry press for more, but lighter, squeezing. The sheets were then ready to be dried in the second-floor loft. This was a touchy business. Single sheets hung up to dry would curl and wrinkle, so the lofters hung them in "spurs" of four or five sheets over horizontal poles. European mills

One of William Rittenhouse's watermarks

Pressing the post

Robert's papermaking machine

dried paper on soft ropes made of cow hair so as not to mark the sheets, but the poles seem to have done well enough and Americans had more poles than cows. The lofter carefully adjusted sliding shutters in all four walls of the loft so that air would blow against the faces of the sheets. If it blew against the edges, those would dry faster than the middles and would warp the paper.

Writing paper had to be sized to keep ink from spreading on it as it does on a blotter. Printing paper, too, worked better if sized. The sizer dipped the dried sheets in a hot solution of animal glue and hung them to dry again, this time individually, in a special room known as the saul. John Spellman, a German, was the first papermaker in England; he called this room the *saal*, and his workmen had made a stab at adopting the word.

After sizing and drying, good writing paper was beaten under the flat face of a plating hammer. This face was large enough to cover a whole sheet and the head was heavy enough to need water power to lift it. After 1800, plating was usually done between rollers, which did a better job. The maker wrapped finished sheets in ream-size bundles with coarse paper made from vat dregs and labeled the bundles with his own name and the name of the sheet size.

England made paper in many sizes, each named—from six-inch-square note paper called billet, to double elephant which was 26¾ by 40 inches. American mills stuck to medium sizes useful for printing and writing: demy, 17½ by 22 inches; post, 14¼ by 19 inches; and pott, 12½ by 15 inches. Sheets went to printers full size, since the rough deckle edges would be trimmed in binding, but writing paper was trimmed at the mill. The trimmed paper sold under the same size-name as the full sheet.

Plating hammer

English makers watermarked each sheet with a symbol designating its size: royal, for instance, showed a crown; post, a horn; pott, a chalice. The Americans sometimes did this, too.

In the late eighteenth century, Nicholas-Louis Robert built the first machine to make paper, not because he wanted to make it faster nor because he was interested in producing a continuous sheet, but because he was disgusted with the waywardness of French vatmen and wanted to bypass them. He ran his machine with a hand crank that any strong arm could turn. A cylinder with long buckets on it supplied a shallow trough which poured pulp evenly onto an endless belt of wire cloth. Robert gave the belt a side shake to cross the fibers. Water drained through the belt as it carried the sheet to a felt roller which squeezed out more water and hardened the paper enough to allow a man to take it from the machine by hand. Englishmen copied Robert's device and improved it, first with rollers to take the paper away, then with heated rollers to dry the paper.

The machine mill that Thomas Gilpin built for himself on the Brandywine in Delaware, in 1817, delivered a continuous sheet thirty inches wide at the rate of sixty feet a minute and rolled it up on reels. This, and all machines since, made wove paper. The wire marks on machine-made laid paper are imitations impressed on it with a cylinder called the "dandy roll" which can also handle watermarks.

The Glass Blowers

Though some glass was made at Jamestown as early as 1609, the history of American glass-making in the seventeenth century is one of trials and failures. There may be one exception: Jan Smedes's glass house in New Amsterdam in 1654. He was able to bring artisans and supplies from Holland, to have, in fact, a transplanted Dutch glassworks. The English colonists had no such chance. Mother England didn't mind her overseas children making glass—it was a minor industry at home—but she did mind their getting any fire clay to make it in, and they found none good enough here. The Americans also had trouble getting the skilled workers that were as

important as the clay, and they had to try out native raw materials, to the disgust of the imported glass blowers who were used to materials that would always behave as expected.

Caspar Wistar, who came from Bavaria, gave the American glass industry its real start in 1737, near Salem in South Jersey. Caspar had grown rich making famous "Philadelphia Brass Buttons Noted for their Strength and Warranted for 7 years." He brought in expert glass blowers from Rotterdam and, under their direction, set up a large-scale works on a two-thousand-acre tract that provided plenty of fuel. Almost all American glass was made by immigrant workers before 1800. They were secretive and natives had a hard time learning the trade from them. For forty years Wistar's factory made most kinds of glass and experimented successfully with new processes. The first American flint glass was probably made there and the first articles with two colors of glass fused together certainly were. But Wistar's most profitable product was window glass. It was scarce and was expensive to import. The colonies weren't too far from the medieval time when a householder going on a long journey took the valuable panes out of his windows and stored them.

A colonial glassmaker's first problem was pots to melt his glass in. Every glassworks had its own pottery which it set up and got into operation before even starting to build the glass furnace itself. The fire clay had to come from Europe. The potters pulverized it and piled it in the open for a full year to "ripen." When it was ripe,

whatever that may mean, they tempered it by adding a fifth of its weight of ground-up baked clay—old pots or even bricks. They wet this mix down and "bugged" it by stomping around in it with their bare feet. Then they left it another six months, under cover this time, to ripen further.

It took three weeks to shape a pot three feet in diameter and equally high which would hold thirteen hundred pounds of glass. No potter's wheel would do for this. The potters hammered the flat base on a slab and cut it into a circular mud pie; they built up the sides by slowly adding rolls of clay which they compacted carefully. Very early glasspots, probably those used at Jamestown, had domed tops and small arched openings where the dome met the walls. It's likely that Wistar used open-topped pots such as were common in Europe in his time. It isn't surprising that he made no glass until 1740. After a pot was shaped, it had to dry for a full year before it could be fired. In use, it would last only two or three months before it broke.

Wistar burned wood in his furnaces. That fact, coupled with his Dutch advisers, makes it probable that he followed the European wood-burning dome shape for them rather than the conical English one which burned coal. England, with its island almost stripped of trees to build ships and smelt iron, forbade its glassmakers to burn wood. Archaeologists are now excavating the Amelung glassworks in Frederick County, Maryland. One of the things they hope to learn is the kind of furnace an early American glassmaker used. But it's known that glass furnaces

17th-century pot

18th-century pot

Green glass pitcher, possibly made by Wistar

Shaping a glass pot

Stirrer and skimmer

glass had white salt (potash) as its alkali; and flint glass, now merely a term for good glass, had pearl ash and actual powdered flint in it as well as litharge and sand. It made the best hollow ware. Glass took color from metallic oxides added to it: silver plus aluminum made yellow; copper or gold made red; chrome or iron made green; cobalt made blue.

Up to the second quarter of the nineteenth century, "hand" blowing was involved in the making of all glass in this country. The blower gathered a parison, a "glob" of hot glass, from the pot by dipping the tip of a six-foot blowing iron (tube) into the mass. He then blew his breath into the wood-covered cool end of the tube and inflated the parison into a bubble, small or large, depending on what would be made of it. Blowing glass took a lot more lung power than blowing soap bubbles; hot glass is heavy and viscous. The repeated effort was bad for the blower's heart, and the hot air, inevitably inhaled, was bad for his lungs. A glass blower knew he risked his health and worked no more than nine months of the year, or even only six, to try to preserve it.

The whole job called for many hands. The actual blowing was done by a "servitor" who needed several assistants, and when he and they had done their work, they turned the parison over to other workers for completion. The servitor could shape his bubble. Before he blew it at all, he evened up the parison by rolling it on a polished iron table called a marver. He could lengthen the blown bubble by swinging his blowing iron. He could give the bubble a gourd neck on either end by rolling it against a horizontal iron bar, reheating it at the furnace whenever the glass began to cool.

Say the article was to be a common blown bottle with a fat body, often slightly crooked, and with a long narrow neck: the servitor shaped his parison accordingly, with the neck end attached to his blowing iron. An apprentice gathered a button of hot glass on the end of a punty (pontil), an iron rod some four feet long, and placed the glazed tip against the center of the ball-shaped end of the bottle. It stuck. Then the "wetter-off" dipped an iron blade into cold water and cut the neck free of the blowing iron. The apprentice turned his punty straight up and, with the

were circular. They were built of brick and lined with blocks of the same fire clay that served for pots. The heat of the furnace baked them in place. Fire, burning underneath, roared up through the furnace and smoke escaped from an opening at the top. Small holes around the walls gave the glass blowers access to the pots of glass inside. Pots were moved hot from the pottery kiln and placed in the hot glass furnace, a section of whose wall had to be taken down to admit each one and then built up again. Moving a hot pot was a Herculean job for six men who must have been almost broiled in the doing. The frit that would melt into glass went into the pot through the hole in the furnace wall. As it cooked, at heats up to 12,000° F, furnace men stirred it and skimmed off the salty sandiver that rose to its surface. Common bottle glass was "done" after sixteen hours; fine flint glass might take seventy-two.

Glass is the result of the seemingly miraculous metamorphosis of sand or ground flint, or both, mixed with some kind of alkali or with a metallic oxide like litharge (red lead) plus an alkali. This mixture is frit. None of it is transparent at the start. The quality of the materials and the proportions in which they are used control such characteristics as hardness, clarity, and color. Frit for the cheapest colonial green bottle glass was sea sand mixed with pulverized slag from an iron furnace or alkaline waste that soapboilers had skimmed from their cauldrons. Window

Blown bottle, 11 inches high

138

glowing hot bottle standing on top of the rod, bore it off to the "gaffer" who would finish shaping it.

The gaffer worked in a backless arm chair, its level arms protected with sheet iron. His many tools hung on pegs driven into the sides of the chair. He rested the punty across the arms with the parison outside the right-hand one; by rolling the punty he could rotate his work at will. The chair stood close to a "glory hole" in the furnace where the craftsman or an assistant could reheat the glass if it started to harden. The gaffer could handle far more complicated articles than bottles: footed goblets or wineglasses, for instance, shaping their stems with wooden pucellas and trimming the tops of their bowls with shears. But let's stick to the bottle.

While its bottom was still soft, the gaffer pushed the punty inward, helped by a wooden tool, to make a depression in the bottom that would allow the vessel to stand upright. Then he reheated the neck and gathered a little glass to apply a rough band around its top. Necking shears, plugged into the neck and turned against the new band, shaped it to neatness and at the same time made a taper on the inside of the neck to receive a cork. A boy carried the new bottle to the leer where he snapped the punty off its bottom. The punty mark shows on the bottoms of blown bottles. A leer man stood the bottle on a hot iron tray in the leer.

If glass is allowed to cool quickly, it becomes so brittle that it may shatter at a touch. For strength it must be annealed by cooling very gradually. That was and is the purpose of the leer. The colonial leer was a long, arched tunnel of brick with small iron doors at intervals along both sides. Heat, sometimes taken from the top of the glass furnace, entered one end. That was the end where the bottle found its tray. The leer men used hooked rods to reach through the doors and move the trays down the tunnel by degrees, away from the heat, until he finally took them, cool, from the far end.

Bottles, tumblers, vases, pitchers, and jars could also be blown inside heated molds which shaped them and impressed fluting or other ornamentation on them. Woodcarvers made the models of mahogany, and the iron or brass molds were cast from these in two or three parts which

were hinged together. The blower stood on a platform above the mold and inserted his parison into an opening in the mold's top before he started blowing. Assistants opened the mold to release the article and took it from the blower on a punty as before. The seams between the mold sections showed on the product. Machines now blow milk bottles in just this way. The colonials also made use of one-piece molds from which the inflated parison would not "draw." The blower got it out at hideous risk by sucking it smaller and blowing it up again after it was outside. He could then blow it larger than it had been inside the mold if he wished; any pattern on it would enlarge proportionately, just as a printed design does on a toy balloon.

All early colonial windows were glazed with crown glass and it remained the best long after cheaper ways of making flat glass were introduced. Except at one small point, the surfaces of crown glass touched nothing until it had hardened; hence, it kept a brilliant luster. The blower made it complete; it needed no chair work. He blew a large sphere and had it transferred to a punty. The wetter-off left a two-and-a-half-inch hole where he cut the parison off the blowing iron. The blower took the punty to a large glory hole where he rested it in an iron fork and rotated it to spin the glass rapidly in the heat. As he spun, he stood partly behind a small screen to avoid slow cremation; and as he spun, the hole in the glass grew larger and the bubble widened and flattened. The spinner increased the speed and quite suddenly, with a loud fluttering pop, the hole flew wide open and the artisan found himself spinning a glass disk four feet across. It was of quite uniform thickness except for a rough core in the center around the attachment of the punty. This was the "bull's eye." Cut out and sold as the cheapest of all window glass, it would admit some light but would not permit recognizing a passing acquaintance. It is now expensively copied to give "atmosphere" to quaint restaurants.

The blower withdrew his disk slowly from the fire, maintaining the spin to keep it in shape until it had cooled enough to support its own weight. Like other glass, it had to be annealed in a leer. It was cut into panes when it was cold. The largest possible pane was about fifteen by

Blowing iron and punty

Wooden tweezers

"Tool," or pucellas, the principal forming implement

Neck-forming "shears"

Crown glass

twenty-four inches and only two that size could be cut from a disk. But fourteen or even sixteen eight-by-ten panes, exclusive of the bull's eye, came out of a four-foot disk. Wistar advertised special large panes.

Broad glass, much easier to make than crown glass and much duller and hence much cheaper, seems to have appeared here about 1800. It was invented in Germany and was also made in France. Making it, the blower formed his parison to something like the shape of a straight-sided egg. (They're rare, but they do happen.) No punty was welded to it. When the wetter-off cut it loose, he also sliced it the long way clear around. An expert flattened the two halves into fan shapes on an iron table, presumably a heated one. It was the iron that dulled the surface of broad glass. In France, the best of it was hand-polished and that may have been done here. Cylinder glass was identical, except that the blower swung his parison to a large cylinder shape from which the wetter-off cut both ends before he sliced it lengthwise on one side only so that the whole gather flattened into a single rectangular sheet.

The French made plate glass in the eighteenth century, pouring the melt onto large copper slabs and rolling it flat. It was annealed on the slab over a period of ten days and then arduously ground smooth on both sides and polished. The first plate glass made in this country was poured

in Brooklyn in 1856. Edward Hazen described the process twenty years earlier than that without mentioning where it was made. He may have been reading Diderot who describes it very fully.

The early 1800's brought in the heyday of pressed glass. The Boston & Sandwich Glass Company, operating at Sandwich on Cape Cod, introduced it and it spread quickly to other glass-making centers. As had happened in other crafts, the enthusiasm generated by a new idea led the originators to high-grade performance. No other plant made pressed glass that equaled Sandwich.

A workman named Robinson built the first glass-pressing machine in 1827. There's no evidence that he invented it and one suspects that Deming Jarves who ran the Sandwich plant may have guided his work. Jarves was a re-markable man. He encouraged everybody in the place to experiment. His men worked a forty-hour week in an era when such hours seemed sheer insanity. They made good wages and were kept on the payroll through the frequent periods of financial depression.

Robinson's pressing machine wasn't auto-matic. An assistant ladled glass into the mold; no blowing was involved; the operator used a foot lever to bring a plunger down on the glass and squeeze it into shape. He then opened the mold with handles to release the new piece, which another assistant carried to the leer. Except for annealing, no finishing was done. Molds were cast from carved wood models, as those for blow-ing were. Jarves employed the best carvers and moldmakers he could get; it was said they were the best in the world. As a result, Sandwich glass, sold originally for ordinary household use and even given away as premiums with shop purchases, is now avidly collected. Cup plates, but one of the many items the factory made, are particularly sought after though nobody now puts them to their original use. In their day, even the most elegant lady poured tea or coffee from her cup into her saucer to cool and then, with daintily extended pinkie, drank it from the saucer. She rested her cup on a glass cup plate to save the table cloth.

Sandwich cup plates are three or four inches in diameter; they have fancy borders that catch light attractively. All of the pattern is on the under side. The central design is often patriotic,

Sandwich cup plate

like the eagle on the plate illustrated. Log cabins, ships, and portraits of famous men occur. You may be able still to buy a simple cup plate for ten dollars, but if you yearn for a ship, you may pay three hundred dollars, and George Washington will set you back six hundred or more. The original retail price of all of them was five cents.

The prices of good blown glass outdo Sandwich. Blown glass is rarer, of course, and much of it is handsome. The South Jersey glass of Wistar and his successors has a pleasant squatness. The gaffers decorated some of it by wrapping raised glass cords around it; some they also double-dipped like the pitcher drawn here. Near Frederick, Maryland, from 1785, John Frederick Amelung operated a notable factory making "all kind of glassware, window glass from the lowest to the finest sorts, white and green bottles, wine and other drinking glasses, as also optical glasses and looking glasses finished complete." When Amelung really tried himself on "presentation" work, he made the finest of all early American glass. The value of such pieces as the Maryland Historical Society's footed goblet runs into startling thousands.

America's most famous glassmaker and one of her best for general high quality was Heinrich Wilhelm Stiegel—the "Baron von Stiegel" he titled himself. Only "Lord Timothy Dexter of Newburyport," who filled his front yard with painted wooden statuary, approached Stiegel in pretentious grandeur, and Stiegel lacked any trace of Lord Timothy's saving sense of humor. The Baron built a mansion at Manheim, Penn-

sylvania, and, some miles away, a strange pyramidal guest house with a cannon on top to salute his arrivals. He traveled in a coach drawn by six white horses, attended by liveried servants and outriders, and he paid for the uniformed band that greeted him with music when he reached Manheim. Eight years of these expenses, plus some too-rapid business expansion, did for him in 1774. Old at forty-eight, he taught school for a few years and died poor.

Stiegel's own trade was iron founder, and he had managed to marry his boss's daughter. But he was also an innovator, and he encouraged the German artisans in his glass factory to do remarkable work in engraved and enameled glass.

Amelung presentation goblet   *Stiegel wineglass*

The Braziers

Bronze and bell metal combine copper and tin; brass combines copper and zinc. The alloys resist corrosion and they are harder and stronger than any of the metals that go into them. Brass had many uses in the colonies, but little of it was alloyed here. The raw materials were too scarce: some copper, mined after 1709; no tin at all; no zinc until 1837. So most colonial brass came from England as sheets or ingots. But Philadelphia founders did alloy their own metal to cast bronze cannon for the Revolutionary Army.

The cementation of brass began in England in Elizabethan times. The founders made it by cooking broken-up copper in crucibles with "calamy." This is calamine or zinc carbonate. The English mined it in rocky lumps and ground

Shop figure of a New Bedford instrument maker, about 1830. Redrawn by permission from the Index of American Design.

Forming a bell core

*Brass candlestick,
about 1725*

*Cast
uniform button,
Revolutionary*

Ring punch

it. Until the middle of the eighteenth century, they had no idea that calamine was a metal at all, though they were familiar with the metallic zinc they imported from China. The founders cast brass ingots in sand and also poured molten brass between slabs of slate to form thick plates. These they reduced to sheets of various gauges by battery with tilt hammers. More battery shaped some sheets into pots and pans right on the spot.

The expanding American merchant fleet demanded mathematical instruments: compasses; quadrants; and, after about 1760, sextants for determining latitude. Instrument makers did well in seaports. Their products demanded brass; so did clock parts; so did a scramble of articles known as "furniture": buttons, pins, rivets, wood screws, upholsterers' nails, buckles, thimbles, corkscrews, nutcrackers, candlesticks, curtain rings, turncocks, and valves. Along with grease cups, the use of the last two increased rapidly after steam engines appeared. The founders cast most of these things rough, in sand molds or in iron ones, and finished them by hand.

Churches needed bells for more practical reasons than modern churches need them. They actually summoned people to services; they rang peals on the king's birthday; they tolled the death of any citizen—six strokes for a woman, nine for a man, with an additional stroke for each year of age. Churches with chimes of bells tolled the one called the "taylor." Hence: "It takes nine taylors to make a man": not nine tailors as the old libel has it.

In 1753, at Fairfield, Connecticut, John Witear cast the first bells made from scratch in the colonies. That same year two young Philadelphians, Pass and Stow, recast what we later named the Liberty Bell when it cracked the first time it was rung. Other bell founders followed, including Isaac Doolittle and Paul Revere, who started his still-flourishing foundry in 1801. Bell metal is bronze with a little extra copper in it and sometimes a little zinc to sharpen the tone. The founder first made a clay model of the outside of his bell, shaping it symmetrically with a cut-out wooden template which he rotated on a central shaft. He dried the model, greased its surface, and then formed a refractory clay mold over it. When this was dry, he removed it; the grease allowed the two surfaces to separate. With the same heat-resistant clay and a smaller template, he made a core to govern the shape of the inside of his bell.

This core stood on a flat base at the bottom of a pit in front of the furnace; in fact, it was usually made in the pit. When it was entirely dry, the founders placed the outside mold over it and precisely centered the two; then they filled up the pit except for a tubular sprue that reached the surface. The packed earth reinforced the mold. A channel leading from the sprue to the furnace had a fire maintained in it before the melt was tapped, so that metal running through it wouldn't be cooled. It was a founder's nightmare that his bronze might harden before it reached the bottom of the mold.

At the last moment the channel was cleared of ashes and the master used a long pole to break the clay that dammed the crucible. The metal ran through the channel like liquid fire and disappeared into the sprue to fill the space between core and mold. The cast cooled in the pit for days before the founders dug it free, hoisted it out, and smoothed and tuned the bell in a big lathe.

Cast-brass buttons, being far smaller than bells, cooled faster. The mold for these was iron, made in two halves and held together for casting by an iron belt that slipped over it and was tightened by driving a wedge behind it. The button caster ladled molten brass from a pot and filled the mold. Caspar Wistar probably molded those of his "Philadelphia Brass Buttons" that had ornamented faces. The plain ones he could make by punching disks out of sheet brass with a

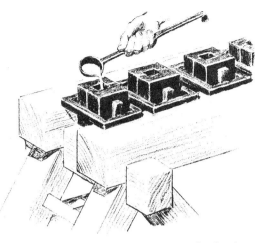

Casting buttons

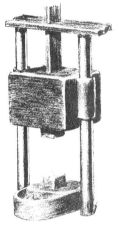

Pin header

device much like a spinning wheel to rotate a stretched wire a little thicker than a pin as if it were a shaft. Its inner end was fastened to the spindle, its outer one to a swivel. As it turned, it wrapped itself with the fine pinhead wire which the spinner then pulled off as a spiral coil.

Boys with nippers cut off two turns of the spiral for each pinhead. Journeymen placed the heads on the shanks and crimped them in place with small foot-powered drop hammers. The anvil and the hammer had matching grooves ending in half-round pockets to accommodate the shank and head of a pin.

The fabricated pin was still raw brass. It had to be washed, tinned in a solution of metal and acid, washed again, and then polished by tumbling with hundreds of its brothers in a crank-turned barrel partly filled with bran. The customer could buy mixed sizes by the pound. Separate sizes came in papers as they still do. The old sizes were designated by numbers—one to twenty—but the smallest were commonly called "minikins," and the next larger were "small whites," which suggests that all sizes once had names.

ring punch and a hammer. Toward the end of the eighteenth century, too late for Caspar, fancy brass buttons were stamped out, cold, with steel dies hit with a sledge. One of the commodities that peddlers brought in was scrap brass for making buttons.

Only a little less important, if any, than buttons were pins; colonial pins were brass. Adam Smith, the architect of industrialism, cited pinmaking to show the advantage of divided labor. A pin passed through twenty-five hands from start to finish, and Smith asked of the wind how long it would take one man to make one pin complete, from sheet brass to final polish.

Without trying to account for all twenty-five hands: Pinmaking began with the drawing of brass wire. Back in Elizabethan times two men made wire by stretching a strip of brass between their wide leather belts. They sat in swings and pushed away from one another by straightening their legs against the "stump," a timber placed between them. Colonial brass wire was drawn much as the silversmith drew his, through a series of diminishing holes, either with a hand-turned windlass or by water power.

A boy cut the lengths of wire for pin shanks with hand snips, half a dozen at a clip. He passed them to workers at grindstones who pointed them, again in batches. Apparently they could roll five or six shanks at once between their fingers steadily enough for the stone to grind symmetrical points on them. An early pin was made in two parts, the head separately from the shank and of finer wire. An apprentice used a

Drawing brass wire

The Clockmakers

Perhaps a clock came over on the *Mayflower*, but hardly more than one because the Pilgrims were poor folk. It is known that a very few of the more prosperous Puritans had "lantern" clocks soon after they had houses in Salem and Boston. A lantern clock was a brass box that stood on a shelf. A bell for striking the hours, mounted on top of the box, gave the effect of a dome. The

143

whole thing was about fifteen inches high. A spring drove the clock's one hand around an unglazed dial which showed numbered hours and half hours marked by fleurs-de-lis, but no minutes. A few minutes one way or the other made no difference to anyone, and the clocks were too inaccurate to make a marking of minutes mean anything.

In 1657, the Dutch physicist, Christian Huygens, knowing that a pendulum oscillates in a fixed span of time, successfully used one to regulate a clock. In London the very next year, John Fromantel started making lantern clocks equipped with short pendulums. Seventeenth-century springs weren't too springy, and it was found that a drum slowly turned by a weighted cord wrapped on it provided a steadier source of power for the new accuracy. A ratchet on the drum allowed the owner to wind his clock. A second drum, separately weighted, powered the "striking train," to use the clockmaker's term.

The hours on the dial could now be divided into quarters instead of merely into halves. It's said that a person used to a one-handed clock could easily tell the time within a minute. Such people preferred one hand to two, hence Nathaniel Dominy of East Hampton, Long Island, still made one-handed clocks in 1778. Some early two-handed clocks had double dials—an outer one divided into sixty minutes, and an inner one with forty-eight quarter hours—to serve the elderly.

The train of time gears in a clock runs through three steps or more, with large wheels driving small pinions, an arrangement which would spin the hands at high speed if it were unchecked. It is checked, however, by the escapement which interrupts the movement. In a pendulum clock, the swinging bob controls the interruptions, stopping the clock completely for an instant at the end of each beat, and causing the clock to tick as it does so. A grandfather clock with a seconds pendulum 39.138 inches long ticks very deliberately at the end of each second: over-*tick*; back-*tick*. The lantern clock's short pendulum swung energetically behind the clock, four times —*tick-tick-tick-tick*—for each second. It controlled a "crown wheel" up under the bell by means of two cams, called pallets, fixed on an arbor which was rocked to and fro by the

Crown wheel

Anchor escapement

17th-century "lantern clock"

pendulum. The pallets also transferred a slight push from the crown wheel to keep the pendulum swinging. The crown wheel passed out of use, but the more accurate "anchor" escapement, which replaced it, operates on the same basic principle.

The new pendulum clocks soon came to America, and English-trained clockmakers, who arrived in the late seventeenth century, converted many of the old spring clocks to pendulums and weights. There are fewer lantern clocks of either kind left in America now than there are hour glasses. American collectors wanted only tall clocks at first and they allowed English agents to buy up all the lantern clocks and take them back where they came from. The first colonial clockmaker known by name seems to be Abel Cottey, who worked in Philadelphia so early that he must have come over on the boat with William Penn. Abel and some others also made new clocks, melting down old kettles to get brass for gears and hammering and filing it into shape.

The town records of Boston account for the cost of maintaining a public tower clock in 1650. This one was doubtless made in England, but the town's second tower clock Benjamin Bagnall made locally in 1718. He is believed by experts also to have made the first American tall clock. A grandfather clock, we would call it, but Bagnall's patrons knew it as a "coffin clock." The type evolved in England about 1675 as a natural result of the wish to enclose the long pendulum and the driving weights—if only to keep the children from playing with them.

Few Americans could afford a clock of any kind and still fewer could stand the cost of an imposing one eight feet high. Some makers in the thirty years or so before 1750 provided such people with small one-handed clocks of the kind the Scots called "wag-at-ta-wa'." Clockmakers sold only the works of grandfather clocks, which the buyer could mount on a bracket, pierced for the pendulum and the weight cords, to serve as a wag-on-the-wall until he could afford to have a cabinetmaker build a case for it.

In addition to the taller clocks, there were also "grandmother" clocks about five feet high, controlled by shorter, half-second pendulums. These are much sought after nowadays, partly because they are "cute" and fit well into modern houses, and partly because they are scarce. The makers built comparatively few of them, but they made a great many fine grandfather clocks between 1750 and 1850, and the best cabinetmakers in the land built cases for them. Many old clocks sound chimes as well as hours, some even offer a selection of tunes. Chime clocks have a third weight.

Clocks of this kind sometimes show the calendar date in a small opening near the center of the dial and often show the phases of the moon in the arched "tympanum" over the dial. They accomplish this last trick by the slow rotation of a largely hidden disk with two moon faces (they usually have human features) painted on it. Twenty-four hours after the old moon disappears at the right side of a curved opening, the second face enters at the left to show the crescent.

Sometime after 1770, David Rittenhouse, the Philadelphia mathematician, great-grandson of William, the papermaker, built what might be called a great-grandfather clock, though he hadn't his ancestor in mind at the time. It is nine feet high. Its chimes cover two complete octaves and offer a selection of four tunes. It shows not only the moon phases but also the positions of the planets. Four small dials around the main one give other astronomical information. This clock now stands in the Drexel Institute in Philadelphia, but it stands silent. The full time of an expert would be needed to keep it running.

In East Hartford, Connecticut, from 1750, the brothers, Benjamin and Timothy Cheney, made excellent brass-clock mechanisms, and, to supply the demand for something cheaper, they also built clock works with mechanisms made of wood except for the escapement. About 1760, the Cheney brothers took as apprentice one Benjamin Willard. As soon as he finished his training, Benjamin hurried home to Grafton, Massachusetts, set up shop, and taught his three brothers, Simon, Ephraim, and Aaron, all he knew. The four soon found Grafton too small for them and moved successively to Roxbury, to Lexington, and then to Boston where their factory throve.

The Willards never made cheap clocks. Though they made grandfather clocks, they are best known for their fine shelf and wall clocks, especially Simon, who, in 1802, patented his famous eight-day "banjo" clock. This was a non-striking wall clock with a short pendulum enclosed in a glass-fronted case which was tapered to accommodate its swing. The glass was painted on the inside—limners did well painting dials and case fronts—but a small opening was left clear near the bottom to let the motion of the pendulum be seen. This was to show that the clock was running, but also, it seems, to add quietly to the life of a room. Simon Willard was a master craftsman. Legend credits him with the ability to space the teeth of a gear by eye alone and to file them accurately to shape with only the same guide.

Wealthy eighteenth-century gentlemen carried watches, fat fellows an inch thick, for which they paid large sums. A man wound his watch with a key carried on his watch chain or on a ribbon fob that hung from the watch pocket of his "small-clothes," as he called his breeches. The key, which a member of the honorary Phi Beta Kappa fraternity still wears, originally wound his watch. It took constant tinkering to keep a watch running and watchmakers did well in large towns. These men didn't actually make watches.

A gentleman's silver-cased watch and its key, made in London in 1760

"Wag-on-the-wall" clock made in New England, about 1750

"Banjo" wall clock by Simon Willard, about 1810

"Pillar-and-scroll" shelf clock by Eli Terry, about 1817

Apparently, shaping the small parts was beyond them. This is borne out by the fact that, as late as 1835, American watchmakers still bought parts in Europe and merely assembled them in their shops.

As population increased, so did the market for cheap clocks. Only one house in ten had a clock of any kind in 1806 when Eli Terry started to do something about it at Plymouth, Connecticut. He hired some help and began making thirty-hour wooden works for grandfather clocks, cutting all the gears by hand with saw and jack-knife out of quarter-sawn black cherry, and turning arbors and pinions, as units, from laurel wood on a foot-powered lathe. Peddlers and retail stores sold his mechanisms uncased for twenty-five dollars each. Terry made some four thousand of them. Two years later he had a better idea, so he sold his grandfather clock factory to Seth Thomas and Silas Hoadley.

Perhaps his idea was the result of a hint from Eli Whitney, who had made interchangeable gun parts for the army. Anyway, the new Terry factory used water power to make wooden clock parts cheaper and better than before. Terry went further and cased his clocks in a plain glass-fronted box which, with only the dial painted on the glass, exposed some of the works. A man could now buy a complete Terry clock for fifteen dollars. Perhaps because he couldn't improve the mechanism, Eli improved the case and in 1814 brought out the famous "pillar-and-scroll" model that most people think of as a Terry clock. It looked well on anyone's mantel—and still does. Thousands were sold and hundreds are still striking the hours with a sound like a spoon hitting a saucepan and keeping respectable time, even with their once-round gears shrunk to lopsided ovals. These clocks were so popular that Terry's plant couldn't meet the demand for them, and he had to license Seth Thomas to make them, also.

Both the time train and the striking train of a Terry clock are driven by weights wound up by a key. The weight cords run over pulleys and the weights descend inside the case on either side. Obviously, not every part of a practical working clock could be made of wood. The hands were metal; so was the pendulum which, in the early models, swung in *front* of the dial. The brass

escapement, also, was clearly visible on the face of the clock. Inside there were very few metal parts and anyone who unwarily removes the front plate of a Terry clock will suddenly be confronted by what looks like a heap of spools that come rattling out.

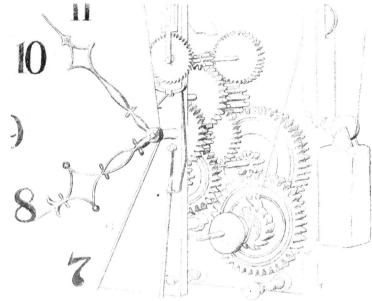

The time train of a Terry clock. This is a late model with the pendulum and escapement behind the dial.

The Ironmasters

George Washington's father, Augustine, was an ironmaster. He helped to establish Bristol Furnace in 1722 on the Rappahannock River some forty miles below Fredericksburg, Virginia, and was active in its management. In 1726, Augustine became a partner in the much larger Principio Furnace at the head of Chesapeake Bay, and, acting for his English associates, he managed a subsidiary smelter on his own land along Accokeek Creek. Only ruins remain of these three furnaces, but at Hopewell Village near Reading, Pennsylvania, the National Park Service is finishing the restoration of an iron furnace that is built much as they were and that originally functioned as they did.

Fireback from Accokeek

Pennsylvania grandfather clock by Jacob Gottshalk, about 1770

Hopewell Furnace began operations in 1770 and is typical of the many "iron plantations" in the colonies. Hopewell is called a "village" because the workers and their families who lived on the premises made it one. The management operated a store to provide for their needs. The ironmaster and his family lived in the "Big House" scarcely two hundred feet from the smoking stack; smaller dwellings, a blacksmith shop, and a school clustered nearby.

The first requirement for locating an iron furnace was, of course, ore, though when the local deposits ran out at Principio, long barges, rowed by gangs of slaves, brought ore to the furnace from mines along the shores of the Chesapeake. The bog iron that the earliest settlers dredged out of ponds was insufficient for the larger operations of the eighteenth century and the iron founders at Hopewell and elsewhere dug ore from veins near the surface of the ground. A second necessity was a lime flux which would combine with the non-metallic parts of the ore to make a brittle glassy slag. Either limestone or oyster shells would serve. As vital as the ore itself was the fuel to heat it. In the colonies, this was exclusively charcoal and no man started an iron furnace unless he owned several square miles of standing timber around the site. Since eastern North America was almost solidly wooded, such a stand wasn't hard to find. The destruction of the Eastern virgin forests—hardly a hundred acres now stand—was the work of the charcoal colliers far more than of the lumbermen, the tanbark grinders, or the farmers.

The axmen worked from October to May felling everything with bark on it. They cut the trunks into four-foot cordwood lengths and split them into "billets"; they also cut up the saplings and limbs, even quite small ones, to make "lapwood." The colliers themselves usually worked as axmen in winter for the eight shillings and sixpence a cord they could make while their coaling operations were closed down. In April they went back to the hearth. They called it a "pit," from an unconscious memory of the time when charcoal was really burned in holes. An eighteenth-century pit was a flat circle, thirty or forty feet in diameter. The colliers first repaired the conical earth-covered hut they slept in, and then raked up last year's charcoal dust into a low embankment around the edge of the hearth. Because he needed this dust, the collier clung to the same pit long after the wood cutting had left it in a treeless barren.

Haulers brought wood to the pit on pungs (sleds) drawn by horses, mules, or oxen. They brought the light lapwood first and piled it around the hearth on the bank of charcoal dust. They piled more of it in the center of the ring and then stacked the billets in a circle just inside the dust bank. The total was as much as fifty cords, but before it was all in, the collier and his helper had made a good start at "setting the pit."

They began with the fagan, a four-inch-thick green pole eighteen feet long, which they set up in the exact center of the hearth and around which they started a three-cornered crib of lapwood to serve as the chimney, carrying it at first

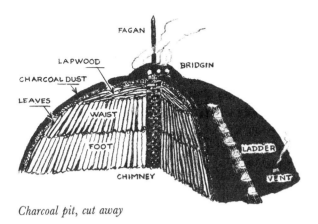

Charcoal pit, cut away

only a little higher than the four-foot length of a billet. The chimney opening wasn't more than eight inches on a side; with nearly half its area filled by the fagan, it made a small flue.

All around the chimney the colliers stacked billets on end, vertically at first but gradually leaning the tops inward as the "foot" grew. They packed the billets as solidly as possible and filled any accidental pockets with lapwood. When the foot spread far enough from the chimney to provide standing room on its top, the men built the chimney four feet higher and started stacking the second tier of billets called the "waist." From there on, foot and waist moved outward together until the base neared the bank of charcoal dust. Then, with three feet more added to the chimney, the colliers covered the "head" and "shoulders" of the pile with lapwood from the dust bank, pointing the sticks toward the fagan. The pile gradually took on the shape of a flattened dome. A ladder, made by notching a log, was needed to reach the top. The men spread leaves four inches deep over the whole surface from chimney to ground and, using very long-handled shovels, they spread charcoal dust on the leaves, four inches deep over the sides and a foot deep on top.

Finally, the colliers filled the chimney with dry kindling nearly to its top and covered it with a "bridgin" made of three billets. That evening they opened the chimney, poured in a shovelful of hot coals, replaced the bridgin, and covered it with charcoal dust. Then they turned in in the hut for the only full night's sleep they could expect for the next two weeks.

The object of this preparation was to char all the wood evenly by allowing the fire only a restricted oxygen supply. For this the fire had to be kept under the surface, and if it burned through, the damage had to be repaired at once. That kept the colliers constantly alert. The fire would die completely without some air. To get this, they opened vent holes in the foot, always on the side away from the wind. When the pile was burning well, blue smoke curled lazily from these vents. If the wind changed, the holes had to be closed at once and new ones opened where the wind couldn't blow into them. If the pile got too little air, it could accumulate gasses and explode violently. Just before sundown every day the master collier climbed the pile and risked incineration by jumping up and down on it to locate "mulls" that might burn through in the night. Mulls were soft spots caused by burned-out cavities. Small ones could be merely stamped down, but large ones had to be dug out and filled with wood.

Finally, as the collier knew by instinct and by poking with a pole, the fire burned all the way to the ground and before dawn one morning he and his helper started "ringing out" charcoal, a little at a time, from the bottom. They used long rakes set with a few iron teeth to do it. Each hole they made created a draft and, as soon as they saw fire, they closed that hole and opened a new one. They stopped when they had removed the two hundred bushels or so that would fill a high-sided wagon and spent the rest of the morning quenching any fire that showed up in the coal they had extracted. When the six-mule wagon arrived, the colliers filled their special two-bushel baskets with charcoal and helped the teamster load it. He took the load to the coal house on "the Bank" above the iron furnace. More wood came in as soon as the hearth was empty, and the colliers started a new pile and repeated the process all summer. Hopewell Furnace used five thousand cords of wood a year. Stacked to four-foot cord-height, this would reach more than seven and a half miles.

Colonial ironmasters sold pig iron "at the Bank." The furnaces were always built at the foot of an embankment; if it was on level ground, a bank was created. This allowed ore, flux, and charcoal to be hauled to a level where it could be

Gutterman's clog. This one is 15 inches long.

Collier's splint basket

carried across a bridge and dumped into the top of the stack.

The stack of Hopewell Furnace is a stone structure built on a base twenty-two feet square. It is thirty-two feet high and narrows upward on all four sides in a series of steps like an Assyrian ziggurat. This general form is usual, though most furnaces had sloping walls and fewer steps than the one at Hopewell. Thirty-five feet was about the maximum height possible; with a higher stack, the weight of the iron ore crushed the charcoal and choked off the draft. There are two recesses in the masonry at ground level: on the front, the casting arch, some twelve feet high and wide and half as deep; and on the Bank side, the somewhat smaller tuyère arch through which the air blast reaches the stack. In the Hopewell furnace, neither has the actual shape of an arch and they seldom had elsewhere. Their purpose was to reduce the thickness of the walls to allow workers to get within tool-reach of the crucible.

The cut-away drawing will explain the inside of a furnace better than many words can do. At Hopewell, ore and flux were stored in the bridge house, a shed built on the bridge; charcoal came to the bridge in hand carts from the coal house on the Bank. Fillers dumped the three materials into the stack, filling the bosh with successive layers and keeping it full day and night. Later furnaces had an opening, the tunnel head, below the top. Two and a half tons of ore, a ton and a half of flux, and 180 bushels of charcoal made a ton of iron. The bosh, egg-shaped to support the weight of the materials, was the actual furnace. It was lined with sandstone as a rule, though firebrick would have been better. Here the fire, fanned by a constant blast of air, raged for thirty or forty weeks on end, though this could be shortened by many mishaps: the supply of ore, fuel, or flux might run out; the lining of the bosh might burn through and have to be replaced; ice might stop the water wheel.

Up to the late 1700's, all iron furnaces got their air from bellows like the blacksmith's but much larger and pumped by water wheels. Cams on the water-wheel shaft compressed two bellows alternately. Both delivered their air to a leather bag from which it was piped to the tuyère. The bag equalized the pulsations to deliver a more even flow. Originally such a pair of bellows blew

*Tuyère—
4 feet long*

Hopewell furnace, but sometime before 1822, possibly thirty years before, its present, more advanced, "double cylinders" took over. These stand on a platform above the water wheel and under the bridge. They are coopered with wooden staves and metal hoops. Cranks on the wheel shaft slowly raise and lower pistons in the cylinders and a system of flap valves makes each cylinder inhale at one end while it exhales at the other. Thus, the two give the effect of four bellows. A rectangular, equalizing chest stands between the cylinders. Air under a pressure of about three-quarters of a pound per square inch passes from the box to the tuyère through a large copper duct.

The tuyère is a nozzle about four feet long, tapered to speed up the blast. Ironworkers commonly called it the "tooyer," or, like the blacksmith, the "tue arn." It pierces the wall under the tuyère arch a foot or so above the level of the liquid iron in the hearth and its blast is directed upward through the burning charcoal in the bosh.

As the iron melted from the ore, it ran down into a small crucible called the hearth, part of which extended beyond a curtain wall (the tymp) into the forehearth under the casting arch, where the liquid metal was held back by the dam stone. A hole in the dam, stopped by an easily breakable clay plug, allowed the furnace to be tapped, usually twice in twenty-four hours. A larger plugged hole, the "cinder hole," in the tymp, above the forehearth and at one side (not shown in the drawing), was opened every hour or so to rake out the slag that accumulated on the surface of the iron in the hearth.

The principal product of an iron furnace was pig iron sold by weight for remelting and casting in various forms by the purchaser or for refining by him into wrought iron. The tapping of the furnace was for the purpose of casting pig. The gutterman made the pig bed with a triangular hoe in the deep sand that floored the casting arch and the shed beyond it. Starting below the plugged hole in the dam, he scraped a trench that ran straight out. Smaller ditches, the "sows," branched from this and still smaller ones, for the "pigs," branched from them. The founder broke the clay plug and the liquid iron flowed from the hearth into the trench, filled all

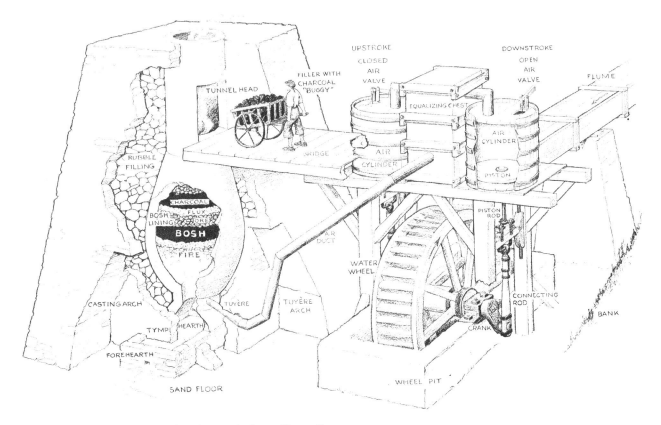

Diagram of a late 18th-century iron furnace similar to Hopewell

the branches, and lay in them bubbling. When all were full, the crucible was empty and the hole in the dam was replugged to accumulate another run.

The founders broke the pigs off the sows with hammers when the metal cooled, and broke up the iron in the other trenches into portable pieces. The thick piece from the main trench was the sow. It weighed upward of two hundred pounds; a pig weighed sixty or seventy. The whole run was weighed on a steel-yard scale and sold as pig iron.

In addition to pigs, most of the furnaces cast simple articles right at the hearth. Firebacks were a continuing product. These flat plates stood against the rear walls of fireplaces, protecting the brickwork from heat and also radiating heat into rooms. A shallow depression in packed sand served as a fireback mold; iron could be run into it just as it was run for pig. The upper side, which would face the bricks, could be rough and unfinished; the front could readily be made ornamental by pressing a

carved wooden pattern into the sand floor. Augustine Washington cast tombstone-shaped firebacks at Accokeek from patterns dated 1728—the date of a pattern is, of course, no guarantee of the date of the casting.

Hopewell cast firebacks, too, but by the time it started smelting, people had begun to heat their houses with stoves made of flat iron plates bolted together. The plates could be cast as simply as firebacks, and Hopewell made hundreds of them. An elaborate one survives, decorated with a two-handled vase and a lot of iron flowers. Across its top, a three-part iron ribbon announces: MARK BIRD / HOPEWELL / FURNACE, with the date, 1772, below it. Mark Bird started Hopewell.

Many foundries cast iron pans and pots, in spite of the English law against their doing so. A potter made a separate clay mold for each pot, including a solid core that had to be broken out when the metal cooled. He hardened his molds over a slow fire, but in no sense fired them as pottery. The diagram shows how the

Pig

mold was buried in sand to reinforce it, and how the sprue and the risers, or air vents, were made with tapered sticks pulled out after the sand had been tamped down. What is not clear—and what it is hoped some reader can resolve—is how the caster got the outside mold over the core and kept the two evenly separated. Obviously the mold could not be made separately and then slipped over the core, unless it were made as two halves, and it doesn't seem to have been. A small pot of this kind exists, cast at the Saugus Iron Works about 1641. For such casting, the founders didn't tap the furnace. They poured iron into the sprue with a ladle filled at the forehearth after first being dipped in semi-liquid clay to keep it from melting.

As early as 1730, some foundries which bought their iron from the furnaces—and some of the furnaces themselves—began to use the sand-flask method for casting articles which, like pots, had to be shaped accurately on all sides. Pots and curved stove plates were best cast in flasks, and so were the strange objects needed for steam engines.

Sand for use in flasks was fine-grained and had some clay mixed naturally with it. The flask was a topless and bottomless box made in two separable parts, the lower drag and the upper cope. Wooden pins matched to holes allowed the edges of the two parts to be set together precisely. Specialists made the wooden patterns for flask-casting, as they still do. Patternmaking as a craft has hardly changed at all except that the modern worker's speed is greater because of help from machines. The pattern was a duplicate of the casting that would result from it, but was slightly larger all over to allow for the shrinkage of cooling metal. The artisan had to make the pattern in two halves with guide pins and holes to allow their being joined accurately.

Small flask

In casting, the founders set the drag on a level "follow board" and placed the lower half of the pattern in the drag with its flat "parting face" on the board. They filled the drag with slightly damp sand, tamped it down tight, and struck off the top by passing a straight edge across it. Then they put a second board, the "bottom board," on top of the drag, inverted the whole business, and removed the follow board to expose the flat face of the pattern lying flush with an equally flat surface of packed sand. This surface they dusted with very fine, dry, parting sand that had had all the clay washed out of it.

Now the workers set the cope on the drag and carefully placed the upper half of the pattern on the lower. They rammed the cope full of sand and pushed a tapered tube down until it touched the pattern, withdrawing it full of sand, to cut a sprue hole. Then they lifted the cope carefully straight up and set it aside. Its sand had a dent in it exactly the shape of the top of the pattern. Delicately they stuck a sharp pin into the pattern and lifted it out of the drag. Here was the test of the patternmaker's skill: his pattern had to draw. If it had a projection that, on lifting, would disturb the sand, it was useless. Some complex patterns overcame this with loose parts which could be removed separately after the main pattern was out. While we are on complications, hollow objects can be cast by setting a supported core in the drag after the pattern is out. Cores are now made of sand held together with a binder; early cores were clay.

Sometimes a little parting sand ran into the mold and had to be blown out with a small bellows; sometimes, through no fault of the maker, removing the pattern damaged the mold slightly. The founders then used iron tools to repair it before they put the cope back on and ladled hot iron into the sprue hole. Large castings required more than one sprue, but vents

Flask tamper

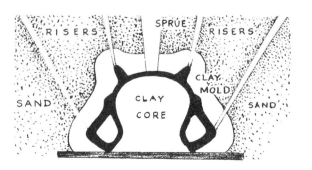

152

Casting ladle, clay-lined

were seldom needed; the sand was porous enough to absorb the air in the mold cavity and leave no pockets. A good shake would free the cooled casting, and it needed only to have its sprue cut off and to be touched up a little with a file.

The Saugus Iron Works, started in 1643 on the Saugus River near Lynn, Massachusetts, has been meticulously restored. Strictly, Saugus isn't the colonies' first ironworks. Captain John Smith's "little chissels" were made from native iron in 1607, and fourteen years later the Jamestown settlers built a furnace, probably much like Hopewell's, eighty miles up the James River at Falling Creek. They smelted iron in it for a year or so before the Indians destroyed it and massacred all the workers.

All through the colonies in the seventeenth century, men set up little "bloomeries" to make wrought iron directly from ore. These were only slightly larger than blacksmith's forges. The founders heated ore in them—with flux—hot enough to become a doughy mass (bloom). This they attacked with sledge hammers to beat out the impurities. What resulted was wrought iron, but of low grade because they never got all the impurities out.

Saugus was another matter. It was a great technical achievement for its time. Trained ironworkers from England built and operated it and its equipment was as advanced as any in the world. Its smelting furnace supplied a companion enterprise, Hammersmith Forge, which turned pig iron into wrought-iron bars and had a water-driven rolling-and-slitting mill to make nail rods from the bars.

Pig iron, or cast iron, is hard and brittle because its metal is mixed with carbon and, to turn it into malleable wrought iron, much of the carbon must be removed. Getting the carbon out was the job of the finery at Saugus. It ran two forges used successively for the process; both were open fire boxes burning charcoal with forced draft from water-powered bellows. There was a small crucible in the bottom of the first forge. The finers filled it with old slag and built their fire on top of it. They pushed pig iron into the forge and melted it to run down into the crucible and displace the slag. It cooked for an hour while a finer stirred it with an iron bar to

bring carbon to the surface where contact with air would burn it. The melt was gradually cooled to a mushy lump which the finers called a loop. They tonged it out of the crucible on to an iron plate and "shingled" it by hitting it with sledge hammers to knock off slag and cinder. Shingling had its hazards; when a hammer hit a pocket, still-liquid metal spurted in unpredictable directions. The men next moved the loop, still hot, to the tilt hammer, which beat it into a thick, square bloom. The bloom went to the second forge, where it sat on top of a fire that heated it to white-hot welding temperature. The finers cut it in half and each part went under the tilt, the men holding it with long tongs and changing its position as necessary to forge it into the curious square dumbbell shape that was an ancony. Only the connecting bar of an ancony was neatly finished; the ends were rough, and one, the mocket, was always larger than the other, the head.

The finers turned their ancony over to the chafery to be finished. The chafery workers had their separate forge in the same area with those of the finery and they shared the one tilt hammer. They beat the head and mocket of the ancony down to the same dimensions as the connecting bar and then lengthened and flattened the whole thing until it was three inches wide, an inch and a half thick, and about eight feet long. This was "merchantable bar-iron," the principal product of Hammersmith.

Though details of the machinery improved

Split wooden pattern for casting a pulley

Hammersmith, restored: the forge and the rolling-and-slitting mill

153

with time—iron shafts instead of wooden ones, threaded nuts instead of wedges to hold down bearings—the processes changed hardly at all. Edward Hazen's description of them, published the year before Victoria became queen of England, parallels all the Hammersmith procedures.

The restored tilt hammer at Hammersmith uses the original 500-pound iron head which archaeologists dug up at the site. It falls upon an anvil that is a replica of one found in Sussex, the home county of the original workers. The butt of the foot-thick oak helve of the hammer is gripped in an iron hurst whose trunions turn freely in holes bored into heavy supports. A post two feet square stands behind the hurst; and mortised into it is an oak timber that extends over the helve and bends to act as a spring to throw the hammer down when it slips off the cam that has raised it. There are four of these cams surrounding the thick water-wheel shaft which turns alongside the helve and slightly below it. The cams strike the underside of the helve a couple of feet back of the hammer head.

Seven-eighths of the bar iron that Hammersmith made was shipped out as a finished product for the use of blacksmiths; the other eighth went to the rolling-and-slitting mill to be made into nail rods. The same machine did both rolling and slitting. Parallel shafts, upper and lower, turned rollers on one end and slitting knives on the other. In most later colonial rolling mills—there were many even after England forbade new installations and they had to be hidden under grist mills—each shaft had its own water wheel, with one on each side of the building. At Saugus, both wheels revolve in the same pit. One drives the lower shaft directly. The other's thick shaft extends across the building to drive the upper mill shaft from the opposite end with a large cogwheel engaging a lantern wheel. The mill shafts are oak heavily collared with iron. Both the polished rollers and the meshing rings of the slitter have bearings set close to them so that the stresses will not break the wooden shafts.

The operators first cut the bars into thirds with big shears. They heated the pieces four hours to white heat and then passed them through the rollers two or three times to double their length but to reduce their thickness to a quarter of an inch. After the last draw, a flattened bar went through the slitter without reheating and came out as a dozen or so nail rods, each a quarter of an inch square and five feet long.

The rolling-and-slitting mill. The man is drawing a bar in the rollers.

INDEX

(Asterisks after page numbers refer to illustrations)

156

ABOUT THE AUTHOR

EDWIN TUNIS, well-known artist, illustrator, and muralist, was born at Cold Spring Harbor, New York. At present he lives and works at Shawan, Maryland. His most ambitious art project was a mural depicting the history of spices, which took two years to paint and is 145 feet long. His articles have appeared in various magazines, and his work has been exhibited at the Baltimore Museum of Art, Society of American Etchers, National Academy of Design, Victoria and Albert Museum, and other galleries. His first book, *Oars, Sails and Steam: A Picture Book of Ships*, was followed by pictorial histories of *Weapons*, *Wheels*, and *Indians*, all of which were highly praised by critics both for content and design. In 1958 *Colonial Living* received the Thomas Alva Edison Foundation Children's Book Award for special excellence in portraying America's past. A companion book, *Frontier Living*, was first runner-up for the Newbery Medal, 1961.